Warman's

Civil War
Collectibles

FIELD GUIDE

John F. Graf

Values and Identification

©2005 by KP Books

Published by

kp books
An Imprint of F+W Publications

700 East State Street • Iola, WI 54990-0001
715-445-2214 • 888-457-2873

Our toll-free number to place an order or
obtain a free catalog is (800) 258-0929.

Library of Congress Catalog Number: 2004113665
ISBN: 0-87349-981-6

Designed by: Kay Sanders
Edited by: Tracy L. Schmidt

Printed in the United States of America

CONTENTS

Introduction 4

Chapter 1: Accoutrements 15

Chapter 2: Bayonets, Knives, and Pikes 76

Chapter 3: Belt Plates and Buckles...........100

Chapter 4: Bullets, Cartridges,
           and Projectiles 136

Chapter 5: Buttons...............................190

Chapter 6: Ephemera............................211

Chapter 7: Firearms 225

Chapter 8: Flags and Musical Equipment ..306

Chapter 9: Medical Instruments 330

Chapter 10: Photographs.........................348

Chapter 11: Swords...............................391

Chapter 12: Uniforms 429

Glossary..480

Civil War Memorabilia Resources.............495

Index 502

As is often the case, many people contributed to this work. We would, however, like to note with great appreciation the contributions of the following: Larry and Debbie Hicklin of Middle Tennessee Relics, Murfreesboro, Tennessee, who graciously shared their time and collection; the Wisconsin Veterans Museum, Madison, Wisconsin, and the museum's curator, Bill Brewster. Mr. Brewster readily shared his Civil War expertise and his enthusiasm for bringing history to life; and, as always, the fine work of photographer Paul Goodwin.

INTRODUCTION

What is it that causes a deep stir within the spirit of some at the sight of a tattered Confederate flag under glass or the bright steel of a cavalry saber? Perhaps such items evoke a long-forgotten school lesson about how nearly four million men answered the call to serve either the Union or the Confederacy between 1861 to 1865. Or, maybe these relics clarify a moment in time when the romantic image of a pioneering America ended and the modern age began. Whatever the reason, more than 300,000 Americans currently categorize themselves as Civil War buffs.

The Civil War's Longevity

Between the bombardment of Fort Sumter on April 12, 1861, and the final surrender of Confederate troops on May 26, 1865, the way wars were fought and the tools soldiers used, changed irrevocably. When troops first formed lines of battle to face each other near Bull Run Creek in Virginia on June 21, 1861, they were dressed in a widely disparate assemblage of uniforms. They carried state-issued, federally-supplied, or brought-from-home weapons, some of which dated back to the Revolutionary War, and marched to the orders and rhythms of tactics that had served land forces for at least the previous 100 years. Four short years later, the generals and soldiers had perfected the art of warfare on the North American continent, having developed such leaps as the use of the repeating rifle, moving siege artillery by rail, extensive employment of trenches and field fortifications, ironclad ships to engage in combat, the widespread use of portable telegraph units on the battlefield, the draft, organized use of African American troops in combat, and even an income tax levied to finance the war.

This change took a toll from the nation, however, in the form of more than one million casualties (over 620,000 war-related deaths). At that rate, nearly one in four soldiers experienced the pains of war firsthand. It was impossible that this did not impact every one of the 34.3 million residents of the United States and former Confederate States. Over the ensuing years, the pain, for most, subsided, but the memory remained strong. Families still pay homage to their veteran ancestors, grade school students memorize the Gettysburg address, we bow our heads on Memorial Day, and hardly a NASCAR event occurs where a Confederate battle flag isn't prominently and defiantly waved.

The Civil War Experience

Many Americans satisfy their desire to feel connected with the Civil War by exploring battlefields or cemeteries or researching their own family ancestors who served. Some people read countless biographies, regimental histories, or battle accounts, even joining Civil War study groups or "Round Tables." For many, these very private explorations are enough to satiate their need to learn about the conflict and the lives of its participants.

For others though, simply memorializing the war isn't sufficient to satisfy that need to remain connected to the events of 1861-1865. Some will painstakingly recreate uniforms and equipment to don on weekend campaigns and refight battles, this time firing at their fellow countrymen with muskets and cannons charged with powder and paper instead of canisters of grape shot or loads of buckshot. For these reenactors, such events help them come close to experiencing the daily work, inconveniences, and feelings of Civil War soldiers. Of course, at the end of the weekend, these modern "Sessesh" and "Billy Yanks," return to their twenty-first-century lives, leaving the recreated image of maimed fellow soldiers, dysentery, and lice-infested clothing behind.

And finally, for another group of Civil War enthusiasts, the best medium for understanding the heritage and role of thousands who served is by collecting war relics. For these collectors, holding an 1861 Taunton-produced Springfield rifled musket, studying the detail of a Nashville Plow Works' foot officer's sword, or admiring the style of a Confederate artilleryman's kepi are a fast connection. They represent direct links to a comprehensive understanding of the depth of commitment, sacrifice, and engagement that the soldiers felt.

Collectors and Accumulators

Collecting mementos and artifacts from the Civil War is not a new hobby. Even before the war ended, people were already gathering remembrances. The first collectors, as with any period of warfare, were the participants themselves. Soldiers sent home scraps of flags, collected Minié-ball shattered logs, purchased privately marketed unit insignias, or obtained a musket or carbine for their own use after the war. Civilians wrote to prominent officers asking for autographs, exchanged photographs ("cartes de visite") with soldiers, or kept scrapbooks of items that represented the progress of the conflict.

After the war, the passion for owning a piece of it did not subside. Early collectors gathered representative weapons, collected battlefield-found relics, and created personal or public memorials to the veterans. For nearly eighty years following the end of hostilities, veterans would gather for annual reunions to swap stories and pay homage to their fallen comrades. When these old soldiers gathered, collectors were right there to acquire any tidbits or mementos that the veterans would release.

Simultaneously, and not unlike the time following any major conflict, a grand scale of surplus sales emerged. This was the heyday of Civil War collecting. Dealers such as Francis Bannerman made hundreds of Civil War relics available to the general public. For as little as $3.50, a person could buy a Springfield musket. Ten dollars would secure a Confederate Richmond-made version. Unissued Union cavalry shell jackets could be had for $3.85 each (or $1.50 if you ordered a dozen!), and an actual 3" rifled cannon for $350. Though a lot of sales were made to early collectors, much of the surplus was sold in bulk to other governments, outdoors enthusiasts, and a lot was sold simply for its scrap value.

Following World War II, a new wave of collecting emerged. Reveling in the victories in Japan and in Europe, Americans were charged with a renewed sense of patriotism and heritage. At the same time, the newspapers started to track the passing of the last few veterans of the Civil War. As the nation paid tribute to the few survivors of the Rebellion, it also acknowledged that the 100-year anniversary of the war was fast upon them. In an effort to capture a sense of the heritage, Civil War buffs began to collect in earnest.

With the high profile of the Civil War Centennial in the 1960s, thousands of outstanding relics seemingly emerged from closets, attics, and long-forgotten chests. Collectors eagerly bought and sold firearms, swords, and uniforms. It was during this time when metal detectors first played a large role in Civil War collecting, as hundreds donned headphones and swept battlefields and campsites, uncovering thousands of spent bullets, buttons, belt plates, and artillery projectiles.

By the 1970s, as this first wave of prominent and easily recognized collectibles disappeared into collections, Civil War buffs discovered carte de visites, tintypes, and ambrotypes. All of the early photographs of the period were fantastic, visual documents of personalities, uniforms, and weapons. With a fervor matched only by collectors of baseball cards, these wonderful items were bought and sold. Simultaneously, more interest turned to the common soldiers. Accoutrements started to reach prices that far outstretched what surplus dealers could have only hoped for, just a few years prior. The demand for letters and diaries written by the soldiers forced people to open boxes and drawers to rediscover long-forgotten manuscript records of battles and campaigns.

By the end of the twentieth century, Civil War collecting had peaked. Some thought all the good stuff was gone. Little did these skeptics realize, collectors are not the end user. Rather, a collector is merely the caretaker who provides a good home for an object until that time when they choose, or no longer are able, to care for the item. Then, these relics, thought to be gone, suddenly reemerge on the market. And it is this era of Civil War relic reemergence in which we currently live.

The fabulous collections of early relics that were assembled in the late 1940s and early 1950s are reappearing. Granted, the prices have increased considerably, but nevertheless, relics like no one has seen available for fifty years are suddenly appearing at auctions, shows, and in private dealer's lists.

Today, we benefit from the many years of research that has resulted from the earlier collecting frenzies. Books that the first generation of collectors could only have dreamed of are now available on specialized topics such as Confederate saddles, Gwyn & Campbell carbines, or Federal shelter tents. At no time since the Civil War, has so much information and material been available at one time.

As we enter this "glory period" of Civil War collecting, though, many lessons need to be relearned. Whereas an old-time collector could look at a saber and recognize offhand that it was the product of the Griswold factory or quantify the variations of percussion conversion done to flintlock muskets at Federal arsenals, many of these outstanding artifacts have not been available for study for many years. Collectors are learning many of the nuances that affect desirability and value for the first time (often at the expense of the old-timer's patience!).

Using the Book

This book deals only with items made before the summer of 1865 when the last troops of the Confederacy laid down their weapons. The items listed are typical of what a soldier would have carried or encountered on a daily basis. It does not address items primarily used by civilians from this period (such as furniture, glassware, toys, or other decorative arts) or produced after the cessation of hostilities. Therefore, there are no veteran group items (for example, items issued by the Grand Army of the Republic (G.A.R.) or the United Confederate Veterans (U.C.V.) listed in this book. Similarly, commemorative items or publications produced after 1865 are not covered.

Availability, Price, and Reproduction Alert

At the beginning of each chapter, there is a rating chart. Three ratings are represented: Availability, Price, and Reproduction Alert. An attempt has been to make a general rating for each category. Each rating is represented by one to five stars with the meaning as follows:

Availability:

★ = Very rare, available through advanced dealers.

★★ = May find the items through private sales lists.

★★★ = Encountered with frequency at Civil War relic shows.

★★★★ = Commonly found through online auctions or through most dealers.

★★★★★ = You should be able to find these items at a general antique show.

Price:

★ = Less than $50

★★ = $51-$250

★★★ = $251-$1,000

★★★★ = $1,001-$5,000

★★★★★ = $5,001-and up

Reproduction Alert

★ = Items in this category rarely, if ever reproduced.

★★ = Reproductions might exist, but most often, misidentification is of more concern.

★★★ = Be careful. Reproductions are known to exist and misrepresented.

★★★★ = Be extremely careful. Reproductions are misrepresented as original on a regular basis.

★★★★★ = Extreme care needed. It is safe to assume that the item you have encountered is a reproduction. Get proof that it isn't before making a purchase.

In each category, you will find items listed using the language from the seller's descriptions. Claims of rarity, condition, or value are that of the original seller. Price may depend on how willing a dealer is to part with his item

Several pros and cons for collecting the items represented in a particular chapter are also listed. These are not provided as a definitive list of reasons to collect or not collect that group of objects, but rather, to cause the reader to learn to consider things such as liability, storage, and fraudulent representation before making a purchase.

Provenance—"Whose was it?"

Provenance will almost always dramatically affect the price of a Civil War relic. Both dealers and collectors like to refer to such items as "identified," meaning that the name of the original Civil War soldier who owned the object is still known. Although it has always been important to collectors to know who carried or used what items during the war, now, more than ever, premium prices are being paid for an item with history. Not only are items being touted as to who originally used an item during the war, now the item's subsequent owners are affecting prices as well. Pieces that once sat in a prominent collection have gained a degree of legitimacy (and value) greater than an identical object with no known history.

Provenance has probably affected price more than any other factor in recent years, so it stands to reason that many items have "acquired" a provenance. When you are paying for an item and its history, be careful. It is easy for a seller to tell a story when handing over an object, but it is a lot more difficult to verify or prove it. The best provenance will be in the form of period inscriptions or written notes attributing an object to a particular soldier.

A boon to the provenance-oriented collector has been the thousands of excavated items that have flooded the market in the last fifty years. A collector who would generally be afraid to purchase an oval "C.S." belt plate will gladly consider a dug example. The patina acquired by years of being underground is more reassuring than any number of stories from a fast-talking dealer. Some very important collections have been assembled consisting of only dug items. But like any deal that is 100% foolproof, collecting excavated relics is no longer devoid of danger. Unscrupulous dealers have found ways to age good reproductions into looking like excavated originals. Also, it is not out of the question for a dealer to strengthen an item's history. Who is to say the sword blade represented as having been dug near the Sunken Road at Antietam didn't really come from a trash pit of an Oregon Territory outpost? Collecting excavated relics with provenance requires that the buyer trusts his dealer.

Though many dealers and collectors like to segregate dug from non-dug items, this book does not differentiate these items other than stating their current condition and price at time of the sale. Therefore, a reader should quickly determine the effect on the price of similar items (such as an excavated cartridge for a Burnside carbine versus a non-dug example).

The Artifact's Context

Finally, it is the goal of this book to help the collector understand the context of the artifact. Depending on how it is viewed, the context can be varied. For example, a 10-lb Parrot shell dug at Stone's River is, in the most base of contexts, an item worth about $250. Stepping up the ladder, it represents the strides in rifled artillery development made in a few short years of the Civil War. Even higher up the ladder of consciousness, it might represent the need of a modern society to feel connected with its past. Context is, obviously, a very personal consideration. Feelings and emotions aside, however, it is factually correct that these items represent a time in the United States' history when a pervasive feeling of states' rights and isolation from its government caused a people to sever themselves from the nation. What ensued was the overwhelming willingness of the masses to die to protect that right or to protect the integrity of the Union. This is the context that we, as collectors of relics of this great struggle, can never forget.

KP photo/Wisconsin Veterans Museum collection

*From mugs to coffee boilers, Civil War tinware can
be purchased for $65-$200 apiece.*

CHAPTER 1

ACCOUTREMENTS

Accoutrements provide collectors with a feeling of direct connection to the Civil War soldier. These were, after all, the tools of his trade—the very trappings that he wore on campaign, in battle, on the drill field, and the souvenirs of his service he decided to take home.

All accoutrements did not survive at the same rate. Nearly every Union foot soldier was issued a haversack, canteen, cartridge box, cap pouch, belt, knapsack, blanket, shelter half, and rubber blanket. However, one doesn't find the same proportion of these items today. Cap pouches, cartridge boxes, canteens, belts, and even knapsacks have passed down through the ages by the thousands. Original blankets, haversacks, shelter halves, and gum blankets, though, are exceedingly rare.

Any Confederate accoutrement with provenance is seldom encountered. Because much of the South's hardware was confiscated from Federal arsenals, it is often difficult to assign a Southern provenance to an accoutrement. Once the war commenced, however, some Southern manufacturers did produce equipment for the Confederate army and navy. When a legitimate, Southern-made, or Confederate-attributed piece is located, adding it to your collection requires a thick pocketbook full of cash.

The abundance of some items (like cap pouches or cartridge boxes) enables a collector to specialize in one particular

8" brass Civil War powder flasks (pair), $350-$400.

accoutrement by seeking out variations and various makers' marks. Others find it satisfying to amass all of the trappings worn by a typical officer or enlisted man.

It is a common practice with dealers to assign the term "Confederate" to accoutrements that are not regulation U.S. issue. Approach such items with caution. If a specific item does not have solid Confederate association, you may not want to pay the higher price by including "C.S." in the title. Just because a canteen may be a "tin, drum-style," does not mean that it was carried by a Confederate solider. Many states (both northern and southern) purchased tin drum-style canteens and issued them to their volunteers.

The color of leather goods is one point to consider when determining an item's origin and authenticity. However, it should not be the sole determinate. For example, a brown-dyed leather belt is not automatically a Confederate-issued piece. Similarly, an oval "C.S." buckle attached to a black, buff leather belt should not immediately be dismissed as a married item. Color should be considered as only one of several clues when examining original leather items.

Civil War-period bullet extractor, $30-$45.

Civil War-period inkwell, $55-$85.

Collecting Hints

Pros:
- Fakes are not as prevalent, because it is extremely difficult to fake the age and patina that most leather or tarred goods acquire naturally.
- Due to the volume of equipment produced during the Civil War, there are a wide variety of variations and manufacturers for most accoutrements. Therefore, assembling a wide study collection is fun.
- Accoutrements, by their very nature, have a "personal" feel to them. By collecting the complete trappings of a soldier, a collector can develop a keen sense of a typical Civil War soldier's burden.

Cons:
- Leather and metal accoutrements can be hard to properly store. Leather requires special treatment and is prone to flaking and dryness. Ideally, it is stored in a slightly humid environment. Metal items, especially tin-dipped iron such as canteens, are prone to rust, and must be kept dry.
- Different types of accoutrements survived at disproportionate rates. As an example, cartridge boxes have survived by the thousands, but very few haversacks have passed down through the ages. Therefore, assembling a complete soldier's kit is costly.
- Many interesting accoutrement variations are often mislabeled Confederate resulting in artificially high prices.
- Union accoutrements are relatively inexpensive, but anything concretely identified as Southern manufacture bears an astronomical price. Assembling typical kits of both Union and Confederate soldiers is difficult.

Availability ★★
Price ★★★
Reproduction Alert ★★★★★

Union, carbine-bore brush, $50-$75.

KP photo/
Wisconsin Veterans
Museum collection

A Confederate plain leather belt with ring and hook for carrying a sword. A small brass buckle is attached to leather straps on left side. A rectangular brass buckle with oval insignia of victorious Roman warrior over fallen enemy with the inscription "Sic Semper Tyrannis/Virginia." Inside of belt, handwritten "J.W.C. Booth," $5,900.

Belts

U.S.

Buff Leather

Artillery belt, no buckle. From a small lot that surfaced years ago from a G.A.R. post. **$395**

Regulation Civil War U.S. infantry belt, fine condition, brown buff leather with brass adjuster or keeper. **$245**

Regulation NCO waist belt (designed to accept the rectangular eagle buckle with silver wreath), mint condition with sliding loop adjuster and brass hook. Early war example with brass keeper secured by stitching only (no rivets). **$295**

Cavalry, top-notch, all straps present, including "over-the-shoulder" strap, beautiful silver wreath buckle, serial number matches keeper. **$1,975**

Harness Leather

Just the belt (no buckle), excellent condition with 98% of original black finish, complete with brass adjuster. Nicely marked with an oval inspector's cartouche. **$275**

Buff examples of these are getting hard to find, samples in black harness leather are virtually impossible to purchase. Complete with brass adjuster and crisp maker's and inspector's stamps, slightest handling age on belt edges.... **$675**

M1855 accoutrement belt with a stamped brass "US" plate with lead-filled back. The black harness leather belt is 40" long, $395.

KP photo/
Wisconsin Veterans
Museum collection

Accoutrements that can be definitively identified as having been made in the Confederacy are extremely rare. This Selma, Alabama, produced cap box is worth, $1,250-$1,700.

The square shaped front and lead-finial are two characteristics often associated with Confederate cap boxes.

Cap Pouches

Confederate

Extremely rare, lead-finial, nice condition with crude, hand-sewn construction, Soldier's initials, "J.W.H." cut into the underside of outside flap. Except for the tip of the leather closure tab, this is a nice lead-finial C.S. pouch. **$1,250**

Box brought home by Michael Moyer, 46th Regiment Illinois Volunteers. Separately applied latch tab, strong hand-stitched seams on all edges, single, wide belt loop on the reverse, cast-lead finial, constructed of excellent-condition, brown-russet leather with excellent finish. The latch tab is connected to the front flap by being sewn to the outside with two rows of vertical blonde stitching, then the tab passes through a bottom slot on the front flap to engage the lead finial. In addition, the side ears of the cap pouch are sewn directly to the front flap with blonde thread. The latch tab is missing, the very end having broken off at the hole that accepts the finial. **$1,495**

Rare, single-loop, lead finial Confederate cap pouch made of hand-stitched, dark-brown leather. Closure tab's tip is missing, as are two small sidepieces attached to the inner flap. Otherwise, a solid, pliable C.S. pouch. **$1,150**

Percussion cap pouch manufactured using leather reclaimed from an S. Isaac, Campbell & Co., London, marked accoutrement. S. Isaac, Campbell & Co. supplied numerous articles of war to the fledgling Confederacy. Occasionally, knapsacks, cartridge boxes, belts, cap pouches, swords, buttons, and firearms of English manufacture are encountered bearing Isaac & Campbell's mark. This is the only truly Confederate-manufactured accoutrement bearing the Isaac & Campbell mark. This is a case of their having reclaimed their own damaged material. Confederate armory workers reused the leather from damaged accoutrements to make new ones. This remanufactured cap pouch includes the classic Confederate lead finial and the wide, single belt loop. Box in excellent condition throughout, even retains its vent pick. **$3,600**

Federal cap box, Confederate factory converted to CS box, **$550-$750.**

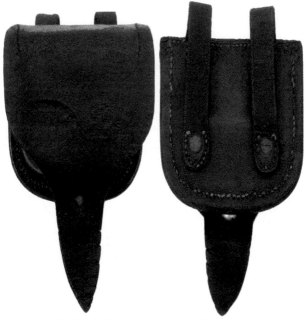

*The classic Federal cap pouch had a shield-shaped flap
and two belt straps, $165-$195.*

The maker's stamp is still visible on this cap pouch flap. Such examples will sell for between $165 and $195.

U.S.

1863-dated, brown, cap pouch with Maine maker's stamp, near-mint condition (no wool or pick inside). The leather is a pretty brown color with much life, stamped on the inner flap, "Carcelon & Covell 1863 Lewiston Me." **$235**

Regulation mid-war cap pouch with a Model 1839 small "US" cartridge box plate attached to the front flap by means of the plate loops being bent over inside the flap. **$245**

Excellent regulation Union specimen, maker unknown, super finish on leather, embossed decorative edge line impressed around the perimeter of outer flap—an added feature not seen on government contract boxes. **$169**

Excellent, russet-brown Union army cap pouch with remnants of lamb's wool still inside. Leather is somewhat dry, and the overall condition rates very good. Inside the inner flap is a name written in pencil (perhaps "Williams"). **$150**

Early war-style black leather cap pouch, front flap subtly shaped to resemble the shield profile of the cartridge box flap, base with brass finial, and reverse with sewn and riveted belt loops, closure billet intact. Leather shows expected wear, but remains pliable. Interior has worn remains of lamb's wool cap barrier and retains original wire cone pick, no visible markings. **$125**

Stamped, "Watertown Arsenal 1864," complete with interior wool, missing pick, light crazing on outside leather, very-good condition. **$325**

Marked, "CS Storms," shows use and age. **$135**

Black saddle leather percussion with the shield-shaped front and the applied closing tab stitched on with a single early-style line of stitching. Two narrow belt loops at the back with no reinforcement rivets, leather and tab excellent, no wool inside. **$250**

KP photo/Wisconsin Veterans Museum collection

*From clockwise starting upper left: Union issued highly finished leather box for percussion caps (3" tall by 3" wide), **$275;** Union issued black leather box for percussion caps (3-1/2" tall by 3-1/2" wide), **$275;** Union issued black leather, shield-front flap percussion cap box (3-3/4" high by 3-3/4" wide), **$250;** Confederate black leather box for percussion caps (3-1/2" tall by 3" wide), **$2,850.***

Union cavalry pistol cartridge box, $165-$250.

Cartridge Boxes, Muskets and Rifles, Confederate

Confederate
Cartridge Box

A Confederate-made cartridge box carried by Private Daniel W. Kline of Company F, 25th Virginia Infantry, into the flap of which he carved his name, "D.W. Kline." Very-fine condition, with the leather in good shape and the original leather strap still intact. Pvt. Kline served with the 25th Virginia and was captured in the very early days of the war in the Battle of Rich Mountain, Virginia, in July 1861. He was under the command of Confederate Colonel John Pegram who led his men against 2,000 of General McClellan's federal troops. Pegram was forced to surrender 555 Confederates on July 13 due to the fact that he was outflanked by McClellan's men. Private Kline was one of these 555 men. He was paroled and exchanged in August 1862. This identified Confederate cartridge box is beautifully homemade with crossed "X-"style harness straps. **$4,500**

Large 8" x 9" tarred leather box for .69-caliber smoothbore musket, round brass finial, excellent condition, white linen strapping sling with original leather reinforced buckle ties. (You can see where they laid across the tar on the box's front.) The two tin liners are reproductions, but otherwise 100% original. Wonderful, early Civil War cartridge box with very strong Southern/Confederate association (superb collection provenance). **$5,000**

U.S.

.58 Rifle Enfield

Classic example of what many U.S. and C.S. soldiers carried with their Enfield rifle muskets. Rig is in superb condition, box is near mint and marked inside outer flap with maker's name and 1861 date, original tin liner, buff leather latch tab, and all the straps and buckles are firmly in place. Standard U.S. example shoulder strap, oval U.S. inspector's cartouche visible near where strap meets box, shows slight handling age, never cut for the eagle "breastplate." **$1,395**

.58 Rifle Mann's Patent

Large 7" x 8" box for rifled musket, clear "US" oval embossed on flap, "Mann Patents" around the edge, retains pull-up tin liner with finger loop, torn closing strap. Complete sling strap arrangement, several pieces need restoration. **$475**

Model 1855

Dark leather box has no maker's mark, leather is dry with surface crazing; seams and tabs are intact, sling has lots of crazing and a repaired break, box has oval brass U.S. plate, and sling has circular brass eagle plate. **$175**

Model 1861

Fine example, early-war-pattern .58-caliber cartridge box. Latch tab secured by single row of stitching only (no rivet), the belt loops are sewn and riveted, and the bottom buckles are stitched in place. Box's finish is very good with just some light surface scuffs and crazing, unmarked in any fashion, the front flap is cut for the box plate (not present). **$435**

Model 1863

Manufactured by, "Edwin A. Crossman & Co., Newark, NJ." 1864 contract for 15,000 sets of "Infantry Accoutrements." This is complete with U.S. sub-inspector stamp, leather is in absolutely excellent condition. **$1,250**

Excavated, Enfield combination gun tool, $85-$95.

Model 1864

Standard 1864 box with the latch tab, buckles, and belt loops all secured by rivets and stitching, front flap nicely embossed with the "US" in an oval panel, overall condition very-good to fine with nice leather finish, tin liners inside, embellished with the soldier's name, "Hilliard," scratched into inner flap. Also remnants of two old paper tags inside the outer flap, neither legible except for one which has, "17 W?M?" The outer flap shows evidence of once having a box plate (no longer present) over the embossed "US" mark.

.... **$365**

.58 Rifle

Very solid and strong box, excellent finish on leather surfaces, inner flap deeply and largely stamped, "J. Boyd & Sons Boston/Manufacturers of ARMY Accoutrements." Front flap has large-size "US" oval cartridge box plate with lovely light age patina secured with original leather thong. "US" plate design is the Boyd & Sons die style. Box has soldier-removed roller buckles and back belt loops show obvious evidence that box was worn on the waist belt, not from a shoulder strap during the war. This box definitely saw service during the Civil War. **$435**

Very solid, faint "Condict" maker's stamp and shows evidence of actually being used with a rack number stenciled inside. **$425**

The Model 1864, cartridge box is distinguished by having an embossed "US" on the flap (shown on page 34) rather than a separate brass plate. These late war boxes, with slings, sell for $650-$950.

Cartridge Boxes, Carbines

Confederate
Carbine
Inscribed, "W B H, CO E 11 RE VA CALV ROS BRE, MAY 1 1864." William
  B. Hoover enlisted at New Market, Virginia, on January 2, 1863. Co. E
  was initially known as, "Potomac Mounted Riflemen or Valley Mounted
  Riflemen," and established as a mounted rifle company, near-mint condition.
  .... **$9,900**

U.S.
Carbine, Burnside
Black leather carbine box for the .54 cartridge. Complete with wood block for 20
  cartridges and both inner flaps and one horizontal belt loop on back. The two
  buckles with button have been removed so it could be worn on waist belt, has
  maker, "JE Condice 57 White St. New York," on inner flap. **$325**

Manufactured by W.H. Wilkinson, Springfield, Massachusetts. Box is in excellent
  condition with no flaking of leather, closing tab complete, and original wood
  interior complete. Strong, "US Ordnance Dept.," mark on front flap.
  .... **$1,295**

Maynard
Maker-marked "Hoover Calhoun & Co. New York." The wooden block liner holds
  20 rounds of Maynard carbine ammunition. Some crackling to the surface
  finish on the leather, but solid and 100% complete. **$395**

Carbine
Kittredge & Co. cartridge box complete with lid spring and belt attachments on
  back. Said to have been issued with Henry rifles and Frank Wesson carbines.
  This box has no dents and has a wonderful mellow patina. **$1,295**

Mann's Patent cavalry carbine box, has patent date, "1864," but was later converted into an Indian War Cavalry box with a wood block that accommodated 32 .45/50 cartridges. The box is in good condition with only one small end panel that fastens to the front flap missing. **$350**

Union cavalry carbine leather cartridge box in solid middle grade condition. The outside flap is pliable and complete, but has surface flaking. Both iron roller buckles are intact, but the end of the leather closure tab is missing. The wood cartridge block remains intact inside. The box is crisply marked, "E.A. Crossman & Co. Newark, N.J.," on the inside flap. **$295**

Carbine cartridge box in outstanding condition. Measures about 9" x 2" x 5", leather in near-perfect condition. **$475**

Regulation box for holding 20 rounds of Joslyn or Spencer ammunition. Crisp, "J. Davy," maker's stamp on outer flap, wooden block liner inside, both buckles firmly in place as are all the straps. Excellent condition with only the lightest wear. **$365**

Cavalry soldier's cartridge box nicely marked, "J Davy & Co/Newark NJ," on the front flap. Very worn, but a really good display item. Damaged latch tab, no bottom buckles and no wooden block inside. Both belt loops intact with damage on one. **$65**

Really fine condition regulation Civil War cavalry carbine cartridge box. It is all complete with undamaged belt loops, buckles (with about all the japanned black finish), and latch tab. It has its original wooden cartridge block. Inside it is maker-marked, "DINGEE & LORIGAN MAKERS NEW YORK." Implement pouch is fine as is inside flap. Just minimal crazing on the front flap. ...**$256**

Model 1855, .58 caliber, cartridge box and shoulder sling with two plates, $750-$1,150.

KP Photos/Wisconsin Veterans Museum collection

Black leather cartridge container with brass finial, two japanned iron roller buckles and five-compartment interior of tinned-iron. Two rear sling loops. Front of box is incised "T.B. Thaxton, A/L." The box was recovered from the Antietam battlefield by a soldier who sent it home. It was most likely carried by a member of Laws Brigade. Because of the Confederate association, this box would sell for $3,500-$4,000.

Brown leather cartridge box with double tin insert attached to leather shoulder strap with brass eagle breastplate attached by leather thong through metal loops. Cartridge box has double closure flaps with inside flapped implement pocket. Main flap is scalloped, no fastener, with oval brass "US" plate on front. Box has horizontal and vertical loops on back, with two buckles on bottom to fit either shoulder or waist belt. The box held 40 rounds of .58 cal. Minié ball paper cartridges. A complete cartridge box like this will sell for $650-$1,100.

KP photo/Wisconsin Veterans Museum collection

Cartridge Boxes, Pistols, and Revolvers

U.S.

Pistol, Navy

Externally, looks like tall version of USN fuse box. Single, wide belt loop on the back, the box's inside has an envelope or implement pouch and inner flap. The front cover is embossed "USN," the inner flap is marked, "Navy Yard Phila 1861." Box's finish is excellent as is overall condition, missing tin liner, small tear in latch tab. **$49**

Day's Patent

This box is quite ingenious. It consists of a wooden revolving cylinder drilled with holes that rests inside a tin carrier that, in turn, rests inside the leather box. The revolving wooden cylinder is designed to accept cartridges in the drilled holes. The user rotated the cylinder to remove each cartridge. Appears designed for revolver ammo or possibly Henry rifle ammo (holes appear to be roughly .45 caliber). The leather box itself is 4-1/2" by 4 1/2" by 1-7/10" in size, and is shaped with a rounded bottom, leather cover flap accepts brass finial centered on box's front, back has two leather upright belt loops with small extensions of leather strapping at top with small buttonholes in extension ends. Condition is good to very good with some finish wear and flaking. The patent for this device was issued during the Civil War. **$975**

Revolver, Navy

5" x 7" black saddle-leather waist-carried cartridge box. "USN" stamped in crisp oval on the outer flap. Outside of box is dry, but fairly smooth, crazing on extended belt loop, but still solid, retains inner flap, closing tab, and the oft-times missing oval accoutrement pouch with cover. Box is lined with a six-compartment tin liner for the Colt .36-caliber cartridge blocks. This box could use a coat of leather preservative, but it is quite presentable and very rare, because most of these had the accoutrement pouch cut out and wooden block tacked in for cartridge weapons. **$650**

Revolver

Plant's, rare box designed to be used with Plant's cartridge revolver, looks just like a miniature carbine-style cartridge box with a delicately scalloped front flap outline. It is roughly half as wide as a carbine box and 80% as tall. It has two belt loops on the reverse and a brass finial. It was made with no inner flap nor an inner implement pouch. The condition is excellent with good finish (just some light surface crazing). The front flap's bottom portion is shaped in a semi-shield shape (coming to a point). The left and right sides of the box are rounded at the top to meet the front flap's contour when closed. **$345**

4" x 6" black saddle-leather cartridge box for two wooden block packets of .36 percussion cartridges. Smooth black leather, only the slightest crazing, crisp, "T.J. Shepard," cartouche over script "US" on the front flap, two or three large areas of crazing on the box's inside face, this does not show nor detract, excellent closing tab with brass acorn finial and belt loops at back. **$350**

Navy, 5" x 7" black saddle-leather waist carried cartridge box. "USN" stamped in crisp oval on the outer flap. Outside of box is dry, but fairly smooth, crazing on extended belt loop, but still solid, retains inner flap, closing tab, and the oft-times missing oval accoutrement pouch with cover. Box is lined with a six-compartment tin liner for the Colt .36-caliber cartridge blocks. This box could use a coat of leather preservative, but it is quite presentable and very rare, because most of these had the accoutrement pouch cut out and wooden block tacked in for cartridge weapons. **$650**

Black saddle-leather cartridge box, front heavily crazed, inspector's cartouche in center, good tab and belt loops. **$165**

Made for the .44 revolver, this is the scarcer of the two patterns being about 15% larger than those made for .36-caliber revolvers, overall excellent condition. **$195**

Fuse Pouches

Confederate

About the size of a regular cartridge box, scalloped front flap, finial is brass, but more of a fat button, inner flap with ears, softer and thinner than the outer flap, box sides are rounded at the top and the sides taper in toward the bottom, just two narrow belt loops sewn on the back, some surface cracking and flexing on the flap top. Inside were two Civil War envelopes that were addressed to a woman in Vicksburg, Mississippi, both of them stamped, no letters. Box is in great condition and has no maker's marks. Belt has been married to the box. The buckle is an old roller-type buckle that is indicative of C.S. use. **$950**

U.S.
Navy

Regulation USN fuse box used to carry fuses by the sailors on their waist belts. Overall fine and solid marked, "Navy Yard/NY/1863," on the front flap, finish has alligator crackling. **$149**

Deeply marked on the outer flap, "Navy Yard/NY/1862," has a rack number "33" stamped into the leather, excellent condition, leather finish has a little crazing. **$225**

Black saddle-leather belt pouch, 3" x 3-1/2" x 2". Shield-shaped front flap, inside crisply stamped, "U.S.N.Y./Boston," within a cartouche, fine condition with closing strap, brass finial, and single belt loop. **$375**

> **"One Maryland lady said she 'could stand the shells if one, nice dressed soldier would kill all the durn Rebs'."**
>
> —*Sgt. M.O. Young,*
> *9th Georgia Infantry*

Leather, U.S. navy fuse box, $250-$325.

On this particular example, the embossed maker's mark was found under the flap on the body of the box. Marked examples are always more valuable than unmarked specimens.

Confederate, regulation, tin-drum canteen, $750-$1,150.

Canteens

Confederate
Tin Drum
4-1/4" d, 1-1/4" w, japanned tin (sheet iron), convex front and flat back with large belt loop, complete with cork, japanned finish 80%, excellent condition. **$200**

Drum style, a bit over 4-1/4" d, flat backside with tall belt loop soldered on, front has convex face, screw cap spout, fine condition, no dents. **$165**

Nice condition, original linen sling, flat on one side and slightly convex on the other, soldier's initials and lots of faint writing on both sides. This style of canteen is often attributed to Confederate usage. **$1,150**

Wood Drum
Cedar, completely untouched with original, coarse cotton sling, pencil identification of "Lt. Col. Benjamin Thompson," a New York officer who ultimately served in the U.S. Colored Troops. Probably a battlefield pickup as there are numerous other names on the reverse. **$3,200**

Excellent Confederate Gardner-pattern cedar canteen, fine overall with only minor shrinkage, partial old initials carved in one side, complete with tin spout and original, coarse cotton sling, beautiful patina overall. **$2,650**

Excellent condition, 7-1/2" d, one side in crude carving says, "Look Out Mt. Nov. 28, 1863 Tenn.," other side says "C A 4th C.S.A.," intact leather strap. .. **$520**

U.S.
Model 1858
Nice example of concentric ring Civil War issue canteen, brown wool cover shows only light age, original stopper (no shoulder strap). **$350**

KP photo/Wisconsin Veterans Museum collection

This Confederate wooden-drum canteen has 11 short barrel staves on obverse and reverse wooden disks and is held together with two steel bands. It has a wooden spout at top, three iron stap bands and a leather strap with two buckles. With no solid provenance, a wooden-drum canteen will sell for about $2,500.

KP photo/Wisconsin Veterans Museum collection

Confederate wooden-drum canteen made like a wooden barrel with short staves at bottom and lid. Staves are held in place with an iron band on each end. Three iron loops held strap. A 3/4" hole was drilled in side with turned wooden mouthpiece, $2,500.

KP photo/Wisconsin Veterans Museum collection

Confederate tin-drum canteen made of three-piece construction. A bull's-eye, "CS" and one concentric ring are stamped on the two end pieces. Three tin loops are soldered to the sides for a strap. A leather cavalry sword knot runs through these loops and is probably not original to the canteen. A bullet entry hole is on side of the canteen and an exit hole is on the other. Though this style of canteen has been widely reproduced, a solid example with plausible provenance will sell for $3,500+.

KP Photo/Wisconsin Veterans Museum Selection

Confederate tin canteen features three tin loops soldered to the side. A coarse sewn canvas strap remains in the loops but has been cut off. Metal stopper and cord do not appear to be original to the canteen. Tin-drum canteens without provenance are often represented as Confederate and may sell for $800-$1,150.

Model 1858, Union, bull's-eye canteen with butternut cover, $400-$525.

Model 1858, smooth-type canteen with butternut cover, $250-$325.

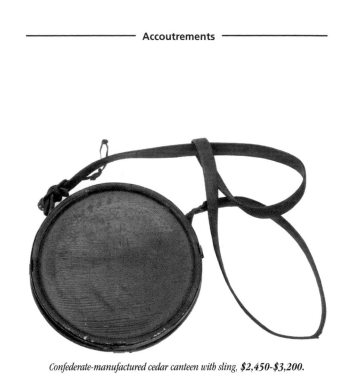

Confederate-manufactured cedar canteen with sling, ***$2,450-$3,200.***

*Even though the stopper is missing, the complete leather sling added
dramatically to the value of the Confederate-styled canteen.*

Regulation M1858 U.S. army smooth-side canteen complete with all three brackets, pewter spout, brown wool original cover, repeated rectangular pattern designs in the cloth. Much more interesting than the common brown wool specimens. This one was covered by the soldier in the field just as prescribed by directive when canteens were issued without covers, great example (no stopper). **$295**

Nice solid bull's-eye with very scarce dark blue wool cover in very good condition, a couple small age/wear holes, but very appealing, 80% of the original cloth shoulder strap which is broken and frayed, Philadelphia maker's mark stamped into spout. **$550**

Spherical tinned-iron canteen with smooth-sides, three strap loops, and tin spout. Painted white with owner's initials, "MHH," in a floral design worked in red and green, worn finish, body holes rusted through the base on both sides, retains remnant of a crimson tassel and old address label, which may aid in identification. **$125**

Very good condition with cotton strap, original plug, and guides for the carrying strap. Believed to be from the New Jersey National Guard, circa 1860, nice brown wool jean covering. **$312**

Excellent example (no stopper) of regulation Model 1858 smooth-side army canteen complete with the full brownish-gray wool cover and the full length (unbroken) "folded and sewn" cotton shoulder strap. Interestingly, this one was actually issued and is not a surplus example. Faintly visible on one side of the canteen in worn black stenciled letter "E" and what appears to be a worn "6." **$455**

About perfect condition standard smooth-side canteen, original stopper still attached to top bracket with chain, tin spout pattern (as opposed to pewter) attributed to manufacture in St. Louis or Cincinnati. **$169**

*Model 1858, Union, bull's-eye canteen with blue cover, **$400-$525**.*

*Model 1858, bull's-eye canteen without cover, **$165-$200**.*

Model 1858, smooth-type canteen with butternut cover (St. Louis Arsenal soldered tin spout), $275-$350.

Holsters

Confederate
Revolver

Sound, brown leather holster, 12-3/8", missing flap tab and bottom belt loop loose. **$495**

Nice condition, hand-stitched, brown leather holster for a .44-caliber revolver. The impressions in the leather suggest it probably had an Adams or Kerr-type revolver in it, the leather remains very pliable. **$550**

Holster in great condition, no maker's mark found, but came from an estate in Georgia, back loop torn in the past and fixed with hand brass rivets..... **$300**

.36 caliber, overall fine condition, hand-sewn, full-flap holster, made entirely of brown-finished pigskin. Constructed with the flap cut so that it ends in a strap passed through a sewn loop on the holster's body (not made with a finial). Superb condition with no flaking, just showing light honest age, missing back belt loop. **$650**

Griswold, authentic Confederate revolver holster from famed Ted Meredith Confederate collection, "found in an old Gettysburg Museum collection with a Griswold and Gunnison revolver." This tooled-leather holster with full flap and closing tab has a rear belt loop riveted in place. There is a brass closing stud, the leather is soft and pliable, one visible area of repair is held with age-old wire reinforcement. Very rare and interesting piece with solid provenance. **$800**

KP photo/Wisconsin Veterans Museum collection

*At left, black leather holster, pattern 1851 for Colt Revolver, **$450.***
At right, glazed black leather pistol holster belonging to Col. George Bryant, 12th Wis.
*Vol. Inf. Because of the association with Col. Bryant, the value is close to **$1,500.***

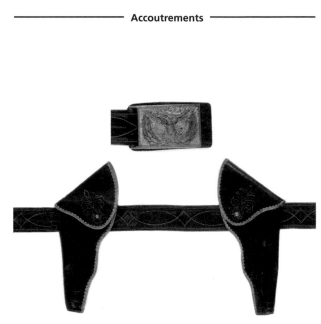

This belt and holsters was worn by Assistant Surgeon William A. Gordon, 10th Wisconsin Volunteer Infantry. The set consists of a black leather belt and two black leather holsters. The belt also features a brass officer's belt plate: an eagle clutching arrows and olive branches in talons, $2,500.

*Model 1851, sword belt rig with holster (upside down buckle, Confederate-made holster), **$1,400-$1,650.***

The crude stitching on the closing strap is unusual on this Confederate holster. Items manufactured in the South generally reflect good workmanship.

*Confederate, .36 caliber, leather
holster, $650-$795.*

U.S.

Model 1849 Colt

Made for Colt's pocket revolver, large flap and brass stud closure, complete with belt loop and barrel plug. **$195**

This was for a revolver with a 5" barrel, excellent condition, good solid body contour. Not limp or flat. Has 90-95% original surface finish with a very shallow network of drying cracks on the face. Rear of holster, flap, and belt loop have no cracks, flap has deep finish cracking along the top bend, 1-1/2" break in the flap at bend's rear, full-length closing strap with flexed finish. **$395**

Model 1860 Colt Army

Very-good condition with minor flaking, but pliable leather, closing tab is complete. All seam stitching is strong, missing bottom plug, "S J" and five-pointed star carved into flap. **$595**

Maker-marked, "Wm Kinsey & Co. Newark–NJ." Holster has bottom plug and original closing tab, very-good condition leather, could easily still be used. Pencil identification on inside of flap, "James Kelly 1861-5." **$695**

Holster and waist belt with brass hardware, no belt plate. **$432**

Model 1851 Colt Navy

Complete with very nice russet-brown saddle leather, small single belt loop on rear, closing tab appears to have been re-riveted a long time ago and is complete, holster has plugged bottom. **$725**

Appears to be made of pigskin, Army-style flap and front pouch for percussion caps. Appears to fit a Colt Navy revolver, stitching is weak and in some places, gone, belt loop is missing on rear. **$295**

Original revolver holster that fits the Colt M1851 Navy perfectly, holster in great condition and comes with an original U.S. belt and belt plate with arrow hooks, rear belt loop is intact, but slightly curled from hanging. **$600**

Regulation cavalry holster with clear "Condict" maker's stamp on flap, overall very good with tear in belt loop and missing plug, otherwise quite nice with good leather finish. **$275**

Saddle

Pair of pommel holsters 12-3/8" and 5-1/4" x 1-3/4" at the top. There is a copper 7/16" band around the bottom. The 4-3/8" connecting strap has been re-stitched by a previous owner. Other than that, the holsters are very good.

.... **$325**

"We rubbed our guns & accouterments and cleaned about our tents ready for inspection...I went on duty today and drilled like thunder."

—*Adjutant A.L. Pool,
19th Mississippi Infantry*

Slings and Boots

U.S. and Confederate

Carbine Boot, U.S.

Black saddle leather "doughnut" with strap and buckle, fine condition, held the muzzle to the saddle of a variety of Civil War carbines. The firearm was attached to the carbine sling over the cavalryman's shoulder. **$85**

Sling Buckle, U.S., Carbine

Excellent condition, dug, Union cavalry carbine sling buckle. This buckle was excavated from Wilson's cavalry position at the Battle of Nashville, Tennessee. It has perfect form and both hooks intact, buckle is uncleaned as dug. **$145**

Sling, U.S., Carbine

Nice example of classic carbine sling, a Bannerman surplus example that has had the leather shortened by 4". **$495**

Sling, Rifle, Confederate

Made from cotton during the South's leather shortage. Two-inch cotton was folded double and hand stitched down each edge. Small amounts of leather were then sewn on to form the end loop and adjustment strip. A doubled iron wire keeper was then sewn onto the end to serve as adjuster. The completed product was totally Confederate-made, excellent condition. **$1,050**

Sling, Rifle, Enfield

78", leather in good condition with some flaking and cracking, sling is a little weak at brass hook, pliable leather. **$350**

U.S., regulation issue, enlisted man's belt rig, 1855 pattern, $295-$350.

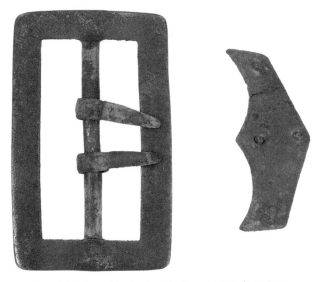

Excavated, Union carbine sling brass buckle and belt tip, $145-$170.

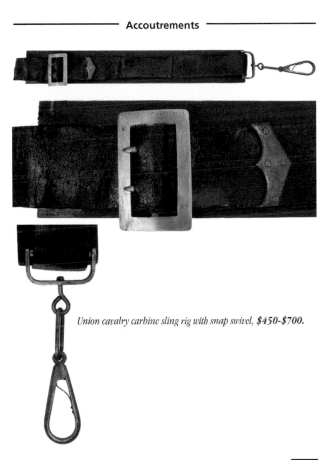

Union cavalry carbine sling rig with snap swivel, $450-$700.

Spurs

Confederate

Clearly a southern spur of undetermined origin, it's a variation of the so-called
"Mississippi" spur. More are found on Virginia sites than Mississippi sites,
neck missing off this excavated example, recovered in the Shenandoah Valley.
.... **$75**

C.S. Richmond Arsenal spur that may have been excavated, and then cleaned
many years ago. Very dark reddish-brown patina left in places, signs of heavy
usage. **$345**

Early pick-up from Tennessee, complete with rowel, several file marks and
irregular-cut strap slots. **$325**

Enlisted Man

Nice, non-excavated, cleaned specimen complete with rowel, many file marks on
strap plates. Many have been dug in Virginia. **$345**

Richmond spur dug in the Antietam Campaign area, super nice with attached
leather remnant. **$395**

U.S.

Enlisted Man

Beautiful condition, Tennessee dug, regulation issue Union enlisted man's
cavalry spur, slick brown patina with practically no ground action. **$75**

Brass with steel starred rowel, cavalry and horse artillery standard issue spur.
A single in excellent condition. **$75**

Excavated, Leech and Rigdon Memphis, Tennessee, CS-marked officer's cavalry spur, $1,850-$2,000.

"Rooster neck" Union cavalry spur dug from the Union cavalry camps at Murfreesboro occupied by General David Stanley's troops after the Battle of Stone's River. **$75**

Nice matched pair of dug, regulation spurs with rowels rusted. **$135**

Pair of regulation cavalry enlisted spurs with rowels intact and nice brass color. **$259**

A nice pair of regulation cavalry enlisted spurs with beautiful aged-brass color, still have the rare leather straps and buckles present for attaching to a pair of boots, very-fine condition, one spur lacks rowel. **$285**

Officer

Style of spur advertised in the 1864 Schuyler Hartley & Graham catalog. It employed the "box" locking device popular in European period designs. A box fit in the shoe, the spike fit into the box. Note the screw heads on the side were purely ornamental. The rowel is also pure ornament, as the rotating hole is intentionally way too big, so that whatever angle is used it never protrudes to jab the horse. This great looking pair is a true "gentleman's" spur. Non-excavated pair, everything intact. **$250**

Nice set complete with original belts/buckles, nickeled brass, essentially the same as enlisted spurs except for the bright silver finish, some minor spotty age to finish, most probably cleanable, leather flexible, lacking finish, pair. **$295**

Steel with steel starred rowels, typical pair of officer's spurs, excellent condition. **$195**

Excavated, regulation Union cavalry spur, $85-$100.

CHAPTER 2

BAYONETS, KNIVES, AND PIKES

Blades of one variety or another hold the fascination of many Civil War collectors. The idea of soldiers marching into battle with bayonets affixed or brandishing large D-Guard Bowies and pikes in bloody hand-to-hand combat are hard notions to dislodge from the spirited collector's mind. Even though blade-related wounds of any variety (including sword or saber-inflicted) were minimal during the war, the weapons that could have delivered such a wound are at the top of many collectors' "premium pieces" list.

Bayonets are a rather straightforward item to collect. Rarely reproduced, plentiful, and with an endless variety, a collector can step into the bayonet arena with a minimum amount of cash and proceed to assemble a very engaging collection.

Knives, on the other hand, get a bit cloudy. It seems that most dealers have forgotten that the Bowie-style blade was available to folks both south and north of the Mason-Dixon line. In fact, a great many actually were manufactured in England. Nevertheless, most Bowies are sold as "Confederate" and if not, very few dealers are quick to deny that these were favorites of Rebel troops. Furthermore, since knives were not an issue item, it is extremely difficult to ascertain whether or not a blade actually campaigned with a soldier or sat on a shelf back in some upstate farm.

.577 caliber Enfield saber bayonet, $185-$225.

Pikes are even more difficult to directly associate with Civil War service. Apart from the documented specimens manufactured in Confederate arsenals, many pikes spent the war propped in armory racks. Regardless, there exists a powerful romantic image of the citizen soldier picking up a pike (in the absence of a more potent weapon) to defend his nation and his rights. Therefore, even though there are very few documented incidents of pikes being used in combat during the Civil War, they are one of the most sought-after edged relics.

Collecting Hints

Pros:
- Due to the materials involved, bayonets, knives, and pikes are plentiful.
- There is a wide variety of items.
- A lot of primary research has been done to identify various knife and pike makers, making authentication easier.

Cons:
- Hand-forged items such as pike heads or D-Guard Bowie knives are easily reproduced and aged to appear like authentic, period items.
- Because iron is the primary material, these items are prone to rust if not stored in a very dry environment.
- A lot of nostalgia is attached to the notion of the Bowie knife-wielding Confederate. Therefore, dealers are quick to assign a Rebel attribution to any blade that vaguely resembles a Bowie. A collector may have to pay premium prices simply to acquire a representative knife carried by either a Confederate or Yankee.

Availability ★★★★★
Price ★★
Reproduction Alert ★★

.577 caliber Enfield triangular socket bayonet and scabbard, **$85-$115**.

Bayonets

Confederate

Boyle and Gamble saber bayonet with adapter for use on the Model 1841 rifle.
....**$2,850**

Saber bayonet made by Cook & Brother, New Orleans in 1861 or 1862, marked
"1472." Research suggests that this piece was issued to one of the Alabama
regiments: 20th Infantry to 30th Infantry or thereabouts. Condition is superb,
bayonet lightly cleaned, pleasing appearance, side spring intact, fastening
button missing. **$2,150**

Made into body hook. Dug from the battlefield area of Richmond, Virginia. Rare
Confederate-manufactured by Tredegar Iron Works of Richmond. **$395**

.58 Rifle

Uncleaned, original condition, 19-5/16" x 1-1/8" V-ground blade with very heavy
patina with medium rust overall, short blade tip, perhaps 3/16" (worn, not
broken). Solid brass handle, 4-1/2" long, number "39" stamped near the
guard is the only marking present, which is typical of this bayonet pattern.
....**$850**

Fayetteville Armory, Confederate Fayetteville Arsenal bayonet recovered in
Fredericksburg, Virginia in the late 1960s, good condition, blade intact with
small pits and rust (dug condition), stamp on handle, "M," as several of them
were. **$2,250**

Georgia Armory, made by the Georgia State Armory in Milledgeville, Georgia,
in 1862, this saber bayonet has a heavy 22-3/4" blade and measures 26-1/2"
overall. The single fuller blade is smooth and semi bright from hilt to point,
near-mint brass hilt with beautiful untouched patina, working lock spring
and release. It was manufactured in the old state penitentiary at Milledgeville.
The armory converted sporting rifles, altered flintlocks, and manufactured

the rare Georgia Armory Rifle based on the Model 1855 Harpers Ferry. The armory also manufactured saber bayonets for its rifles. Lower serial numbers 16, 17, and 32 are brass hilted. Higher numbers, 127 and 135 are wooden hilted. The armory never returned to the brass hilted model, so at most, only one out of four were brass hilted. The armory continued using wood slabbed hilts for the remainder of its full production of less than four hundred rifles and bayonets. It is reasonably estimated that less than ten survive of all models combined. The armory manufactured weapons as opposed to altering for only four months, from December 1862 until March 1863, most likely due to a lack of raw materials. The changeover from brass to wooden hilts would tend to support that theory. **$5,800**

U.S.
.54 Rifle, Model 1841
Ames brass-hilted saber bayonet for a New Hampshire state contract alteration of the Model 1841 rifle measuring 26-1/2" overall, with a 22" semi-yataghan iron blade. Crisp Ames address at left ricasso, blade tarnished but fine, mustard colored brass hilt with spring release, no scabbard. **$450**

.58 Rifle Musket, Model 1855
Bright steel triangular bayonet with crisp, "US," at the ricasso. Black saddle leather with sheet brass drag has slight crazing on bottom third, otherwise excellent. Buff leather frog with the 1864 eight-rivet reinforcing arrangement. **$325**

.58 Rifle Musket, Model 1861
A good, cleanable, old, brown 1861 pattern socket, end of socket has small crimp prohibiting it from passing over the gun's muzzle. Scabbard present, but lacks frog and tip. **$69**

A super example for the Models 1855, 1861, 1863, 1864, and Special Model 1861 rifle muskets, shows just light age. **$155**

*Confederate manufactured Boyle and Gamble saber
bayonet (bullet struck in battle), $900-$1,350.*

*Normally, a damaged item will not sell for as much as an
unmolested example. This is not the case with this bayonet with
the collapsed Miniè ball still imbedded in the handle.*

Three bayonet scabbards all made of leather and brass. The scabbard attached to a belt with a move-able leather loop sewn to top of scabbard. Bayonets have a much higher survival rate than the leather scabbard. Values range from $80-$150 for just the scabbard.

KP photo/Wisconsin Veterans Museum collection

Cleaned, bright and shiny condition, .58 caliber bayonet with "US" stamped on ricasso. **$89**

Really shiny bayonet in a top-notch, black harness leather scabbard of seven-rivet design. **$425**

Standard .58 caliber bayonet with faint "US" stamp on the ricasso and a small "J" below the "US." Clean steel color overall, with light age patina. **$135**

.58 Rifle, Model 1841
Saber bayonet for the Colt conversion of the Model 1841 rifle, a very-good to fine condition example with great steel blade marked with crisp "1861" date on the ricasso, the brass handle is a nice mellow brass color and it has a serial number of 6,854 stamped into it. Complete with spring catch and button. **$289**

.58 Rifle, Model 1855
Saber bayonet, brass-handled for Model 1855 rifle. The 21-7/18" blade is slightly rounded at the tip, missing lock and spring, sharpened blade has a smooth dark patina, no scabbard, very-good condition. **$165**

.58 Rifle, Model 1863 Remington
Brass-handled saber bayonet and scabbard for the Model 1863 Remington "Zouave" rifle measuring 26" overall with a brilliant 20" semi-yataghan blade. Bayonet about mint. Scabbard very good with old repaired crack in leather about 6" from the drag. **$375**

.58 Rifle, P.S. Justice
Rare, brass-handled saber bayonet for the P.S. Justice two-band rifle measuring 26" overall with a tarnished 21-1/2" semi-yataghan blade, mellow brass hilt with spring catch, no scabbard. **$435**

.69 Musket, Model 1795
Quite rare 1795-1812 pattern .69 friction-fit triangular socket bayonet, smooth, brown, never-cleaned patina. **$125**

.69 Musket, Model 1816

19-1/4" overall, triangular 16-3/4" blade, "US" stamped ricasso, bayonet is smooth plum and steel mix patina. **$185**

Early .69 Model 1816 triangular socket bayonet picked up at Stones River in the early 1900s, very solid with the "U.S." marking still visible. **$125**

Marking of "U" above the "US" stamp on the ricasso and has an "E 43" mark on the socket. Does not appear to have any significant pitting mixed with the brown patina. **$135**

Overall very-good condition with a medium age patina and light patches of pitting. Has large "US" stamp on ricasso which tends to indicate earlier manufacture date.. **$120**

Socket bayonet for the Hewes & Phillips conversion musket, bright and shiny with "US" stamp at the ricasso, 1816-style socket (but longer) and long-length blade. **$145**

Friction fit triangular .69 socket bayonet in leather shaft portion of original scabbard. The bayonet has a smooth dark, never-cleaned aged patina. **$195**

South Carolina-marked Model 1816 socket bayonet in overall very-good condition with deep-brown age patina and deep "SC" stamp on the ricasso, pattern with the "S" above the "C" on the ricasso (the markings were put on by South Carolina by obliterating the "U" in the original "US" stamp. Also marked on the shank, "LWK," or, "LAK," and marked on the socket." "Z59." **$325**

.69 Musket, Model 1835

21" overall with a triangular 18-1/2" bright blade, crisp "US" at the ricasso. Square shoulders at the elbow differ from the Model 1855, .69 bayonet. **$195**

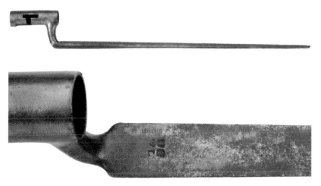

U.S. Model 1816, .69 caliber, friction-fit, triangular-socket bayonet, **$150-$185.**

.69 Musket, Model 1842

Overall fine condition with clean steel color and good US stamp on the ricasso.
.... **$195**

.69 Rifle Musket, Model 1835/42

18" socket bayonet has scalloped corners, face flute, back flutes carried through the elbow, socket complete with locking ring, ricasso has heavy, "A" stamped over and obscuring any U.S. surcharge that may have originally been there. The stamping is in the style of those attributed to 1835/42 bayonets refurbished for issue with the U.S. Model 1847 Musketoon. This bayonet maintains its original 18" length, however, with the 1847 Musketoon bayonets being shortened to 15". Bright finish in good polish has only a few age spots.
.... **$125**

.69 Rifle Musket, Model 1842

Really a fine example with clean steel color overall, clear "US" stamp, and nice pointy tip. **$145**

.69 Rifle Musket, Model 1855

21" overall with 17" triangular blade, good to fine condition. **$135**

For the Model 1842 Rifled Musket and used on the conversions, smooth plumbrown patina, would clean to fine, crisp "US" stamped on the ricasso. . **$155**

Scabbard, .58 Rifle, Musket, Model 1861

Attic brown, seven-rivet pattern, very solid with a good "just-found" look to it.
.... **$185**

Scabbard, .58 Rifle, Model 1863

Remington, near-mint example of the leather scabbard with brass mounts for use with the Remington "Zouave" rifle, brass-handled saber bayonet. Outstanding leather finish, great bright brass mounts, only defect is lightly separated back stitching, which does not affect the soundness of the scabbard.
.... **$195**

.69 Rifle, Plymouth/Whitney

Extremely rare, Navy 1862 Ames Dahlgreen bayonet from the ironclad gunboat U.S.S. Cincinnati. These bayonets are Bowie-style, made by Ames Swords for the Plymouth/Whitney Rifle. This was fashioned from a single brass casting. This bayonet has the original scabbard, blade is marked, "U.S.S. Cincinnati Cairo," "U.S.N. D.R. 1862," on the other side, "AMES MFG. CO. CHICOPEE MASS." Brass end on handle is marked "D.R." Scabbard is intact with plaque of Landsmans Mame who owned this bayonet. The piece is in original condition and has not been cleaned. Bayonet measures 17 1/8" from tip to back of handle. **$1,750**

Fine condition, Ames Dahlgren, crisp example dated and inspected 1864, excellent blade, fine grip, and sheath. Never polished or altered—missing only a couple of tiny brass pins on the drag. **$2,050**

Import

Bayonet, .54 Rifle, Austrian Lorenz

Four-sided Austrian bayonet recently excavated from the Confederate battle line at Stones River. **$85**

Complete with locking ring, unique four-sided bayonet with the spiral mortise, goes on the .54 caliber Lorenz. **$125**

Four-sided Austrian socket bayonet with a smooth, never-cleaned, attic-brown patina. **$150**

The quadrangular socket bayonet for the Lorenz rifle with overall gray and brown patina, some surface pitting in the socket. **$89**

Lorenz Bayonet in very-good condition with an excellent scabbard. **$475**

.577 Rifle Musket, Model 1853 Enfield

A nice brown metal triangular socket bayonet for the Enfield rifle with nice patina and areas of surface scale. **$85**

.58 caliber, Springfield, triangular-socket bayonet and scabbard, $150-$200.

Solid example of the Enfield socket bayonet for the Tower Enfield rifle muskets. Good steel color with no rust or pitting. **$125**

This one is brown and has some age crud on the socket, very solid, and should clean. **$79**

.577 Rifle, Model 1858 Enfield
Bayonet for the two-band Enfield rifled musket with both pressed leather grips intact and a smooth, dark, never-cleaned patina. **$195**

Enfield-pattern saber bayonet and scabbard measuring 28" overall with a bright 23" semi-yataghan blade. British proofs at the ricasso, hilt and pommel are iron, hard black leather, two-piece grips have diamond checkering. Good, solid black-leather scabbard with iron mounts. This bayonet was made for the P1856 Short Rifle. **$225**

.58 Rifle, French Import
Brown patina with age crud and light pits, this bayonet fits an imported French rifle. It looks like a Fayetteville, but the socket is a little smaller in diameter. **$85**

.70 Rifle, Brunswick
Saber bayonet with brass handle and 22" blade. The British Pattern 1845 Brunswick Rifle was purchased during the Civil War only by Confederate purchasing agent Caleb Huse. There are no known U.S. purchases of this musket and bayonet. Nice example with "G 640" stamped on the grip and light sharpening marks on the blade, no blade markings. **$175**

.69 Musket, Enfield
Enfield triangular-socket bayonet in original leather scabbard. The metal is smooth with an aged gray patina. The leather scabbard is very nice, no breaks or weak spots. **$295**

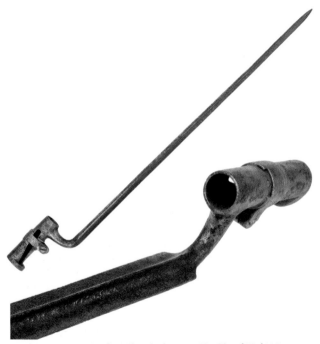

*Import, Austrian four-side socket bayonet, .54 caliber, **$85-$125**.*

Knives

Bowie

A hefty and substantial Civil War Sheffield Bowie that has a 7" spear-point blade. The ricasso is deeply marked, "IXL," in large characters. The grips are a lovely aged stag horn and the left slab has a wonderful silver escutcheon plate (oval, narrow and 1-1/4" wide) which is beautifully engraved, "M.A. O'Brien Co "B" 13th Regiment N.Y.S.M." This knife dates to 1861 when the 13th was organized under Colonel Abel Smith and left the state on April 13, 1861, under Lincoln's first call for troops. It served as infantry at Annapolis and Baltimore and was mustered out of service on August 6, 1861. The cross guard on this knife was intentionally removed during its period of use.
....**$1,150**

Excellent condition, dug, 13" Bowie knife. This knife was excavated from General Polk's 1863 winter camps along Duck River near Shelbyville, Tennessee. This knife is 100% complete lacking only the wooden grip. The blade was forged from a file, and numerous file teeth are still visible. .. **$650**

D-Guard Bowie

From Texas, 21" overall length with a 16-1/2" l double- edged blade, oval iron guard 3-3/4" l, tapered tang with copper or brass riveted walnut scales, copper or brass buttplate secured by two non-ferrous screws. Dark patina on all the metal, negligible pitting, handles are fine. **$500**

Authentic, non-excavated, blacksmith-made D-guard Bowie knife. Blacksmith-forged from old file blade. Teeth of the file are very prominent, somewhat crude, but very solid. A large and heavily constructed knife, overall length is 17-1/2" with a 12" dark blade. Multiple heavy hammer marks over entire blade. Semi-taper clip point blade. Grip looks to be made of pecan or walnut. The "D" itself is a thick, heavy hand-hammered forged iron guard. All in all, very typical of many of the D-guards that Confederate troops had made by local blacksmiths before they marched off to war. There is no doubt about this knife. This specimen is definitely *not* a Philippino- or Mexican-import such as are often encountered in the market, as well as being sold as original. Nor is this knife a postwar cane or field knife. This is an authentic specimen, and was manufactured to be carried off into the Civil War by Southern soldiers. **$2,275**

Confederate States Armory Bowie knife that is a rare product of the Confederate States Armory, Kenansville, North Carolina. This massive 16" spear-point Bowie is 100% authentic and original. This weapon is a piece of 1862-1864 Southern-made steel and walnut, with a unique tarred-leather grip covering, perhaps indicating its use as a Naval Cutlass. **$3,500**

Knife, Confederate

11" overall with a double-edged, spear-pointed, 7" blade made from a file. Still has the turned file handle with brass tang ferrule, fine condition, from the Bray Family, Fincastle, Virginia. **$1,250**

12-1/2" long with a hand forged, heavily used 7-3/4" single-edged blade and oval iron guard. Two-piece wooden grips held by three rivets. Knife came from the Howard Family of Rockingham County, Virginia. **$650**

Pikes

Confederate

Augusta Arsenal pike head that is complete with retainer bands and rivets in place. Wooden pike handle was either burnt out or rotted away. Metal pieces are all in attached position. **$1,195**

*Confederate, Bowie knife made from Confederate saber, **$1,250-$1,500**.*

Beautiful condition Georgia pike head, original brass cuff, several inches of original pole intact. Blade has a smooth, aged, gray-brown patina without even a single nick, brass cuff is perfect with a rich uncleaned patina. .. **$975**

Original Confederate "Richmond-style" pike on the original haft measuring 8'7" from tip to bottom of grounding iron. 13-1/4", double-edged, spear-pointed blade that enters into a brass 2" ferrule, which has a rolled edge for strength. Iron rivet through the ferrule holds the blade, 17-1/2" blackened iron reinforcing straps on either side to strengthen the ash haft. Haft has turned almost black with age, but is still in excellent condition. Grounding iron is of heavy folded and hammer welded iron riveted through the haft. Overall the entire pike is in excellent condition. Collectors and historians consider this style pike to be a product of Confederate shops in and around Richmond, Virginia, from the early days of the war. **$3,295**

Superb, identified Confederate, Richmond Armory pike, full-length pole, missing bottom cap, excellent blade. Name clearly inked in wood, "Cap. H.A. Coursen." Coursen served with distinction with both the 7th and 23rd New Jersey Infantry, seeing action at Williamsburg, Seven Pines, Malvern Hill, 2nd Bull Run and Fredericksburg! Excellent overall condition, 96-1/2" tip-to-tip.
....**$3,500**

U.S.
Navy
8' long overall with a 12-1/2", four-sided, spike-style blade, 3" langets run down the sides of the haft for reinforcement, one langet marked with an "L," fine, original handle appears to be of ash. This pattern of pikes was used as early 1797, but continued in service through the Civil War, fine condition.
....**$1,650**

*Confederate, Bowie knife and scabbard
made from bayonet, $3,500-$3,900.*

Blacksmith-made Confederate side knife, $600-$800.

Excavated, Confederate Bowie knife, $350-$400.

CHAPTER 3

BELT PLATES AND BUCKLES

Collecting Civil War belt plates can be very satisfying: The pieces look really nice on display, are readily available, and offer many levels for collection growth. Both Union and Confederate troops wore a variety of belt buckles and plates, so it is advisable for beginners to first assemble a representative collection (perhaps consisting of a U.S. oval plate, C.S. oval plate, pattern of 1851 plate, and a frame buckle), and then focusing on a particular variety or style.

Reproductions abound, however, so great care should be exercised when purchasing buckles and plates. Because of the demand by reenactors, even low-grade, common plates have been reproduced in abundance. One would assume that dug buckles would guarantee authenticity, but this is not the case. Because some Confederate buckles can sell for tens of thousands of dollars, a forger has a lot of incentive to make their handiwork look as convincing as possible. On the other hand, a dug U.S. buckle, pattern of 1841, isn't probably going to pose too many authenticity concerns to a buyer—it simply isn't worth a forger's time to artificially age the common plate.

Collecting Hints

Pros:
• Belt plates and buckles are still widely available.

• It is easy to assemble a large collection that does not require a lot of space.

- Belt plates and buckles display well, as they are not adversely affected by light.

- Many belt plates can be purchased for under $150 each.

- Belt plates are very impressive when on display.

Cons:

- Many belt plates have been restruck, reproduced, and faked.

- Variety is virtually unlimited and overwhelming.

- Advanced items require tens of thousands of dollars.

Availability ★★★
Price ★★★
Reproduction Alert ★★★★

Excavated, large-sized, plain-edge Confederate, Georgia, frame buckle, $550-$575.

*Excavated, pewter, CSA, waist belt plate made by Noble Brothers
of Rome, Georgia, **$5,500-$5,700.***

Buckles and Plates

Confederate, General Issue
Belt Buckle, Frame

"Baby cavalry" Georgia frame that was recently dug from Bragg's C.S. camp
near Shelbyville, Tennessee, perfect and not cleaned. **$625**

Beautiful condition, dug, Confederate cavalry Georgia frame buckle from the
camp of the 51st Alabama Cavalry. Pattern manufactured by McElroy &
Hunt of Macon, Georgia, but is unmarked. Buckle has a pretty, slick, green
uncleaned patina. **$550**

Cast brass. Fine, excavated condition, brownish patina. **$785**

Frame buckle with the hooks raised was a popular pattern that could be
produced inexpensively. **$500**

Excellent, dug, large-size C.S. Georgia frame waist belt buckle that is uncleaned
and retains a brown-green patina. Dug from Bragg's camps following the
Battle of Stones River. **$550**

Beautiful, dug, smooth-type, large-size Confederate Georgia frame buckle, slick
brown wood patina dug from C.S. camps along Duck River near Shelbyville,
Tennessee. **$550**

C.S. Georgia frame that is the guttered back style, recently dug from Bragg's C.S.
camps near Shelbyville, Tennessee. It is a perfect buckle with an uncleaned
brown-green patina. **$575**

Belt Buckle, Fork-Tongue Frame
Classic Confederate forked-tongue brass belt buckle, non-dug example in perfect
condition, and guaranteed original with letter of authenticity. **$1,250**

*Excavated, small-sized, beveled edge, Confederate cavalry, Georgia,
frame buckle, $575-$625.*

Large-size Confederate "wishbone" or "fork-tongue" frame buckle dug along the Confederate retreat route out of Shiloh towards Corinth, Mississippi, very attractive with a thick pea-green patina. **$650**

Scarce, medium-size, Confederate fork-tongue frame waist belt buckle. It has a nice wood brown-green patina, and has not even been washed off. **$695**

Belt and buckle known as a "forked-tongue frame" waist belt. This style accoutrement belt was widely manufactured and issued throughout the Confederacy. Despite their widespread use, very few of the belts survive. Example is strong and supple, stitching is intact, original, and tight. **$8,500**

Plate, Belt, Oval

Called the "rope-border" style because there is the faint outline of a rope just inside the rim, these plates were stamped, never lead-filled, and the attachment hooks were individually fashioned from sheet brass. All three hooks are original and intact. Plate shows good bit of wear from actual use. There was a bend in the middle, now straightened, but it was not broken or cracked and has not been repaired in any way. The red color is from having been cleaned with lemon juice at one time, a technique used by some to remove oxidation and other crud. **$2,500**

Dug, rope-border-style stamped-brass oval waist belt plate. Buckle has nice brown patina and all three hooks intact. Plate has a couple tiny hairline freeze cracks, as is typically the case with thin die-struck southern plates. It is, otherwise, a complete, quite solid, very pretty example. **$3,250**

Leech and Rigdon 11-star C.S. oval is untouched with nice patina, perfect body curve, and all three hooks intact. **$22,500**

*Excavated, large oval, die-struck, Breckenridge pattern, CS,
waist belt plate, $2,850-$3,350.*

Excavated, large oval, cast-brass, CS, waist belt plate, $3,500-$3,800.

Excavated, "gutter back," large-sized Confederate, Georgia, frame buckle, $575-$600.

Egg-shaped, C.S., oval, waist belt plate excavated from N.B. Forrest's Confederate cavalry camp near Spence Springs located at Murfreesboro, Tennessee. Plate is very solid and has been professionally straightened where it was bent downward on each end. This is the stamped-brass, non-lead-filled, western theater variety. **$1,250**

Western theater-style Confederate (egg) belt buckle. Dug directly behind the Confederate trench line at the Siege of Port Hudson, Louisiana. The plate is very strong and has a lot of character to it. **$620**

Dug, rope-border, C.S. oval waist belt plate. This plate was dug near Shiloh and has a smooth, brown-green patina, perfect body curve and all three hooks intact, small amount of professionally-restored chipping along the rim to the lower right of the S. **$2,850**

Rare, stamped brass "Breckinridge style," C.S., oval waist belt plate. This buckle was dug at the Battle of Franklin, Tennessee, and was on display in the Lotz House Civil War Museum in Franklin, Tennessee, for a number of years. The buckle still has the museum's accession number on the back. The plate is very solid with all three hooks intact on the reverse and a green-brown patina. **$3,850**

Scarce Army of Tennessee, Confederate, solid, cast oval border "CS" plate, belt, all hooks intact, but tip broken from one. Recovered in a field near a hospital site in Kinston, North Carolina, where the military battle of Wyse Forks took place, fine deep-green patina. **$3,000**

Very nice, dug, solid cast-brass, Army of Tennessee round-corner C.S. waist belt plate dug from a C.S. camp near Mobile, Alabama. Very attractive, uncleaned, brown-green patina, approximately 80% black enamel still visible in the background, all three hooks intact on reverse with nice deep spun downs around each. **$3,250**

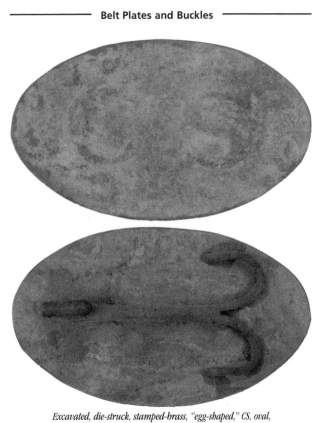

*Excavated, die-struck, stamped-brass, "egg-shaped," CS, oval,
waist belt plate, $3,000-$3,500.*

Excavated, thinner Tennessee pattern, brass, rectangular, C.S.A., waist belt plate, $2,300-$2,600.

Plate, Belt, Rectangular, and Belt

Beautiful condition, cast-brass, Atlanta-style rectangle "C.S.A." on original Confederate brown leather belt. Plate has prominent file marks and a rich, never-cleaned patina. **$5,500**

The letters "C S A" are well shaped and well defined. Sand casting, using a brass with a high copper content, has resulted in its having a patina with a pleasing reddish hue. It appears to be on its original waist belt, which remains strong, soft, and supple. There is an illegible name inked into the russet side of the belt. **$18,500**

Plate, Belt, Rectangular

"CSA" Army of Northern Virginia pattern rectangular, excavated just south of Richmond. Fine overall condition, solid hooks, smooth face; pleasing light-brown patina. **$2,500**

Absolutely beautiful freshly dug cast brass rectangular "C.S.A." waist belt plate, dug near Vicksburg, Mississippi, and has an uncleaned wood brown-green patina. Plate has nice body curve, all three hooks intact, and a good-size piece of original leather belt remaining under the hooks. This is the thinner early-war, Tennessee style with the rim notched for the period after the "A." This is a relatively uncommon pattern in the best of the best condition. **$2,850**

Very attractive, non-excavated, cast-brass, Atlanta-style, rectangular C.S.A. plate with a rich aged-bronze patina and all three hooks intact. One hook is a little shorter than the others due to an air bubble casting flaw in the end of the hook. The letters are nice and tall, making the "C.S.A." really stand out. **$3,250**

Plate, Belt, Two Piece

A beautiful, two-piece Confederate belt buckle considered to be made in Richmond, Virginia. This buckle has a soft, mellow brass patina that has never been cleaned or polished. It is a non-dug example and is in perfect condition. **$3,600**

*Excavated, thinner Tennessee pattern, brass, rectangular, CSA, waist belt plate, **$2,300-$2,600.***

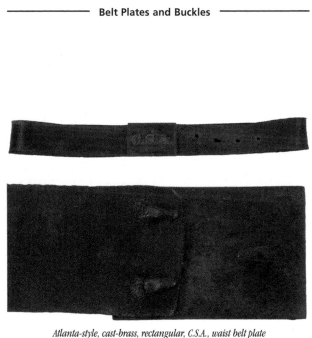

*Atlanta-style, cast-brass, rectangular, C.S.A., waist belt plate
on original belt, **$4,500-$5,000**.*

The Atlanta-styled C.S.A. differ from the Tennessee variants by being thicker and heavier.

Absolutely beautiful and perfect Richmond Arsenal-style C.S. two-piece officer's sword belt plate. This plate was dug near Brandy Station in the early 1970s. Both pieces were dug together and fit perfectly. The plate has a nice deep chocolate-brown patina and literally could not be prettier. **$2,450**

Flawless condition, wreath portion of a heavy pattern coin-type C.S. two-piece buckle. This wreath was dug from Forrest's and Van Dorn's camps near Spring Hill, Tennessee. It has a smooth, dark brown-green patina. **$950**

Plain face excavated tongue portion of a two-piece tongue and wreath sword belt plate. This buckle was excavated from an 1863 Confederate camp along Duck River near Shelbyville, Tennessee. It is perfect with a smooth, chocolate-brown patina. **$175**

Very pretty, dug, two-piece C.S. Richmond Arsenal tongue and wreath sword belt plate. The fit is excellent, and the two pieces were dug in the same area, but were not interlocked. Both halves have a nice uncleaned woods, brown-green patina. **$2,450**

Two-part Virginia style is noted for the convex curve and straight serif. Beautiful dug example, both halves dug together. **$2,700**

"I got up at daylight and cooked coffee. We were then ordered to put on our cartridge belt and to be ready to advance the skirmish line."

—*Clinton Hogue,*
19th Indiana Infantry

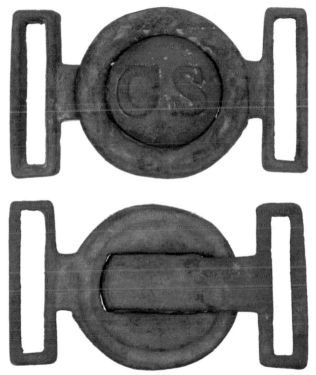

Excavated, interlocking two-piece, CS, sword belt plate, $2,450-$2,700.

Belt Plate

"Rope border" C.S. waist belt plate. **$7,500**

"S S" belt plate. **$5,500**

Brass or bronze, excellent condition. No damage or repairs. 3-1/4" x 2" when
buckled. No maker's mark. **$1,875**

C.S. belt plate in the "Atlanta Style." Very fine example with one hook half
missing, recovered at Marietta, Georgia... **$3,300**

Die-stamped, 1850-era "star" militia plate. This is a very beautiful and ornate
plate that was carried over into the Civil War. Due to its star motif and prewar
availability, this plate often is excavated from C.S. campsites, especially Texas
and Mississippi. The plate has a perfect face, and the main hook is intact on
the reverse. It is, however, missing the belt loop bar. This is a beautiful plate
that would look nice in any collection. **$450**

Confederate, State Issue
Plate, Belt, Alabama

Alabama Volunteer Corps waist belt plate. **$7,900**

Plate, Belt, Georgia, and Belt

Extremely rare, non-dug, lead-filled, Georgia, oval state seal waist belt plate on
the original leather waist belt. The leather belt is 1-1/2" w. The Confederate
soldier customized the Georgia oval to the inner circle to make it smaller
to better fit the belt. The leather belt is complete, but stiff. This belt rig was
purchased directly from a central Georgia estate and has since been displayed
in a Tennessee museum. **$4,850**

This accoutrement belt buckle was manufactured by Emerson Gaylord under
contract to the great state of Georgia. Georgia bought 1,000 of this type belt
for issuance to her native soldiers. These were acquired in the fall of 1860,
assuring that virtually all saw subsequent Confederate service with the first
wave of Georgia patriots who rushed to defend the South. **$6,800**

Plate, Belt, Louisiana, and Belt

Sword belt consists of a two-piece belt plate and a belt of patent leather over cotton webbing. This alone makes this a very rare and desirable belt. The die-struck disc is mounted upside down and the belt is notched in order to allow the sword hanger to be reversed. The belt is in excellent condition, being strong and supple throughout. The long sword hanger is in excellent condition, but only about 4" of the short hanger remains. **$12,500**

Plate, Belt, Mississippi

Oval Mississippi Belt Buckle. This plate was dug in the summer of 1976 at the Fraser's Farm Battlefield. Plate in very-good condition, minor rim repair.
.... **$6,500**

Plate, Belt, North Carolina

6th North Carolina Troops, cast-brass buckle with black-enamel background and three brass-soldered belt hooks. Only marked regimental plate worn by Confederates. These were made at a small railway shop in Greensboro, North Carolina, as the 6th Troops prepared to embark for the front. **$4,500**

Plate, Belt, Virginia, with Belt

Manufactured by James Smith & Sons of New York, circa 1860. It was used in conjunction with two web belts that supported a cartridge box and a bayonet. The cross belts were pinned together at the breast and locked into position at the waist with this belt. The plate bears the Virginia coat of arms, a Victorious Virtus wearing the Liberty cap, standing over an uncrowned and defeated Tyranny. The Latin motto, "Sic Semper Tyrannis" or "Thus Ever to Tyrants" arches around "Virtus" or Virtue. **$5,900**

Plate, Belt, Virginia

Absolutely beautiful, dug, die-struck Virginia State Seal waist belt plate with a smooth brown patina with crisp, sharp detail. Solder marks remain on the reverse where the bar and hook once were. **$2,850**

From the late 1850s until the fall of Fort Sumter, the Commonwealth of Virginia purchased sword belts from Emerson Gaylord of Chicopee, Massachusetts. Gaylord produced a very high quality plate by first casting and then die stamping to bring out the detail in the Virginia state seal. After casting and die stamping the face, the tongue was brazed on and a keeper was fitted. Both the keeper and the plate were then struck with a matching number. In this case, the number 73. The initials "J W" are carved into the back of the plate, unfortunately this is not enough information to identify its original owner. This particular example shows a lot of wear around the tongue where the keeper rode, indicating long hard service. **$3,850**

Stamped-brass, rectangular, Virginia waist belt plate with bar and tongue back. This particular plate came from the collection of Norm Flayderman and it still retains his number and identifying card: "Orig Confed Va Buckle, bought from estate of Capt. T. Halan 5th US Vols. In CW from New Bedford Mass. & 3rd Mass Cav'ly & 82nc Col. Inf." **$5,700**

Virginia two-piece sword belt plate. **$7,500**

Stamped brass Virginia belt plate with the familiar seal of Virtue triumphing over Tyranny. The state motto, "Sic Semper Tyrannis" is around the scene. Both belt attachments are off the back. **$2,800**

Has 76 stamped in corner on back, dings on top and bottom edges, light-brown patina, non-dug plate with nice body bend. **$3,950**

Plate, Cartridge Box Sling, Virginia

Few southern belt plates can be attributed to a specific maker, and fewer still to a specific unit. This exceedingly rare, die-struck Virginia State Seal Cross belt plate is an exception. By comparing the die-strike with waist belt plates marked James Smith & Sons, New York, it can be identified as a circa 1860 Smith product. There are several images of "Southern Guards" wearing this distinctive cross and waist belt configuration. These cross belt plates are exceedingly rare, and there are no known links to any other unit. Other Virginia units did, however, use the James Smith & Sons' waist belt.

.... **$14,500**

U.S., General Issue
Buckle, Belt, M1855 Rifleman

An attractive, non-dug example of the interlocking solid brass Rifleman's buckle complete with the two cast-brass keepers that flank the buckle on the belt for use with the knapsack hooks. **$395**

Plate, Belt, Pattern of 1839, and Belt

White buff leather accoutrement belt with brass supporting rings inserted to hold the buff leather scabbard frog for an M1832 Ames Foot Artillery Sword. Beautiful cast "US" spoon and wreath-style buckle. Belt is complete with both buff keepers and brass hook adjuster, top-notch condition with only some very slight frog staining. **$1,500**

Beautiful, white buff early belt with leather standing loop, small U.S. brass buckle with single arrow hook on back. Belt and buckle unmarked but definitely original. **$800**

Fine example of the earliest plate made, oval studs on back instead of arrowhead hooks, and a wide, tapered, and serpentine silvered tongue, instead of a flat sheet brass one. Face has even light patina, shows use, but not dented and very sharp. It is on an original well-used Civil War leather belt. All finish flaked and torn a bit at the keeper end. The reverse has original, faded stenciled unit information: "Co. G. (s?) REGT. G.R. 39," a rare plate these days. **$395**

Plate, Belt, Pattern of 1839

An excellent non-dug specimen belt buckle, face has crisp U.S. strike and back has full solder fill with the single arrow and prong, fine, light age patina.

.... **$325**

An excellent, non-dug specimen of this highly desirable belt buckle. The face has a crisp U.S. strike and the back has full solder fill with the single arrow and prong, fine, light age patina. A really fine buckle correct for display with Mexican War or Civil War plates. **$325**

Beautiful condition excavated 1839 small, oval U.S. waist belt plate. Rare pattern with hooks made of iron and barely enough lead to hold them in place. An early find, and the face couldn't be nicer. There are rusty remnants of what once were the iron hooks on the reverse. **$275**

Plate, Cartridge Box, Pattern of 1839

Excellent condition, non-excavated, small-size, oval U.S. cartridge box plate with an attractive aged patina. The reverse has full lead and both loops perfectly intact. **$295**

Dug, small-size circular "Burnside" breastplate with excellent face, crisp detail, and a smooth chocolate patina, full lead in the reverse, but the two iron loops are rusted away. **$195**

Plate, N.C.O. Sling, Pattern of 1839

The rare Eagle plate with arrow hooks on the back, like a belt buckle, lead filled, for the over shoulder N.C.O. sword sling. Mint example has a nice, light age patina, rare version with the arrow hooks on the back. **$395**

Exceptionally nice condition, dug, three-wire hook, circular Union N.C.O. eagle plate. This plate has sharp detail and a smooth chocolate patina, lead is full and smooth, and all three hooks are intact on the reverse. **$295**

Plate, Belt, Pattern of 1841, and Belt

Regulation U.S. oval buckle w/arrow hooks (very pretty) on original waist belt with original brass adjuster, very solid and supple, with much finish loss, a very solid example. **$295**

Excavated, large size, lead-filled, U.S. belt plate, $185-$250.

A scarce piece of Civil War equipment, very early black harness leather waist belt with the standing leather loop adjuster (keeper). A large U.S. oval buckle with the round "puppy paw" studs (not the later oval studs), attaches in a left to right fashion from the wearer's perspective. This buckle is likely an early product of Boyd & Sons of Boston as the die style of the "U.S." is identical to theirs though this plate is not marked. Condition is very good with a small expert repair on the belt where the buckle attaches. **$395**

Regulation Union issue oval buckle with arrow hooks and buff leather belt with brass adjuster. Absolutely mint condition never having been put together. Just the way shipped from factory, with the belt holes (for arrow hooks) never touched. **$595**

Plate, Belt, Pattern of 1841

Beautiful, dug, Smith Contract, oval U.S. belt plate with puppy paw studs. Great patina on this plate with no bends or dents and most all of the lead back is intact, "W.H. Smith, B." Smith was a contractor for the U.S. Government during the Civil War. This belt plate was dug in Tennessee around the Fort Donelson area about 15 years ago. **$285**

Regulation oval U.S. buckle with arrow hooks in excellent condition. This one bears maker's stamp of "S Peters" in the lead back. **$245**

U.S., oval, arrow-hook, dug out of an old roadbed used by Rosecran's Army of the Cumberland on their way to Chickamauga. Plate is complete with full lead and all three hooks. It must have been run over by every wagon and every cannon in Rosecran's army to get mashed this flat. **$125**

Plate, Cartridge Box, Pattern of 1841

Identical to the U.S. oval belt buckles but having two iron wire loops on the back for securing to the flap of the cartridge box, fine, non-dug condition.
.... **$225**

Model 1839, small-sized, stamped-brass, U.S., dual-waist belt plate, $275-$345.

*Regulation issue, lead-filled, large, oval, U.S.,
waist belt plate, non-dug,* ***$200-$275.***

Regulation-size, U.S., oval plate with high-quality plate, gilt finish, a few minor scratches. Under "US" is stamped small "MS." Back in excellent condition.
.... **$695**

Beautiful excavated, backmarked, large, oval U.S. cartridge box plate. This plate was dug at Resaca, Georgia, January 27, 1960, perfect smooth brown face, full lead, both loops, and a super crisp, "W. H. Smith Brooklyn," backmark.
.... **$195**

Beautiful, non-excavated, large-size, U.S. oval cartridge box plate, face is perfect, reverse has full lead and both wire loops intact. **$195**

Plate, Pattern of 1851, and Belt

A perfect Civil War eagle buckle with silver wreath. This one shows how the plates continue in service for years after the war, as it resides on a white patent leather waist belt that was probably worn by a New York militia soldier just after the war. **$395**

This piece is most intriguing, possessing a most ingenious repair. The buckle is an officer's pattern M1851 rectangular eagle sword belt plate with cast-brass wreath surrounding the eagle. During its period of service the loop at the buckle's end was damaged and removed. In its place was carefully fitted (and soldered) a replacement loop that was carefully manufactured in copper or bronze. It was fitted so that the buckle appears to not have a repair when viewed from the front. This ingenious plate is attached to a much earlier waist belt (possibly 1830s or 1840s period) by means of two large, crude, copper rivets. It also has the proper brass keeper riveted to the female belt end. The leather belt itself is made of very soft (almost doe skin) brown leather with a hand-stitched, leather-edge border that runs the belt's full length.. **$295**

*Excavated, circular, lead-filled Union eagle breastplate, **$195-$245**.*

Plate, Pattern of 1851, and Saber Belt

Classic Civil War-issue, buff-leather cavalry belt with silver-wreath eagle buckle and matching keeper, both saber hanger straps, the shoulder support strap, all leather adjusters (keepers) and overall in near mint condition. There is a professional (undetectable) repair 4" in from the keeper. **$1,100**

Near-mint, black, buff-leather Model 1851 saber belt complete in all respects including the scarce over-the-shoulder support strap. Fine pliable buff leather, rectangular, brass-eagle buckle with applied silver wreath (number on buckle matches on keeper), both saber straps and all the leather adjusters. Marked, "J. DAVY & CO.," on the inside of the leather near the triangular brass hook that secures the belt around the buckle loop. Made in 1864 with two copper rivets in addition to the three rows of stitching holding the brass keeper in place. **$1,595**

Early war buff leather artillery saber belt (made without provision for shoulder support strap) in very good condition, has three-piece silver-wreath eagle buckle with matched number to the keeper (very pretty). Has both saber straps with all four loop adjusters, just lacks the loop adjuster on the belt portion. Early pattern, the brass keeper is secured to the belt with stitching only (no rivets). **$795**

Plate, Belt, Pattern of 1851, and Sword Belt

Black "folded & sewn" construction, has both saber hanger straps intact (small repair on one) that are affixed to sliding loop keepers. Buckle is pretty eagle with mid-war, medium-wide tongue. **$795**

Model 1851 black, leather, private-purchase sword belt made in the folded construction style. Solid case, eagle belt plate retains shield-shaped, leather coat guard and brass hardware, including both scabbard ring snap hooks. Leather is dry with some crazing to finish, but still supple enough for display. Shoulder sling is broken with some leather lost, saber straps intact, but with one partial tear. **$435**

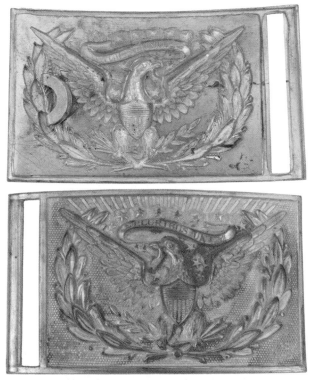

Model 1851, Federal eagle, sword belt plate, gilded, officer, stamped brass, $245-$300.

Excavated Model 1851, Federal eagle, sword belt plate, $175-$245.

The buckle measures 3-1/4" x 2". The belt is approximately 33", leather belt has usual wear for this time period, has the sword hangers intact, very good condition. **$283**

Excellent condition, buff leather sword belt was manufactured by, "Joseph Davy & Co., Newark, NJ." On Sept. 11 and 12, 1863, Davy received four contracts for a total of 60,000 sets of cavalry accoutrements. This features an M1851 Sword belt plate w/applied wreath. Rig is complete with over-the-shoulder straps, absolutely mint condition.. **$2,500**

Plate, Belt, Pattern of 1851

Cast brass with applied German silver one-piece wreath, standard-issue buckle, shows use. **$245**

Eagle belt plate recovered from a fire pit at Stafford Court House, Virginia. The wreath is missing, but the plate is still nice for a dug piece and is hallmarked "806." **$175**

Excellent condition, non-excavated, cast-brass, pattern of 1851, Union eagle sword belt plate with a nice, uncleaned patina. The applied silver wreath is 100% intact, it is marked on the reverse, "832." **$375**

U.S., State Issue
Plate, Belt, New York, and Sword Belt

Identified to George Vail, Union Continentals. The belt has two suspension straps with scabbard hooks and a rectangular cast-brass *N.Y.* buckle with wreath and old English letters *N.Y.* Belt has a small area of scuffing, condition is still fine. **$300**

NY Militia shoulder belt plate of the City Guard, ca. 1855-1865. Gilt-rolled brass plate displaying a die-struck, white metal motif secured by three wire loops through plate. Attachment pin is there. In addition to the 9th Regiment (10th prior to 1859), N.Y.S.M., this style may have been worn by Brooklyn's 23rd Regiment (City Guard Reserve), which was formed from portions of the 9th and 10th in 1859, and reorganized in 1862. .... **$475**

Model 1851, Federal eagle, sword belt plate on prewar linen waist belt, $425-$500.

Stamped brass, solder filled with the early wire hooks. These buckles were manufactured well before the Civil War, were stored in a warehouse in New York, but, due to a classic case of bureaucratic bungling, were forgotten and missed the fighting entirely. Discovered during 1866, they were sold as surplus stock, and loaded on an old merchant steamer enroute to Mexico. The ship sank off the coast of South Carolina in a storm. The wreck was scattered over a large distance, in international water, and many of these plates have been discovered along with muskets, cannons, and other military items. Most of the plates, so discovered, have been in very poor condition as the salt-water environment is extremely harsh on any small metal objects buried on the ocean floor. The brass skin and iron hooks are entirely missing leaving the solder filling fully intact and clearly bearing the motif, "SNY." Relatively good condition. **$200**

Plate, Belt, Ohio Volunteer Militia
Plate was found in 1990 at Camp Jones in Southern Raleigh County, Huffs Knob, West Virginia, hooks are missing, beautiful brown patina. **$1,895**

Plate, Belt, Ohio
Very scarce Ohio Volunteer Militia buckle being the medium-size variety. This was disposed of a few years back by a museum in the Midwest with verbal history that it was dug at Antietam. Edges are chipped, and hooks intentionally removed when displayed decades ago, but a good solid buckle with much appeal. **$595**

Plate, Cartridge Box, U.S., Volunteer Militia of Maine
Constructed of stamped brass, solder filling is missing for this plate, pattern of plate is distinguished by shoddy workmanship. Hooks missing, outstanding example is still dirt covered. **$700**

Excavated large oval "SNY" (State of New York) waist belt plate, **$250-$400.**

CHAPTER 4

BULLETS, CARTRIDGES, AND PROJECTILES

When one considers the sheer volume of lead and iron that was fired during the Civil War, it is not surprising that an extensive variety of projectiles existed. A single armory, or even a system of armories, simply could not provide all of the bullets, balls, shells, and projectiles required by the armies. Therefore, governments on both sides turned to any source they could find to fulfill the demand. In many cases, the companies that supplied contracted weapons also were required to supply the ammunition, thereby, increasing the chain from the Ordnance officer placing the order and the manufacturer producing the product. It is no wonder that standardization was not achieved.

All of this is good news for collectors of bullets, cartridges, and projectiles. Entering this field of Civil War collecting is not going to be mastered with a few key purchases. Rather, there are several extensive studies that have been published identifying thousands of varieties. Further attempts have been made to classify projectiles into "Union," "Confederate," "Western Theater," "contracted," "carved," "imported," "dropped," "fired," or many other categories. The derivatives are so vast, a collector can focus on .58-caliber rounds, carbine bullets, Confederate-used, or any one of several other paths that this field offers.

.36 caliber, Colt Navy revolver bullet, $2-$4.

.58 caliber, type 3 Williams cleaner, $7-$10.

Cartridges are an extremely interesting area of collecting. The Civil War was the last time the United States issued paper-wrapped cartridges to its infantry soldiers. Intended to be bitten off at the end and rammed into the musket, the survival of paper cartridges was small. Most that are available to collectors were leftovers found in cartridges boxes. The same is true for the paper or linen combustible cartridges used in many revolvers and carbines.

On the other hand, metallic-cased rounds have survived in decent quantity to make it possible for novice collectors to easily assemble extensive collections. Dealers will often have both dug and non-dug examples for sale.

Another area of projectile collecting enters a larger scale. Collecting artillery rounds offers some unique challenges. First, and foremost, a collector has to bear in mind that most artillery projectiles (besides solid shot and rifled bolts) were intended to explode. Before lifting one out of a freshly dug hole, a collector should pause to consider why the round he just uncovered did not explode. The second question he/she should ask is, "Will it explode when I handle it?" Disarming artillery rounds is best left to experts. If, however, you decide to collect artillery rounds, you might be best served by buying rounds from reputable dealers that are already disarmed.

The other consideration when collecting artillery rounds is the weight. If you specialize in 32 lb. projectiles, don't count on friends to help you move around your collection!

*Gang mold for .44 caliber, Colt Model 1860
Army revolver, $400-$475.*

.58 caliber, 2-ring, Confederate Gardner carbine bullet, $7-$15.

Collecting projectiles, whether dug bullets or artillery rounds, unfired cartridges, or original, unissued packages can be a hobby all in itself. But, if you are more generalized in your Civil War collecting focus, these items are great complements to a display of weapons, artillery implements, or accoutrements.

Collecting Hints

Pros:

- Collecting bullets or projectiles allows a collector to become peripherally involved in the study of Civil War weaponry for a fraction of the cost of collecting firearms. Consider, for example, a bullet for a .56-caliber Colt Revolving Rifle will sell for about $7.50, a complete cartridge for around $125, an unopened package of cartridges for $600, and the actual rifle for $2,750. It becomes apparent that, for the novice at least, bullets and cartridges are a much more affordable way of becoming engaged with the Colt Revolving Rifle.

- There are a lot of excavated bullets and projectiles available for collectors and new ones are being unearthed every year. The supply will certainly keep up with the demand for many years.

- Both bullets and artillery rounds are relatively stable and do not require a lot of room for storage making it easy for a collector with limited area for storage and display to enjoy the collection.

- Projectiles and cartridges are wonderful adjunct items to display with accoutrements, weapons, or artillery items. The projectiles help put the rest of the items into context for the viewer.

- Excellent references are available in several facets of this area. Standardized numbering has been established within the hobby enabling collectors to effectively sort and categorize their projectiles.

Cons:

- Many cartridges and artillery rounds are live! That is, they can explode. Know what you're acquiring before you take it home. If you are out digging, bear in mind that the artillery round you are unearthing could explode. Exercise extreme caution. Only allow experts to disarm a projectile. There isn't much of a learning curve that allows for mistakes.

- You need to decide a purely ethical question before you begin: Should battlefields be mined for the relics they retain? Some consider a battlefield a sacred area and digging at such a site is considered to be a desecration of it. On the other hand, plenty of relics are dug at non-battle sites, such as camp and bivouac sites.

- Displayed on their own, outside of the context of the associated weapons, projectiles are not the most impressive items. It might be difficult to convey your enthusiasm for a tray of bullets to a viewer who is not intimate with the various idiosyncrasies that so enthrall an expert.

Availability ★★★★
Price ★
Reproduction Alert ★

30 lb, time-fused Parrot projectile, $250-$300.

.54 caliber, Starr carbine cartridges (full unopened packet), ***$750-$950.***

Individual Cartridges

.28 Plant Revolver
In brass casing, non-dug, used in Plant Revolver, .28 caliber. **$18**

.32 National Revolver
Teat-fire cartridge in brass casing, very fine. **$18**

.32 caliber, round teat, in brass casing, VF. **$18**

.35 Maynard Carbine
Excellent condition and quite rare, .35 caliber, non-excavated Maynard sporting
    carbine cartridge. **$65**

.35-caliber "top hat" cartridge with conical lead projectile. Most of the .35-
    caliber First Model Maynard Carbines "went South," so this has a good
    chance of being a Confederate cartridge. Excellent condition in a glass-
    fronted Riker case. **$95**

.36 Colt Pocket Revolver
Manufactured by Colt with combustible paper. **$110**

Manufactured by Eley Hays, English Patent Paper sleeve w/orange label. ... **$95**

Manufactured by Eley Hays, English Patent Paper sleeve w/orange label. ... **$85**

.44 Colt Revolver
A perfect "skin" cartridge being a .44-caliber conical bullet with nitrated paper
    powder bag still attached and full. **$65**

.44 Henry Rifle
"H" on bottom, non-dug, very fine condition. **$26**

Coppery brass cartridge with snow white, flat-nosed lead projectile, excellent
    condition, in a glass-fronted Riker mount. **$35**

.50 caliber, Maynard carbine cartridge, $25-$45.

Excavated, .69 caliber, 4-piece "buck and ball," $10-$15.

.50 Maynard Carbine

Brass casing, non-dug, .50 caliber, very-fine condition. **$25**

Perfect condition, non-excavated, .50 Maynard carbine cartridge.

.... **$45**

.50 Smith Carbine

A single complete cartridge, excellent with light handling age. **$95**

Cartridge in rubber casing, .50 caliber, very-good condition. **$145**

.52 Sharps

Nice condition, complete .52 linen cartridge for the Sharps carbine or rifle.

.... **$125**

A perfect example of the .52 caliber Sharps linen cartridge as issued with the
    rifles and carbines. **$135**

.52 Spencer

Non-excavated .56/.52 round, head stamped "S.A.W.," excellent shape.

.... **$30**

.54 Burnside Carbine

Excellent condition, non-excavated, .54 Burnside carbine cartridge, very-good
    condition. **$75**

A complete brass cartridge and bullet for the Burnside carbine. Once common,
    now quite hard to find. **$65**

.54 Model 1841 Rifle

Three-ringed bullet in paper casing, fine condition. **$95**

Pinkish-brown, paper-tied, .54-caliber Minié ball, excellent condition, in glass-
    fronted Riker mount. **$145**

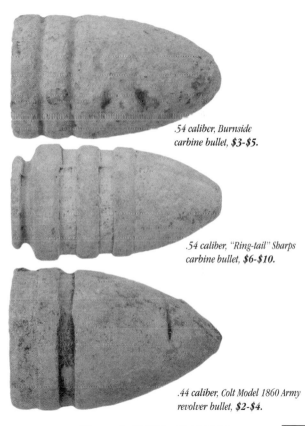

*.54 caliber, Burnside carbine bullet, **$3-$5.***

*.54 caliber, "Ring-tail" Sharps carbine bullet, **$6-$10.***

*.44 caliber, Colt Model 1860 Army revolver bullet, **$2-$4.***

.54 caliber, Gallagher paper/foil cartridge, $45-$85.

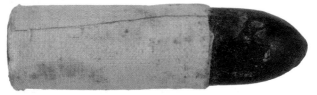

.54 caliber, Starr carbine linen cartridge, $85-$120.

.36 caliber, needle-fire revolver cartridge, $35-$50.

.54 Starr Carbine
.54 caliber, linen casing, very-good condition. **$85**

A perfect complete cartridge for the Starr breech-loading carbine, bullet with
   nitrated linen powder bag. **$135**

.58 Rifled Musket
An original paper wrapped .58-caliber musket cartridge just as was issued,
   excellent condition. **$125**

Bartholow's Pattern #36,066 (repaired). **$450**

Dug Johnston & Dow combustible .58 cartridge. The combustible envelope is still
   present on this bullet—sort of petrified and varnished. **$49**

.69 Ball, Musket
Found in a Confederate cartridge box and appears to be homemade. Heavy
   course paper is all there and has been emptied of all powder. **$385**

The standard Civil War cartridge as issued to all troops equipped with the
   .69-caliber musket. **$65**

.69 Buck and Ball, Musket
An original cartridge, in great overall condition, has one small repair. **$101**

One large .69-caliber ball with three small buckshot tied on top, slight paper
   missing exposing shoulders of the buckshot, otherwise excellent, in Riker
   display. **$150**

Perfect early-war cartridge that came inside a cartridge box. **$185**

7 mm Pinfire
Non-dug, in brass casing, very-fine condition. **$14**

.69 caliber ball cartridge, $65-$110

.58 caliber, musket ball, $1-$2.

*Top: 3-ringed Minié bullets, **$1-$5** each; at bottom: .69 caliber 3-ring Minié complete cartridge, **$105-$130.***

*.698 caliber, 2-ring Prussian Minié, **$16-$18.***

*.69 caliber, 3-ring Minié ball, **$6-$9.***

*.69 caliber, triangular base French Minié, **$15-$20.***

*.58 caliber, Minié ball, **$1-$5.***

9 mm Pinfire

Excellent condition, non-excavated, Civil War-era 9 mm French pinfire cartridge, nice clear "FUSNOT" French base marking. **$15**

Brass casing, non-dug, very-fine condition. **$16**

12 mm Pinfire

Brass casing, as used in the LeFaucheaux Revolver, very-fine condition. **$19**

Copper cartridge for use in such revolvers as the LeFaucheaux, this has a short casing, excellent, and complete. **$22**

.52 caliber, Spencer carbine bullet, $8-$15.

Cartridge Packages

.31 Colt Pocket Revolver, Package

Near perfect condition, label reads, "6 Combustible Envelope/Cartridges/Made of Hazards Powder/-Expressly for/ Col. Colt's Patent Revolving/Pocket Pistol/ Address/Colt's Cartridge Works/Hartford Conn/USA America." **$275**

.35 Maynard Carbine, Package

.35 caliber ammo (10 rounds), which is proper for display with the Confederate-used 1st Model Maynard carbines, still tied with original string, couple of minor wrapper tears. **$575**

.36 Colt Police Revolver, Package

Paper cracked on top, otherwise in fine condition. Label reads, "5 Combustible Envelope/Cartridges/Made of Hazards Powder/ Expressly for/Col. Colt's Patent/ New Model/Revolving/ Police Pistol/.36/100 Inch Caliber/Address Col Colts Works/Hartford Conn/US America." **$295**

.36 Colt Revolver, Package

A mint unopened package of six .36-caliber skin cartridges with a wonderful label which reads, "6 Combustible Envelope Cartridges Made of Hazards Powder For Either Colt's or Whitney's Revolving Belt Pistols 36/100 inch Calibre Warranted Superior Quality." This label is around the interior wooden block that holds the cartridges. **$365**

.36 Whitney Navy Revolver, Package

Two packages, one that is a perfect pack (wood block covered with paper label). Label reads, "Six Seamless Skin/CARTRIDGES/ for Whitney's/Navy Pistol/36/100 calibre/Hotchkiss Patent Feb 11th 1862/Manufactured by/D. C Sage Middletown Conn." The second package is identical, but has had one cartridge removed and that small end section of the package broken off, still has fine label. **$475**

*Original packet of .44 Colt Army cartridges, **$265-$300**.*

.44 Colt Revolver, Package

A perfect empty package with spectacular label reading, "Six Johnston & Dow Waterproof & Combustible cartridges/For Colts Army Revolvers Cal 44-100 Patented Oct 1st 1861 and June 24th 1862/New York." Perfect for display. **$135**

No label remains, just the wooden block and four bullets—the cartridges themselves have disintegrated. **$35**

.50 Gallager Carbine, Package

A fine, empty package with great label on the box's top giving all the data and date. **$125**

Unopened package with label that reads, "10 Poultney's Metallic Cartridges Patented December 15th 1863 For Gallager's Breech Loading Carbine 50/100 Calibre." **$675**

.50 Maynard Carbine, Package

Unopened and wrapped in plain paper wrapper, tied with original string, light wrapper tears, 10 cartridges. **$495**

.50 Smith Carbine, Package

Perfect empty box, full Smith carbine data on top label. **$135**

Perfect, unopened specimen. Label reads, "10 Poultney's Patent Metallic CARTRIDGES Patented Dec 15th 1863 12 caps, For Smith's Breech Loading CARBINE 50/100 Calibre/Address Poultney & Trimble Baltimore, MD." **$1,150**

.52 Sharps Carbine, Package

This pasteboard box contains nine complete cartridges and the pack of caps (one cartridge gone). The box's left end is cut off to open the package, the rest of the box is intact and displays very well. The box's top is labeled, "TEN/ LINEN CARTRIDGES/For Sharps Carbine/Cal. 52 100/With Percussion Caps/ WATERVLIET ARSENAL/1864." The box and label are brown with age but very sound. **$895**

.50 caliber, Gallagher carbine cartridges (full unopened packet), $675-$800.

.52 Spencer, Package

An original cardboard box still containing seven original Spencer cartridges, excellent with one end of the box open. **$95**

Complete box of 42 rounds. Lid label reads, "42/Metallic Cartridges/for the/ Spencer and Joslyn Carbine/No 56 Navy and Infantry Size/ Manufactured by/Crittendon & Tibbals Mfg Co./ Coventry Conn US." Label has small section torn off through name "Crittendon" and town "Coventry." **$675**

.54 Burnside Carbine, Package

Complete unopened package with label "10 Cartridges/ with 12 Caps/For The Burnside Breech Loading Rifle Patented March 25, 1856 Burnside Rifle Co. Providence RI." **$895**

Full wrapper with fantastic label, "10 CARTRIDGES with 12 Caps for the Burnside Breech Loading Rifle Patented March 25th 1856 Caliber .54/100 Made By The Burnside Rifle Co. Providence R.I." Package is empty. **$145**

12 mm Pinfire, Package

For LeFaucheaux pinfire revolver, small cardboard box, label, "Cartouches/12 Millimetr/Houllier-Blanchard/ Arqubusier Brevete/Paris/A Longue Portee," excellent condition. **$165**

> "A Minie ball struck me in the right side just above my hip and knocked me down. I lay where I fell for a while and the rebel bullets were hitting the ground all around me."
> —*David Milburn Haworth,*
> *3rd Tennessee Volunteer Infantry (U.S.A.)*

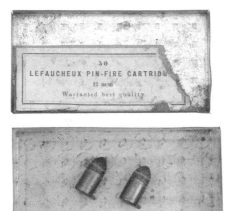

French Lefaucheaux, pinfire cartridges in original tin, **$115-$150.**

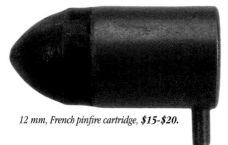

12 mm, French pinfire cartridge, **$15-$20.**

15 mm, French pinfire revolver cartridges (full box), $275-$350.

Bullets

Ball .69 Musket
Found in Potomac Creek. **$7**

.36 Teardrop Revolver
Very attractive little bullet in perfect condition. **$9.50**

.44 Deane & Adams
Non-excavated, spike-base, bullet, rare caliber, still has the leather washer intact
    on spike. **$45**

.45 Whitworth
Mint, flawless condition, freshly dug, drop 45 cal., cylindrical Whitworth
    projectile. Dug from General John Bell Hood's sharpshooter positions at the
    Battle of Nashville, Tennessee; has smooth, perfect white patina. **$275**

.52 Sharps
4-ring as used with Confederate Sharps Carbines. **$75**

Dug, good, dropped bullet with some nicks. **$3**

.54 Burnside Carbine
Flat-based. **$7.50**

Dished-base. **$7.50**

.54 Merrill Carbine
Merrill carbine bullet in non-excavated condition. **$3**

Richmond-style bullet. **$47**

.577 Rifle
Nice white and brown patina with no dig marks, dug at New Hope Church,
    Georgia. **$4.50**

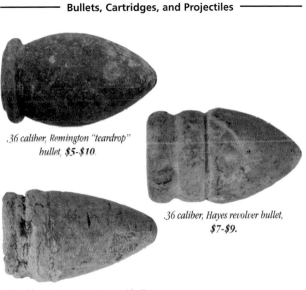

.36 caliber, Remington "teardrop" bullet, **$5-$10**.

.36 caliber, Hayes revolver bullet, **$7-$9**.

.50 caliber, pointed-nose Maynard bullet, **$12-$15**.

.36 caliber, Confederate country rifle bullet, **$2-$4**.

*.54 caliber, Starr carbine bullet, **$2-$6.***

*.54 caliber, Merrill carbine bullet, **$3-$6.***

*.55 caliber, Suhl carbine bullet, CS, **$10-$15.***

.44 caliber, Starr revolver bullet, **$16 $18.**

.36 caliber, Manhattan revolver in original bullet mold, **$55-$90.**

.56 caliber, Colt revolving rifle bullet, **$5-$7.**

*Excavated, .69 caliber, Enfield-Tower projectile, **$25-$35**.*

*.577 caliber, Enfield bullet, **$4-$6**.*

*.54 caliber, Sharps bullet, **$8-$10**.*

*.50 caliber, Smith bullet, **$4-$8**.*

Looks like an Enfield, but has one ring toward the bottom, and a base like a Sharps (hole in the bottom), dug in a C.S. Texas camp. **$35**

.69 Gardner

Deep base. **$325**

Bulb nose. **$125**

Gardner insert, dug at Salem Church. This fired Gardner insert bullet was found in the battlefield along Old Orange Plank Road. **$6**

Very rare to dig, this is a dropped .69 Confederate Gardner bullet. **$85**

Shotgun

Double-end slug. **$75**

Nice condition, dug, Confederate shotgun slug, dropped example. **$55**

A unique way to display some bullets is to lay them into original molds. Closeup of a section on .31 caliber, Colt Pocket Model shows a bullet in bullet mold, $90-$125.

Caps, Percussion

Lawrence Pellet Primers

Little copper or brass tube with a small wooden block holding in what appears to be 25 of the small, wafer-thin fulminates for the Lawrence Pellet Priming assembly on the Sharps Carbine and some other Lawrence equipped firearms, excellent condition. **$65**

Maynard Priming

One original roll of paper caps for use with the Maynard tape priming devices on the 1855 rifles (and others), still in wrapper. **$35**

Roll of famous Maynard caps unwrapped from the original, waxed tissue paper, displayed Riker display case. **$80**

Revolver

Mint pasteboard circular container with label on each side. Top label bears date of 1858 and, "American Manufacture Anticorrosive Percussion Caps by J. Goldmark" along with pictures of two medals awarded for excellence. Other side has label with crossed muskets and a ribbon and is written in French saying 100 caps American Made, etc. **$49**

Tin pistol percussion cap can with lid. **$25**

Yellow Frank Ford Arsenal, 1863, 15-second artillery time fuse packet, $55-$100.

Artillery Fuses

Fuse and Wood Plug

From a siege shell. Very-fine condition, length 2-1/4" x 1-2/5". **$25**

Fits a 30 lb Parrot shell, very-good condition, dug near Vicksburg. **$35**

10-Second

An original, paper, time fuse for an exploding artillery projectile, nicely
displayed in a Riker case with description. **$20**

Original, paper, time fuse used for exploding an artillery projectile. Displayed in
glass case with description. **$20**

Naval

Marked "ORD 1862." Made of brass. **$65**

5-Second, Package

Brown paper-wrapped package stenciled in large black letters on paper "5.S."
Mint surplus example. **$59**

Frankford Arsenal. **$195**

8-Second, Package

Marked "8.S.". **$59**

Paper time fuses from Frankford Arsenal, untied. **$150**

10-Second, Package

Pack of 1864-dated Frankford Arsenal fuses complete with label, tapes, and fuses
in Riker display. **$80**

*Pink Frankford Arsenal, 1864, 5-second artillery time fuse packet, **$180-$200.***

*Green Frankford Arsenal, 1864, 10-second artillery time fuse packet, **$100-$125.***

12-Second, Package

Box of 12-second fuses in their original blue case from the Frankfort Arsenal, 1863. Instructions say "To take a fuse from the package, tear the paper at the top by raising the piece at tape, and press against the small end of the fuse [sic] with the finger," intact and never opened. **$115**

20-Second, Package

Frankford Arsenal fuse pack in mint condition. **$135**

25-Second, Package

Original, unopened, brown-wrapped packet containing two 25-second artillery time fuses. **$45**

Yellow Frankford Arsenal, 1863, 8-second artillery time fuse packet, $125-$150.

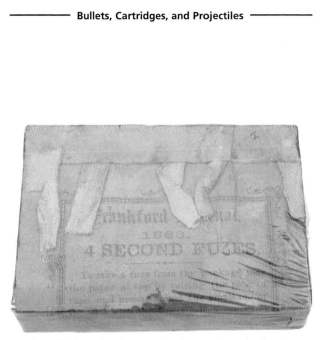

*Pink Frankford Arsenal, 1863, 4-second artillery time fuse packet, **$55-$100.***

*Multi-Time plain paper wrap artillery fuse packet, **$150-$200.***

Artillery Projectiles, Confederate

Bolt

Nice, excavated 3" Archer bolt, projectile dug at Shiloh many years ago. It has been displayed at the Lotz House Civil War Museum in Franklin, Tennessee. Retains the museum's accession number. It is in display ready condition.
....**$650**

3.3" round-nose Selma disc, fine condition, with sabot, cloverleaf design.
....**$1,250**

Case Shot

12 lb, excellent condition, wood, drive-in fuse-type cannon ball. Not only is this projectile in nice condition, but it also has a couple of unusual and rare characteristics. First of all, the wooden fuse plug is petrified and remains 100 percent intact. And secondly, this is a case shot, rather than being a shell, which is typically the case with this type projectile. This was determined by its unusual heavy weight and case-shot ball cuttings during drilling, quite rare C.S. ball.
....**$295**

Grape Shot, 2"

Used in Confederate canister, fine condition, dug at Port Gibson, Mississippi.
....**$19**

Shell
Read Parrot

Shell shows ground action, but is stabilized and mounted to a display board with brass plaque that says "BATTLE OF MOBILE, ALABAMA." **$285**

3" Schenkl combination fused case-shot, $400-$450.

*12 lb solid shot, **$125-$150**.*

*Grape shot (fired in clusters from cannon), **$20-$30**.*

12 lb Bormann-Type

This 12 lb Confederate Bormann cannonball has been nicely sectioned in half to show the powder cavity, brass C.S. underplug, and Bormann fuse. Recovered at Shiloh. **$150**

12 lb Mortar

An excellent item that was brought back after the war by George Frazee of Grant County, Indiana, who was in the 12th Indiana Infantry. This mortar shell is in mint, non-dug condition and measures about 5-1/2" across. This type took the wooden drive-in fuse, mold seam around the middle of the cannonball. **$275**

12 lb Side-Loading

Excavated Confederate cannonball with brass paper fuse plug and leaded loading hole for adding the explosive, fine plum patina. **$575**

Nice C.S. side-loader case shot, cannonball has copper fuse that held the paper time fuse. It also has the lead side plug that was used to fill the ball with iron shot. The ball has a few little chips missing from the side, but that doesn't take away from the total appearance of the cannonball. The ball has been cleaned and disarmed and is completely safe. It was recovered in north Georgia. **$265**

4 lb

No fuse, but has brass underplug, nice iron shell, dug near Vicksburg. **$245**

Wood drive-in fuse cannonball dug at Vicksburg, Mississippi, cleaned and coated. Surface is about average with normal ground action. **$295**

23" Read

Excavated from the Battle of Stone's River, Tennessee. Missing a portion of one side of nose section, but doesn't detract from the shell. Fuse grooves strong and visible, missing the copper sabot, good shape, professionally cleaned and coated. **$295**

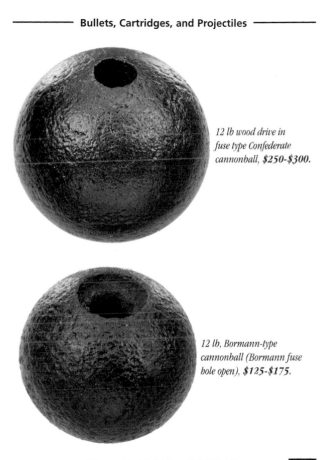

*12 lb wood drive in fuse type Confederate cannonball, **$250-$300**.*

*12 lb, Bormann-type cannonball (Bormann fuse hole open), **$125-$175**.*

Exceptionally nice, dug, 3" Confederate Read shell that has a smooth shell body and a complete brass sabot with deep clean rifling. **$475**

Nice condition, dug, Confederate Read shell with a perfect rifled brass sabot intact, as is, a nice brass C.S. time fuse. Good metal, but was not cleaned well before being coated, the clear coat is actually over rust build-up. **$350**

3" Read-Broun
Exceptionally nice condition, dug Confederate Read-Broun projectile, dug at Petersburg, Virginia. It has already been cleaned and coated. This type Confederate shell usually is quite pitted due to the poor-quality iron from which it was cast. Intact brass sabot with deep, sharp rifling except for one small 2" section that was thrown when fired. **$450**

3" Read-Parrot
This display-ready projectile has a nice, smooth shell body and has been cleaned and coated. It is a wood drive-in fuse-type and was dug at Petersburg, Virginia. About a quarter of the iron sabot is intact, and the remainder was thrown when fired. Characteristic C.S. lathe dimple in base. **$295**

32 lb
Fine iron shell with wood plug dug near Vicksburg. **$250**

4.6" Read
Unlisted Confederate 4.6" Read Shell. Only about 6 of these shells are known to exist, great condition with absolutely no pitting, cleaned and coated.

.... **$3,500**

Archer
Excellent condition Confederate shell, has some of the original wooden drive-in fuse visible. Minimal ground action with no major pitting or flaking. Nice example, cleaned and coated, found near Shiloh, Tennessee.

.... **$645**

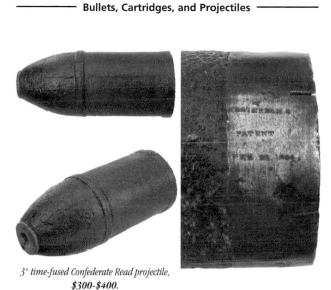

3" time-fused Confederate Read projectile,
$300-$400.

3" Absterdam (Union),
$295-$335.

Solid Shot

Confederate, 8 lb
From the Augusta, Georgia, Arsenal. **$585**

Confederate, 12 lb
Solid shot with a very pronounced seam mark, has traces of gold paint on it,
display base. **$165**

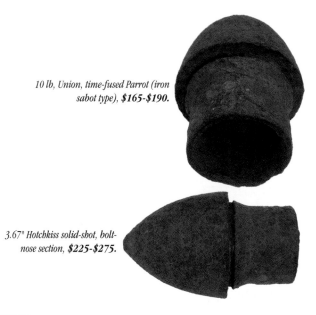

*10 lb, Union, time-fused Parrot (iron sabot type), **$165-$190**.*

*3.67" Hotchkiss solid-shot, bolt-nose section, **$225-$275**.*

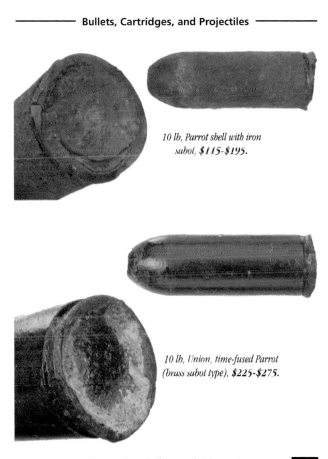

10 lb, Parrot shell with iron sabot, $115-$195.

10 lb, Union, time-fused Parrot (brass sabot type), $225-$275.

Artillery Projectiles, U.S.

Bolt, 2.35" Pattison
Extremely rare short version, measuring only 5-1/4". **$1,550**

Bolt, 20 lb Parrot
3.67" "bottlenose" Parrot bolt dug at Vicksburg, Mississippi, nicely cleaned and
coated. As was commonly the case, the projectile threw the copper sabot when
fired. **$225**

Bolt, 30 lb Parrot
Vicksburg-dug "bottlenose" Parrot bolt. Projectile has been cleaned, coated, and
is ready for display. It has nice condition iron with only a typical amount of
pitting in areas. Rifled brass sabot is 100% intact. This is somewhat rare in
that 30 lb Parrot bolts often threw all, or part, of their sabot. **$350**

Bolt, 60 lb Parrot
Extremely rare, as this Navy caliber was primarily fired over water. This
bottlenose bolt hit something hard and dead-on as the nose is chipped and
the shock sheared a portion of the sabot mount. Some cosmetic work on the
nose and the base has been done to allow it to stand. **$1,350**

> "I remember how we spent the last Fourth of July down
> on the Chattahoochie, exposed to shell and bullets while
> we were throwing up breastworks we made remarks, and
> wondered where we would be on the next Fourth."
>
> —*Charles Berry,*
> *7th Iowa Infantry*

3.67" time-fused Hotchkiss nose section, $100-$150.

20 lb, time-fused Parrot projectile, $275-$300.

Case Shot, 3" Hotchkiss

Complete, dug, 3" flame groove Hotchkiss case shot projectile excavated from
the Battle of Nashville, Tennessee. The shell has been cleaned and coated and
consists of cup, rifled lead sabot, nose, and brass time fuse. Only about one
Hotchkiss out of 10 are dug with all parts intact. **$250**

Grape Shot, Stand

Recovered from a well in Vicksburg many years ago. An extremely fine
specimen, with little sign of its great time buried. Could be cleaned much
more or left as is. Has a thin rust patina, but solid and stable, measures
6-1/4" d, and 8-1/4" h. Weight is approximately 35 lbs. Consists of cast-iron
discs top and bottom, each of which has on its inside face, three depressions
which hold the balls in position. There are levels of 3 balls, held into position
by two iron rings. There is a heavy bolt top to bottom. On firing, the bolt and
the rings break, and the entire thing comes apart. **$1,950**

Shell, U.S.

12 lb Ball

12 lb smoothbore shell with Bormann time fuse. This is a very clean specimen
showing signs of the four tin wood sabot straps and the fuse collar. The
Bormann fuse is perfect. The ball is 4.52" d. **$450**

Bormann-fused cannonball from Honey Hill, South Carolina, near where the
55th Massachusetts battled. Fuse top broken off, otherwise intact, includes
display base. **$165**

10 lb Parrot

Very nice condition, Union projectile, dug at Kennesaw Mountain, smooth clean
iron, a complete excellent brass sabot, and a complete, pewter time fuse
intact. **$250**

20 lb Parrot

Early variety with the high brass Parrots, these sabots almost always threw their sabots and most are recovered without the sabot intact. Rare variant of the 20 lb Parrot projectile, missing threaded fuse. **$375**

3" Hotchkiss

Excavated and still retains nice flame grooves. Has brass fuse intact, but missing the lead band. Good shape, professionally cleaned and coated. **$215**

3" Parrot

A 10 lb shell cut in half showing the powder compartment and a cut-away of the percussion fuse. Mounted on a board with a brass plaque engraved, "3 IN. PARROT/PERCUSSION FUSED." Dug in Richmond area. **$195**

3.25" J.P. Schenkl

About 3-1/4" d, still has most of its lead Bormannn fuse. Nice crusty brown patina. **$175**

Solid Shot

4 lb

Very-early-type solid shot made for smoothbore gun, 3-1/8" d and weighs a bit over 4 lbs. From the Battle of Lexington, Missouri, September 18-20, 1861. Early pick-up, very-good shape. **$115**

12 lb

Nice condition, dug 12 lb solid shot cannonball. This was an early find here at Stones River and has already been cleaned, coated, and is ready for display. **$150**

Very-fine condition, iron, with original wood sabot.................................... **$395**

18 lb

Shell has mold seam, sprue on top, very good example, found in Pennsylvania, and painted black.. **$225**

24 lb

Fine condition, found at Vicksburg. **$225**

5-5/8" d, an extremely clean shot. **$240**

32 lb

Very good condition. **$235**

*3" "flat-top" Hotchkiss nose section, **$150-$195.***

CHAPTER 5

BUTTONS

Collecting uniform buttons can be very satisfying to a collector, whether beginner or expert. Without the expense of collecting cloth items, a Civil War enthusiast can feel a link to individual soldiers by assembling a collection of buttons. The variety of issues, as well as manufacturers, provides for a wide field of available items with a price scale ranging from a couple of dollars for a common U.S. General Service button to several thousands of dollars for a Confederate locally-made staff officer's button.

Like so many areas of Civil War collecting, it is important to specialize if you decide to focus your attention on buttons. Pick a branch of service, a state, (or better, a manageable combination) as opposed to simply buying what comes along. There are far too many buttons available, and you will soon become overwhelmed if you don't narrow the field a bit. Simply collecting Confederate buttons will soon empty your financial resources, whereas a collection of Virginia buttons will provide a wide variety of items at a more affordable collecting pace.

Button collectors have the opportunity to collect non-dug or dug items. Whereas dug items lend a greater sense of authenticity, their usual dull patinas are not the most attractive. Non-dug buttons, on the other hand, can be very expensive for rare examples, and are easier to reproduce. Collecting on the high end of the field should only be done after exhaustive research and examination of buttons in other collections.

Non-excavated, coat-size, Union Navy button, $45 $75.

Non-excavated, cuff-size, Rhode Island, state-seal button, $35-$45.

Non-excavated, coat-size, Vermont, state-seal button, $55-$85.

As is the case in so many areas of Civil War collecting, the button field has been inundated with reproductions and fakes. The same dies that were used to stamp buttons during the 1860s still exist and, in many cases, are used to produce buttons primarily for the reenacting market. It takes very little campaigning to give a newly struck brass button a warm, rich patina.

High prices have prompted some forgers to actually bury or artificially age buttons to achieve a dug appearance. Inspect any button, but especially those priced over more than a few dollars, with attention to detail. Use a high-powered magnifying glass and bright light to make your inspection.

During the Civil War, three button styles were in use: the one-piece button (figure 1); the two-piece button (figure 2); and the staff button (figure 3). It is important to note that the style of button is not an indicator of rank, but rather is a result of different manufacturing techniques.

The one-piece button was very popular during the eighteenth century and the first half of the nineteenth for both uniforms and civilian clothes. It can be found in cast, molded, or die-struck form. The shank, in earlier examples, is often part of the same casting as the face. On later, struck examples, the shank was made of a separate loop of wire and brazed onto the back of the face.

Two-piece buttons were first introduced around 1813 by an English inventor, Benjamin Sanders. The button consists of a front "shell" on which the design is struck and a back "plate" on which the shank is attached. The front shell is attached by rolling it over the edge of the back plate.

The third style is often referred to as a "staff" button. It was first produced in the United States in the 1830s, and became the mainstay of uniform button style through the twentieth century. It is similar to the two-piece button except that the front shell and back plate are held together by a separate rim piece.

Button Types

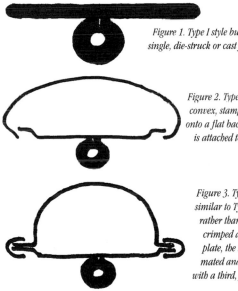

Figure 1. Type I style button consists of a single, die-struck or cast face with a shank.

Figure 2. Type II buttons have a convex, stamped shell crimped onto a flat back plate. The shank is attached to the back plate.

Figure 3. Type III buttons are similar to Type II buttons, but rather than having the shell crimped around the back plate, the two surfaces are mated and bound together with a third, flat piece of metal.

Collecting Hints

Pros:
- There is a huge variety of buttons available for collectors.
- It is easy to assemble a large collection and not require a lot of space.
- Buttons display well and are not adversely affected by longtime exposure.
- Many buttons can be purchased for under $30 each.
- Good references are available.

Cons:
- Many buttons have been restruck, reproduced, and faked.
- Variety is virtually unlimited and a collector can easily become overwhelmed.
- Because of the size, buttons do not easily command a lot of attention when displayed.

Availability ★★★★★
Price ★
Reproduction Alert ★★★

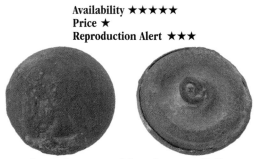

*Excavated, coat-size, Confederate drop-wing, staff-officer
(crude Confederate local manufacture) button, $225-$250.*

Confederate

Branch of Service Buttons

General Service

"CS over A." Rare and unusually nice! Smooth, without shank; most of this variety are dented or heavily pushed, very minor place above the "C" and is an especially fine example, 17 mm. **$600**

"Superior Quality," 23 mm. **$200**

Scarce kepi "CSA" button, "Treble Rich/Standard," 13 mm. **$450**

Artillery

Block "A" with a tin back, a crudely-made local, beautiful chocolate patina.
.... **$750**

Lined "A" "Superior Quality," 23 mm. **$200**

A very nice example of the block "A" button with backmark, "E.M. Lewis & Co./Richmond." Small face dent, back is slightly pushed in, still really great-looking artifact with super character, complete with the shank. **$135**

Cavalry

Lined "C," backmark blank, beautiful copper face. **$625**

Script "C": "Isaacs & Campbell/London/71 Jeremyn St." Dug from low country South Carolina, condition rough, 23 mm. **$85**

Engineer

Manuscript, "E" ".S. Isaacs Campbell & Co./ London/St.James .St.," 26 mm.
.... **$3,000**

Infantry

Beautiful set of three, two-piece Confederate block "I" coat-size buttons. These buttons were dug only a few inches from each other off the same jacket. All three have beautiful faces, full back, and shank intact. **$250**

A beautiful, dug example of a solid cast "I" button with rich chocolate patina. **$125**

Block "I," no shank, nice face, dug at Morton, Mississippi. **$65**

Coat-size, solid cast-brass Confederate block "I." It is very rare to find this button in non-excavated condition, 23 mm-button with shank intact... **$495**

Dug, two-piece Confederate Block "I" coat-size button, iron back, face has attractive smooth brown patina. The back is rusty but intact, and the iron loop is rusted away as usual. A good, solid example of probably the most frequently encountered marked Confederate button in the western theater. **$85**

Navy

A very fine hard rubber or black plastic-type of material. Very attractive Confederate button, backmark, "Courtney & Tennent/Charleston S C/ Manton's Patent." **$1,200**

Confederate Navy medium size. Blank, stand up shank intact, chocolate-brown patina, 18 mm. **$500**

Rifleman

German Text "R" "Van Wart Son & Co.," 23 mm. **$450**

This is a two-piece, non-dug, coat-size button with a stippled Roman "R" with an "H T & B Manchester" backmark, 25 mm d, complete with shank. **$645**

Excavated, Confederate coat-size, solid, cast infantry button, $200-$265.

Excavated, Confederate coat-size, iron-back, 2-piece button, $100-$150.

Excavated, Confederate coat-size, cavalry, iron-back, 2-piece button, $250-$300.

18 mm, Confederate Navy button, $395-$475.

Excavated, Confederate coat-size script "I" button, $135-$165.

Staff

Beautiful condition, non-excavated, Confederate, droop-wing eagle, staff officer's button, 19 mm size, "Treble Gilt Extra Rich" backmark, 100% bright gold gilt and nice straight shank intact on the reverse. **$225**

Coat-size, droop-wing eagle, Confederate staff officer's button dug from General Leonidas Polk's winter camps along Duck River following the Battle of Stones River, smooth, uncleaned, brown patina. Button does have a slight dent, but still looks great, iron shank remains intact on the reverse. **$125**

Dug off Charleston, South Carolina, 15% bright background gilt, shank half broken off by digger, very nice example "droop-wing" eagle button. **$395**

State-Issued Buttons

The distinction is rarely made by button dealers between buttons produced with state seals before the war and buttons produced during the war. Though rarely priced accordingly, it is safe to assume that a button bearing a southern state seal and possessing a northern manufacturer's mark were produced before or after 1861-1865. Whereas, it is likely that these buttons produced prior to 1861 found their way to Confederate uniforms. One should consider place of manufacture before expending large sums of money.

*Excavated, Confederate coat-size script "C" button, **$495-$550.***

*Excavated, Confederate coat-size staff officer button, **$165-$225.***

*Coat-size Louisiana state seal (sideways pelican) button, **$450-$500.***

*Coat-size Louisiana state seal (frontal pelican) button, **$300-$325.***

Alabama

"AVC, has rare, "Lambert & Mast/Philada" rmdc, unusual and desirable mark is easily readable, smooth patina, device highlighted with gilt, 21 mm." .. **$400**

This AVC was found in Caroline County, Virginia, touch of gold gilt above the eagle's head, inside the "V," and front has light touches. The front has light ground action typical of many dug buttons. The backmark is "R W Robinson Extra Rich." The shank is slightly bent which put pressure on the back and slightly kinked it. **$230**

Georgia

Beautiful condition, non-dug, coat-size Georgia state seal, Van Wart backmark, 100% bright gold gilt with shank intact. **$95**

Georgia seal, "Horstmann & Allien/NY" with rays, 24 mm. **$200**

Kentucky

Kentucky cuff, "*Extra*/Quality," 15 mm. **$250**

Kentucky seal, "Horstmann & Allien/NY," mint, 23 mm. **$750**

Louisiana

Dug, coat-size Confederate local Louisiana state seal, smooth brown patina with 80% bright beautiful gilt and dent-free. The back is very solid, but the wire loop is rusted away. **$350**

Louisiana seal, "Horstmann's/N.Y.& PHI," 23 mm. **$450**

A cuff-sized example "Pelican" button, pelican has her head to her left, Scovill backmark, rich dug patina, nice detail, no shank. **$95**

Maryland

Maryland cuff, marked, "*Extra*/Quality."15 mm. **$175**

Unusual Maryland with double-struck backmark, "*Extra*/Quality," 23 mm. **$375**

Excavated, coat-size, Confederate-used floral or pattern button, $5-$10.

Excavated, coat-size, Wisconsin, state-seal button, $95-$125.

Excavated, coat size, New York, state-seal button, $25-$45.

Excavated, Confederate coat-size Virginia state-seal button, $175-$225.

Non-excavated, Confederate coat-size staff officer button, $185-$215.

Non-excavated, Confederate coat-size CSA button, $200-$225.

Excavated, vest-size, South Carolina, state-seal button, $185-$225.

Mississippi

Dug, Mississippi "C" cuff, "Hyde & Goodrich/N.O.," 16 mm. **$375**

Dug, Mississippi Infantry "I" "local" cuff blank, probably produced by C. Rouyer, no shank, attractive patina, 16 mm. **$125**

North Carolina

Absolutely beautiful, non-dug, coat-size Confederate local North Carolina state seal, 100% bright gold gilt front and back, huge crude shank intact but leans to one side. **$475**

South Carolina

75% original guilt remaining, carved lead Palmetto Tree with metal pin.
.... **$385**

Beautiful dug, coat-size, South Carolina state seal button that has 90% bright gold gilt with shank intact, "Horstmann and Allen" backmark. **$185**

Coat size, dug, with shank, good, very-good condition. **$68**

Virginia

Virginia staff, "Horstmann & Allien/N.Y." flat back, 23 mm. **$225**

Non excavated, pre Civil War, one-piece coat button, "Superior Quality" backmark, fine. **$350**

Excavated, coat size, Louisiana, state-seal button, $350-$375.

U.S.

Branch of Service Buttons
General Service
Dug, large-sized eagle button with dark, aged patina. Back is slightly pushed in and still has the shank and Scovill backmark. **$15**

Infantry, silvered, 21 mm, low convex, 2-piece, ".Young. Smith & Co./New York." **$45**

Standard pattern eagle button, size is midway between the small "shell jacket size" and the standard "blouse size" (20% larger than the small-size button). This size is sometimes seen on infantry pattern shell jackets, and is a very scarce variant. **$15**

Artillery
Eagle "A," dug in Central Mississippi, shank present, fine condition. **$29**

Artillery, "W.H.Horstmann & Sons/Phi.," rmdc, 21 mm. **$45**

Cavalry
Backmarked "Waterbury Button Co. Waterbury Con.".................................. **$55**

Civil War cavalry button set of 12 with history, 10 are a bit under 23 mm and the two cuff buttons are just over 16 mm. Larger button backs say, "Extra Quality," cuff button backs say, "Waterbury Button Co." All have the very articulated eagle with the "C" in the shield or center area. Excellent condition, just a couple of bent shanks. Consigner included the following information: "These buttons were from the uniform of William McKendree Snyder. He served in the Civil War enlisting at the age of 12 as a drummer boy for the Union (Indiana Volunteers) side. After the war he became a noteworthy painter. He is a listed artist and his work can be found on the art search sites online. He was born in 1848 and died in 1930." **$385**

Dragoon

Beautiful, non-excavated, coat-size eagle "D," 100% bright gold gilt, WG Mintzer backmark and shank intact. **$125**

Dug, cuff button, perfect condition, "Scovill" backmark. **$55**

Eagle "D," dug in Texas, cuff-size button w/shank, very good condition. **$35**

Engineer

"Scovill Mf'g. Co./Waterbury," 23 mm. **$225**

"Horstmann.Bros.&.Allien/N.Y." 23 mm. **$225**

Infantry

"D. Evans & Co.," backmark. Eagle "I" coat button, lots of gilt left, small push to back at shank. **$20**

Eagle "I," backmark: "R&W. Robinson/Extra Rich," 85% gilt. **$30**

National Guard

"NG" on breast of eagle, 1850s "*Waterbury Button. Co.*/Extra" (in small letters around outside edge of button back), condition excellent, 23 mm. **$100**

Navy

".Scovill Mf'g. Co/Waterbury." rmdc, 23 mm. **$40**

"R&W. Robinson" with eagle, 22 mm. **$75**

One-piece button with backmark, "Treble Gilt/Standard Colour," 100% gilt back and front. **$145**

Rifleman

Dug, eagle "R" Rifleman's cuff button from Richmond, Virginia, full shank, illegible backmark. **$50**

Staff

Backmark, "Extra Quality," 100% gilt. **$45**

Excellent, non-excavated, cuff-size, Union staff officer with 100% bright gold gilt, has the Scovill backmark, intact shank. **$25**

Dug, somewhat squashed, standard U.S. staff officer's button. **$10**

"**R&W. Robinson**/Makers/*Attleborough*/Mass," 23 mm. **$55**

"*Horstmann Bro & Co*/Phila," rmdc, silver plated, 23 mm. **$85**

State-Issued Buttons

California

State seal, wartime and increasingly hard to find, "Scovill Mf'g Co./Waterbury," 23 mm. **$225**

Connecticut

Battlefield-excavated, state seal button, backmark "Scovill Waterbury." **$35**

C.N.G., staff cuff, "*Superior*/Quality," low convex relief, 15 mm. **$25**

Connecticut seal, "*Scovill Mf'g Co./Waterbury," 23 mm. **$60**

Maine

Backmark, "Waterbury Button Co. Waterbury." **$40**

Large-size, coin-style, one-piece button, five-pointed star surrounded by 17 tiny stars on lined field, Imperial Standard backmark, perfect non-dug with shank. **$59**

Maine "R&W. Robinson/Attleborough/***Extra***/ Rich." 22 mm. **$68**

Massachusetts

Beautiful non-excavated, gilt, coat-size Massachusetts state seal with "Extra Quality" backmark, 100% bright gold gilt, no dents, and shank intact. ... **$45**

Boston city guards, "Draper & Sandland/Extra," 23 mm. **$150**

Boston Light Infantry; one-piece convex, "*R&W. Robinson*/Attleborough/ ***Extra***/Rich." Scarce and nice, early example, 21 mm. **$250**

Excavated, coat-size, Union infantry button, $15-$20.

Excavated, coat-size, Texas seal button, $225-$275.

Excavated, coat-size, South Carolina, state-seal button, $125-$185.

Cuff-size staff button with rim, nice prewar backmark, "Robinsons Makers," excellent, non-dug example. **$25**

Cuff-size staff button with rim, nice prewar backmark, "*D. Evans & Co.* Extra." **$25**

Independent Corps of Cadets "*Robinsons*/Extra." Mint, 15 mm. **$35**

Massachusetts, one-piece, plain field; "(16 asterisks in depressed channel)," scarce Peasley-made variant, distinctive die, 22 mm. **$185**

New England guards, cuff, "R&W. Robinson/Extra," 15 mm. **$35**

New England guards, low convex, two-piece, "R&W. Robinson," in ribbon with eagle, 21 mm. **$55**

Michigan
Michigan cuff, "Scovill Mf'g Co./Waterbury," 15 mm. **$45**

Dug, "Extra Quality" backmark, quite a bit of gilt, slight push in back, nice looking, found on Civil War site. **$39**

Michigan seal, "Scovill Mf'g Co./Waterbury," 23 mm. **$200**

New Hampshire
Gold-over-brass state seal button, backmark, "Scovill MFG Co Waterbury."
.... **$60**

Nice, non-dug pair, war date, no shanks, glue remnants where mounted in button display. **$20**

New York
A fine, non-dug, cuff-size example, "Scovill Mfg Co" backmark, excellent with nice gilt. **$15**

Backmark, "Waterbury Button Co./Extra," 100% gilt. **$30**

Big, flat, New York one-piece, silver-plated, blank, 24 mm. **$145**

Brass, state seal button excavated from Sharpsburg battlefield, 7/8" d, backmarked, "Goddard & Bro Extra.".. **$25**

Pennsylvania
Chausseur's button cuff, "Cordier Freres/Paris," 17 mm. **$75**

Pennsylvania seal, "*Superior*/Quality," 23 mm. **$235**

Rhode Island
One-piece, blank, earliest Rhode Island seal known in 13 mm size. **$250**

Coat-size, non-excavated, three-piece staff officer's button, 100% bright gold gilt, intact shank. **$75**

Cuff-sized, backmarked, "Robinson Maker." **$35**

Vermont
Nice cuff-sized example of the Vermont state seal button, nice, non-dug light patina and one tiny face dent, desirable rmdc backmark "Scovill Mfg Co Waterbury."... **$55**

Coat-sized, excellent. **$60**

Vermont Volunteer Militia, light infantry; one-piece, "R&W. Robinson/ Attleborough/.*.*.*.Extra.*.*.*./ Rich." Shows honest use and genuine wear, 22 mm.. **$125**

Wisconsin
Very scarce, coat-sized, non-dug, nice patina, some face wear and a tiny dent, backmark, "Extra Quality." **$95**

Non-dug, nice patina, some face wear and a tiny dent, backmark, "Extra Quality".. **$100**

Wisconsin state seal, "*Extra*/Quality," 23 mm. **$225**

*Excavated, coat-size,
Confederate infantry, iron-back
button, $75-$100.*

*Excavated, coat-size,
N. Carolina, state-seal (crude
Confederate local manufacture)
button, $65-$95.*

*Excavated, coat-size, Union
eagle button, $7-$12.*

CHAPTER 6

EPHEMERA

Ephemera can be loosely defined as paper items documenting a generation's daily lives without the intention of being saved. By that standard, our current ephemera would range from the nightly newspaper to the wrappers on our fast-food hamburgers. In the context of the Civil War, ephemera is the group of items that allows us to peer deeply into the everyday existence of the soldiers. This could range from a set of general orders intended to be read at a morning inspection to a parole, granting a secessionist the right to return to his home in return for a pledge of allegiance. Civil War ephemera is the group of written snapshots of the soldier's life.

Collecting ephemera is a very broad category. It is not as easy as assembling a type collection that includes one of everything. That approach may leave a collector overwhelmed, and eventually, low on funds. Rather, many collectors of ephemera take a thematic approach. Perhaps, a single regiment is the focus of their collection, or a battle, or even, a political theme such as President Lincoln or slavery. The thematic approach imposes a discipline that many collectors desperately seem to need to rein them in from buying every piece they encounter. More importantly though, thematic collecting starts to define a particular idea.

Take for example, a person who is interested in the role a sutler played during the Civil War. Perhaps this interest began by acquiring a rare and expensive broadside touting a regimental sutler's availability of goods. The price of such an item might be in the thousands of dollars, so it will be difficult for the collector to develop a "type collection." Using a thematic approach, however, he will soon discover that he could add sutler's tokens, soldier's letters describing visits to the sutler, documents that tabulate a soldier's accounts, autographs of regimental sutlers, handbills, or even newspapers advertising the availability of goods for sutlers to sell to soldiers in the field. Soon, the collector has assembled a variety of items that afford a much better understanding of the regimental sutler's role than the line or two that most published histories provide.

There is, however, an ethical dilemma associated with ephemera collecting, and it relates directly to manuscript material such as diaries, letters, and other handwritten documents. Though it is with great pride that a collector obtains an original diary or pack of soldier's letters, this does pull the items out of their effective role as historical documents. When stored in a private collection, these items are withdrawn from access to scholarly research. Perhaps, one day, when the collection comes back to the market, a public archive will be able to acquire the pieces, making them accessible once again. But, private ownership does, in many cases, remove important records from a generation's access. It is an issue that only individual collectors can decide for themselves.

Collecting Hints

Pros:
- Ephemera stores in very little space. It is easy to accumulate hundreds of pieces and store them in only one box.

- Ephemera is extremely available. Ephemera dealers, stamp dealers, numismatists, newspaper handlers, and antiquarians are all possible sources.

- Ephemera can be very affordable. Though, like all areas of Civil War collecting, items associated with the Confederacy, President Lincoln, or African-Americans in the service will always be pricey, other items pertaining to less recognizable themes are within the means of a novice.

- Other than autographs, stamps, a few poorly reproduced broadsides, and Confederate notes, there are very few reproductions of documents on the market. This makes ephemera a safer venue for novice collectors. Unfortunately, apart from the above-named collector areas, though, there are very few published references available.

Cons:

- Unless you have lots of wall space, it will be difficult to display much of the ephemera you collect. Most collections are relegated to flat, acid-free boxes, or slipped into archival sleeves and tucked into three-ring binders. It requires lots of flat space to visually enjoy a collection. Furthermore, long-term exposure to light is extremely detrimental to paper items.

- Paper items are susceptible to fluctuations in temperature and humidity. A collection will require a very stable environment.

- Document collecting promotes the dissolution of manuscript collections and removing valuable primary sources from public access. This is one of those ethical issues you have to deal with on your own.

> **Availability** ★★★★
> **Price** ★★
> **Reproduction Alert** ★★★

Confederate Currency, By Year

Notes

C.S.A., $5, 1861
Sailor seated beside bales of cotton, center; C.G. Memminger, left; Justice & Ceres, right. Dated: Richmond, September 2, 1861, good condition. **$50**

C.S.A., $10, 1861
Popular note pictures Ceres reclining on a cotton bale, printing error by Hoyer & Ludwig. It should be dated, "Sep. 2, 1861," and is dated in error, "Sep. 2, 1862." This is a circulated note in solid condition with good print color. **$65**

C.S.A., $20, 1861
Nice circulated condition, issue date September 2, 1861, Industry is seated between cupid and a beehive, it also has a bust shot of A.H. Stephens. ... **$45**

C.S.A., $1, 1862
Steamship, Lucy Pickens, uncirculated, tight margins, bright white paper. **$265**

C.S.A., $2, 1862
South strikes Union, circulated. **$325**

Judah Benjamin at top left, Justice triumphs over tyranny in center, very-good condition. **$33**

C.S.A., $10, 1862
Nice circulated condition, issue date December 2, 1862, fancy blue back with the state capitol at Columbia, South Carolina, and has R.M.T. Hunter at right. **$45**

C.S.A., $20, 1862
Nashville, Tennessee, capitol building, blue reverse, extra fine. **$195**

C.S.A., $50, 1862
Jefferson Davis, C.S.A. president, green tint, very fine. **$395**

C.S.A., $100, 1862
Negroes hoeing cotton, J.C. Calhoun, orange "HUNDRED," circulated....... **$125**

Nice circulated condition, issue date June 23, 1862, railway train with diffused
locomotive steam, milkmaid at left. **$60**

C.S.A., $2, 1863
Judah P. Benjamin, right, Richmond, April 6, 1863, good condition. **$60**

J.P. Benjamin, pink paper, plain reverse, uncirculated. **$475**

C.S.A., $10, 1863
Capitol-Columbia R.M.T. Hunter, blue reverse, circulated. **$125**

C.S.A., $20, 1863
Capitol-Nashville, blue reverse, uncirculated. **$245**

C.S.A., $50, 1863
Jefferson Davis, fancy green reverse, uncirculated. **$265**

C.S.A., $100, 1863
Lucy Pickens, soldiers, green reverse, uncirculated. **$895**

Lucy Pickens, soldiers, G.W. Randolph, green reverse, circulated. **$375**

C.S.A., $1, 1864
C.C. Clay, C.S.A. senator, uncirculated, dark red. **$225**

Clement C. Clay, center, Richmond, February 17, 1864, fine condition. **$72**

C.S.A., $2, 1864
Judah P. Benjamin, right, black with reddish network background overprint,
Richmond, good condition. **$55**

Confederate currency, T-41
$100 note, $75-$100.

Confederate currency, T-67
$20 note, $45-$60.

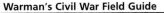

C.S.A., $10, 1864

Horses pulling cannon (Mexican War scene), R.M.T. Hunter, blue "TEN" reverse, uncirculated. **$45**

C.S.A., $500, 1864

Equestrian view of Washington, C.S.A. flag, Gen. T.J. (Stonewall) Jackson, light red, very sharp. **$740**

February 17, 1864, solid, circulated note with a pretty pink color, face of the note is very nice, serial #2142. The note's reverse has "$3,000" written in old brown ink and has a spatter where a drop of ink fell. **$375**

Confederate Currency, State-Issued
Alabama
$1, 1863

Note issued out of Montgomery, Alabama, January 1. The note is in sound circulated condition, serial #89585 .... **$45**

$20, 1853

Central Bank of Alabama, Montgomery, beautiful, spread-wing eagle holding American flag, Ben Franklin, left. Indian maiden in tent, rare, historic "C.S.A." red circular stamp, fine **$105**

Georgia
5¢, 1863

Milledgeville, Georgia, fine condition. **$21**

$1, ca. 1857-1861

Appealing note on the Timber Cutters Bank, Savannah, Georgia, with lithographs of slaves working at cutting timber, carrying cotton, and also a sailor sitting on a bale of cotton. Worn, roughly 7" x 3". **$18.50**

Louisiana
$5, 1862
Soldier striking down Lady Liberty in the center, pelican on the left, Baton Rouge, Louisiana, very-fine condition. **$39**

50¢, 1864
Eagle on left, Navy ship middle, Shreveport, Louisiana, very-good. **$35**

Maryland
$5
The Valley Bank of Maryland. **$28**

Mississippi
$50
Faith of the State Pledged, red, Indian, maiden, left; train center, red "50," beautiful note, extra fine. **$115**

North Carolina
$1, 1861
Dated October 12, 1861, $1 North Carolina note, nice circulated condition. **$45**

South Carolina
25¢, 1863
Bank of the State of South Carolina Palmetto, no watermark. **$30**

Tennessee
10¢, 1861
Quite rare 10-cent Bank of Tennessee at Nashville, dated December 4, 1861, complete but circulated. **$35**

Virginia
$1, 1861
Corporation of Fredericksburg, $2, train and ship center; woman in field right, November 1, 1861, good condition. **$55**

*Confederate currency, T-53 $5 note, **$45-$55.***

*Canal bank note, New Orleans $100 note, **$45-$65.***

Confederate currency, T-68 $10 note, $40-$50.

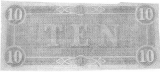

Confederate currency, T-66 $50 note, $65-$85.

Confederate currency, T-20 $20 note, $40-$50.

Corporation of Richmond, 25¢ fractional note, $60-$75.

Confederate currency, T-36 $5 note, $40-$50.

Confederate currency, T 72 50¢ note, $35-$40.

Autographs

Canby, Edward S., general, U.S.A., one page, autographed letter signed with rank by General Edward R. S. Canby. Fine condition, written in period ink on "War Department, Washington City" letterhead. Great content about the condition of the body of General Joseph B. Plummer, and whether it can be transported to Washington City. Edward Canby was the only U.S. Army general to die at the hands of Indians, when he was brutally murdered by the Modoc Indians in 1873. .... **$375**

Davis, Jefferson, President, C.S.A., fine signature penned as "JeffersDavis" on a federal War Department document from 1854. His signature appears just above his printed title, "Secretary of War." The document itself is 7" x 13" and is handsomely framed with a CDV engraving of Davis and a beautiful brass plate with the details of his life. Overall size of the frame, constructed from red burled wood, is 21" square. **$1,250**

Elliott, Washington Lafayette, general, U.S.A., war date document signed (endorsed) by Union General Washington Lafayette Elliott. "No. 40 SPECIAL REQUISITION" dated Sept. 19th, 1863, and signed boldly by Elliot with rank. Also signed by Captain J.W. Hart as acting quartermaster for the 3rd Division of the 3rd Army Corps. Very-fine condition. **$195**

Ellsworth, Elmer Ephraim, colonel, U.S.A., one legal page autographed document signed, Head Quarters, 1st Zouaves, Capital Buildings, May 6, 1861. Special Order giving orders to Lieutenant Barry, Company E. as Officer of the Day, Sergeant Leary as Officer of the Guard and telling him to post the Police Guard with positive orders that no one shall pass unless by order of the Colonel, ordering the Quartermaster to inspect the guns and report the number and kind of each rifle, and finally ordering the Captains of the Companies to hand in a complete roll of their command, more content. Signed "E.E. Ellsworth, Col 1st Zouaves." He wrote this on the back of what is thought to be a fire department form that makes it an extremely rare manuscript. Ellsworth war-dated items are extremely rare, because his war service lasted from April 12 (firing on Fort Sumter) to May 24, 1861, when he was shot at the Marshall House in Alexandria, Virginia, in the process of removing a Confederate flag from the roof. **$11,950**

Forrest, Nathan Bedford, general, C.S.A., clipped signature from a Selma, Marion & Memphis Railroad bond. Signature is on a panel of the bond which measures 4-1/2" h x 8" w, and is darkly penned in brown ink. Railroad bonds are now basically the most affordable format for obtaining an authentic Forrest signature with no risk of deception. Forrest served as president of this railroad and then resigned as a result of the Panic of 1873. The Selma, Marion and Memphis Railroad had been started by Confederate general Gideon Pillow and thus this enterprise was strongly imbued with the energy and vision of southern military men whose role in the war had reduced their wealth, status and opportunities. **$1,695**

Grant, Ulysses, general, U.S.A., letter, dated December 2, 1865, is a recommendation for former Civil War Colonel S.S. Curtis while visiting Europe. The letter is in the hand of Grant and is signed boldly by him, including his rank. Letter measures 5" x 6-1/2". **$762**

Hunter, David, general, U.S.A., war-dated letter signed by General David Hunter, as commander of the Department of the South. "Head Quarters, Dept. of the South, Hilton Head S.C. May 30, 1862." To the governor of New York pertaining to vacated officers from the 46th New York Infantry. Signed boldly "D. Hunter, Maj. Gen." Hunter adds below his name, "It may be remarked that this regiment is now reduced to less than 660 enlisted men and it could probably better spare officers for staff duty than any other in this command." Full margins and in very-fine condition. **$185**

Lee, Robert E., general, C.S.A., document signed and dated May 31, 1842, from Fort La Fayette. Two 8" x 10" pages with two check-size attachments, printed and filled in with Lee's bold blue signature on back of 8" x 10" sheet. Listing of supplies to do repairs on Fort and Lee is certifying that it is correct and that the prices are reasonable. Main document completed by a clerk, other receipts by two different other people. **$4,650**

Logan, John A., general, U.S.A., fine one-page ink "autograph letter signed" (written and signed entirely in the hand of the writer) by Union General John A. Logan. Written in the field, the letter is headed "Head Quarters 3d Division 17th Army Corps On Big Black River, Miss. May 5th 1863." It reads, "Mr. L.I. Cist, Dear Sir, Your favor of April 15th is received, inquiring the date of my commissions as Brig and Maj General. I take rank of Brig General from March 21, 1862 and accepted my commission as Maj General April 19, 1863 to take rank from Nov 29, 1862." It is boldly signed "Very Respectfully/Your Obt Servt/John A Logan". Written on lined paper 8" x 10" in size, entirely on the front of the sheet... **$595**

Porter, David D., admiral, U.S.A., amazing autograph statement signed, one page, quarto, on Navy Department letterhead, dated August 14, 1865, from Washington, D.C. Written to an unknown correspondent, in the form of a patriotic statement of belief, Porter pens (in full): "In fighting for a Country like ours, all personal Considerations should be lost sight of, it is so necessary for the good of mankind that this union should live, that we should give our lives freely to maintain the present form of government under which we have attained a prosperity unparalleled in the annals of history. David D. Porter, Rear Admiral" Mounting remnants on verso; otherwise in fine condition.
.... **$6,950**

Schofield, John McAllister, general, U.S.A., beautifully matted and framed full standing pose cdv and autograph of Schofield. General Schofield is famous for his roles in the Battles of Spring Hill and Franklin, Tennessee.
.... **$295**

CHAPTER 7

FIREARMS

No single group of items better represents the conflict between northern and southern soldiers than firearms. Collectors are fortunate that the pistols, revolvers, carbines, muskets, and rifles have survived in great quantities. Though any single item will set a collector back a minimum of several hundred dollars, the variety of selection and the opportunity to specialize will provide a lifetime of searching and finding additions for a collection.

Collecting of firearms can be broken down into various categories. For example, one may want to collect weapons associated only with the cavalry, or perhaps, just Confederate-made weapons. The most common categorization is by type: carbines, muskets (and rifled muskets), and handguns (revolvers and pistols).

Carbines

The carbine, a shorter-than-normal shoulder arm, was the essential weapon of the Civil War cavalry trooper. Never in large supply before the Civil War, manufacturers rushed to meet the demand of both the Northern and Southern force. By War's end, no fewer than 17 different makes had been adopted by U.S. troops. Secessionist troops were not as fortunate and adopted a wide variety of captured carbines, sawed off shotguns and muskets, imported musketoons and breechloaders, in addition to a few thousand Southern-produced carbines.

Carbine collectors can focus on a variety of areas. For example, one could collect just breechloaders, metal cartridge weapons, Southern-produced, imports, or even variations of one specific make like Sharps or Spencer. Collecting carbines can also be just a facet of a larger collection such as cavalry-related items, or highlighting a photograph or accouterment collection.

Collecting Hints

Pros:
- A wide variety of Civil War carbines are available to collectors.
- Reproductions have been marketed to reenactors and skirmishers, and therefore, are appropriately marked as being reproductions.
- Carbines take a relatively small amount of space to store and are stable if kept in a low-humidity environment.

Cons:
- Firearms are always prime targets for thieves. Civil War carbines are easily sold and not easily traced. Having a weapons-based collection presents new concerns and responsibilities to collectors.
- Actual, documented, Confederate-produced and/or used carbines are scarce. The price range limits these items to advanced collectors.
- A lot of muskets shortened after the Civil War are marketed as "cut-downs" or "Confederate."
- The market for firearms is a bit more fluid than other collectibles. It is very much based on supply and demand.

Availability ★★★
Price ★★★
Reproduction Alert ★★

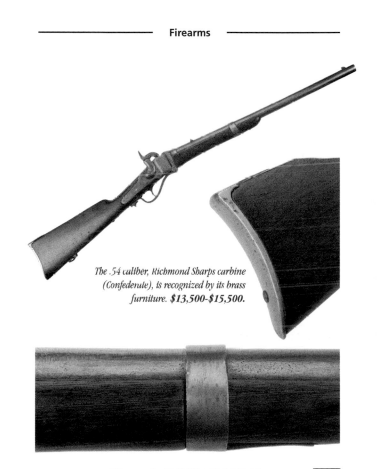

The .54 caliber, Richmond Sharps carbine (Confederate), is recognized by its brass furniture. $13,500-$15,500.

.50 caliber, Maynard carbine, $900-$1,650.

Confederate

Keen, Walker & Co.

Brass-framed, breechloading carbine, estimated that fewer than 25 currently exist. Very good condition, barrel has brown patina and a good sharp "P" proof mark, very-good rifling, saddle ring and bar are replacements. The brass frame has a beautiful mellow patina, excellent walnut stock with only minor chips and abrasions, breech and lever action is smooth and tight. **$24,500**

Extremely rare Confederate carbine (one of only 286 made between May and September 1862, in Danville, Virginia). Gun is 100% original in very good attic condition, has uncleaned, beautiful brass receiver with a rich patina. The barrel has a dark-brown patina with light salt and pepper pitting, "P" marked barrel, which is a proof mark, walnut stock is fine with the letters, "R.H. Harris" carved in it. Complete history of R.H. Harris comes with this extremely well-researched carbine. Lieutenant R.H. Harris was a member of the "Nottoway Reserves," Company F, 1st. Regiment of Virginia Reserves under the command of Captain Benjamin L. Farinholt. **$24,000**

Morse

Interesting period adaptation of this brass-framed carbine, manufactured in South Carolina. Weapon is number "374;" at some point, the carbine barrel was removed and a rifled octagonal barrel added. The gun turned up in Florida in the mid-1980s without much history. Unquestionably original, typical Confederate "make-do" to compensate for lack of the Morse cartridges—musket barrel has nipple threaded at rear of breech to take a percussion cap. **$3,500**

Morse, Type III

Serial no. 437. .... **$17,100**

Musketoon

Confederate Richmond cavalry carbine dated 1863, excellent and mellow example with all original parts and beautiful patina to the brass mounts. Nice bore, perfect "pinch" front sight, superb wood. **$11,500**

Richmond percussion carbine, cavalry pattern, dated 1863. Fine wood and clean metal overall, scattered light pitting, mainly at the breech area. Clear lock markings, strong action, missing butt swivel and ramrod, brass lightly cleaned on nose cap and buttplate. **$7,500**

Sharps, Richmond Pattern

Serial no. 2,812 on the lock, tang, and barrel, very-good condition and rates a fine grading. Smooth metal uniformly covered with a plum-brown color, patch of barrel pitting on the right side near the brass barrel band, and another small patch to the right of the rear sight. No other appreciable pitting except on the lever and frame bottom, marked "Richmond Va.," 100% complete including rear sight, butt sling swivel, sling ring, and bar that are frequently missing. Wood to metal fit is outstanding, bore is fine... **$13,500**

Shotgun

Extremely rare, Confederate-carried 1st Model Maynard, .64-caliber, 26" barrel shotgun. A number of Maynard rifles and carbines were purchased by Florida, Georgia, and Mississippi, and even more were confiscated out of southern arsenals. This particular weapon came out of central Mississippi. The metal on this weapon has a thick, dark, never-cleaned patina. The Maynard markings all remain crisp and clear. The bracket for the long-range tang site remains present, but the site itself is not present. The stock is in nice condition, but does have numerous small dings and marks from actual service. The shotgun is serial no. 7020. .... **$1,250**

> **"The bar-keeper took down a double-barreled shotgun loaded with pigeon shot and banged away at our boys—the shot took effect in the face, arms, and body of a little fellow in Co. A."**
>
> *—Thomas Buchanan Linn, 16th Ohio Volunteer Infantry*

U.S.

Ballard

Serial no. 4431, .44 rimfire, 22-3/8" part round/part octagon barrel, good bore. Gray patina on metal, negligible faint pitting. The forend has a repaired grain crack and the stock shows some normal handling marks. The mainspring is weak, good-plus condition overall. **$600**

"Presented to Cap't D.L. Wilcox, Jr. by the Officers, on Morris Island 1863." Captain Wilcox was the youngest officer in the Navy during the Civil War. At the age of 17, he was assigned as First Officer of the Warship, General Burnside, under the command of Rear Admiral Dahlgren. This carbine was displayed in the Bruce Museum, on loan by Mrs. Lee H. Crittenden, a family descendent. At the exhibit's close, it was purchased by Mr. Norm Flayderman. Captain Wilcox's records and purchased documentation accompany the carbine. **$9,500**

Burnside, 2nd Model

Very scarce, early production that includes 1st Model barrel. These 2nd Models were manufactured without forend wood, and without a hinged breechblock lever. Only about 2,000 of these models were produced, and of that number, roughly one third to one half incorporate parts from two different 2nd Models, or combinations of 1st and 2nd Models with mixed serial nos. This gun has a 1st Model barrel bearing serial no. 333. The frame and breechblock bear serial no. 402 (early 2nd Model), and the buttplate bears number 981 (mid-production 2nd Model). This gun was produced in 1860 or 1861, "good" to "very good" condition, walnut butt stock has good lines and color, shows normal age and use. The metal is uniform, smooth steel mixed with a light-brown patina, and no appreciable pitting (some scattered salt and pepper tiny pits on the frame's front left and barrel breech). The markings are crisp and clear "Bristol Firearm Co." on lock, "G.P. Foster Patent April 10th 1860" on lever, and "Burnside's Patent Nov. 25th 1856" on the breechblock. The sling ring and bar were removed with the screws left in the frame. A small piece of steel is chipped off of the breechblock where the block itself joins the floating small block that carries the nipple (very minor). It is otherwise complete and functional. **$2,150**

Burnside 3rd Model

Serial no. 1463, .54 caliber, standard military configuration, fair condition. Mottled gray metal shows pitting, buttplate has heavy pitting, missing the frame screw and cock. Action needs adjustment, wood has scattered dents, scratches, and bruises. **$400**

Serial no. 13826, .54 caliber, 21" barrel, walnut stock and forend. Wrist with two inspector's cartouches, good condition. Metal has dark patina, some patches of heavy pitting. Stock with scattered light dents and bruises. **$575**

The first Burnside that utilized a wooden forend on the gun, otherwise virtually identical to the 2nd Models including the breechblock lever having no hinge in the middle, very good condition with even steel-gray color on the metal parts, very light surface pitting. It has attractive wood on both the butt and fore stock with good lines and edges showing normal handling and age. There were approximately 1,500 of this pattern produced. All matched serial nos. of 3,320 (the number on the block is nearly illegible due to some nicks and dings.) Gun is 100% original and complete, and is mechanically perfect. Lock marked, "Burnside Rifle Co. Providence RI," breechblock has partially legible 1856 patent marking, and the lever has Foster's patent stamping. **$1,650**

Burnside, 5th Model

Serial no. 16518, .54 caliber, 21" barrel, good bore. Frame and lock are a smooth dark grey, the barrel has a lot of original blue mixing with plum patina. Tangs and sling ring bar have light pitting. Frame markings are clear but lockplate markings are worn. Stocks show usual handling marks, there are two 3/8" circular depressions in buttstock near the buttplate (purpose unknown), and two very-good cartouches, "E.P.K.," and, "R.K.W." Good condition. **$1,250**

Serial no. 38724, .54 caliber, 21" barrel, good bore. The Burnside is entirely gray with even dark freckling overall. The wood has many old handling marks, particularly a large gouge on the comb of the buttstock and several deep marks on the forend. Cartouches still visible under an added oil finish. Fair/good condition. **$700**

Serial no. 5437, .54 caliber, 21" barrel, fair bore. Metal is dark with even light pitting, stock shows normal handling marks and a worn cartouche. Fair overall condition. **$450**

Serial no. 3897, .54 caliber, 21" round barrel, good-plus bore may clean to very good. Gray patina on all the metal with scattered patches of fine pitting, most of the frame marking is clear, but "BURNSIDE" is worn or missing, refinished stocks. Good condition. **$700**

Gallagher

Serial no. 1149, .50 caliber, 22-1/4" round barrel, fine bore, manufactured circa 1861, all original, good-plus condition, stock has no finish and many dings and dents, clear markings. **$800**

Serial no. 133xx, .50 caliber, barrel shows 80% original blue with no pitting, bore is very good to excellent. Frame and lock show sharp markings and 40% original color. Patch box and buttplate show equal amounts of color. Walnut stock is in very good condition. Overall a very nice gun. **$2,795**

Gwyn & Campbell, Type I

Serial no. 1274, .52 caliber. This has a 20" round barrel, good-plus bore, dark patina on all metal, clear markings, pitting near muzzle, removed sling ring, sanded and refinished buttstock has a small chip missing at the toe. Overall good condition. **$1,300**

Serial no. 1744, .52 caliber, 20" barrel, fair bore, dark-brown patina on all metal, good markings on lockplate with clear "UNION/RIFLE" on frame, breechblock and frame top are pitting, broken nipple. The rear sight leaf is slightly bent and the slide and stop screws are missing. The buttstock has a large splinter missing on the right side of the trigger, crack at same place on the left side, sanded and refinished stock. Fair-plus condition. **$600**

Hall, Model 1840, Type II

Serial no. 134, .52 caliber, 21" round rifled barrels, very fine/excellent bores, manufactured 1841, Hall/North carbine retains 95% smooth, brown lacquer finish on the barrel and frame, with 50% on buttplate. Breechblock and hammer show a mottled dark-blue finish with scattered areas of light-brown spotting, and the block marked, "U.S. North Midlin Conn. 1841." Barrel breech stamped with small "EB" and a "B" at frame's left rear. The letters "HA" are punched under the block's front, "134" scratched under the trigger and punched into both barrel bands. One-piece trigger guard with ring, fishtail opening lever and both barrel bands are lightly rusted to a rough brown finish. The wood shows some handling marks and light bruising along with minor chipping below the breechblock on the right side. Two cartouches are lightly punched at the frame's rear, one on either side, with the initials "WB" scratched into the wood at rear of the trigger guard tang. Fine to excellent condition, with a bright bore showing little evidence of use, no pitting or evidence of firing on the breechblock face. A scarce rifled Model 1840 carbine with a production estimate of 6,000 pieces. **$3,650**

Hall, Model 1843

Standard model, .52 caliber, 21" barrel, breechblock marked, "U.S./S. North/Midltn/Conn/1852." Walnut stock, poor to fair condition. Gray metal showing areas of light pitting. Sling ring missing, hammer spur broken, stock shows dents and bruises, hairline crack to right side above trigger guard, chips and losses behind breech. **$850**

NSN, .52 caliber smoother bore, 21" round barrel, good bore, manufactured during 1845. Brown varnish remains in protected areas on all metal surfaces. The breechblock shows a mottled fire blue finish with pitted areas near the percussion nipple, stock has some gouges, dings, and bruises and apparent sanding. The breech is marked, "U.S.S. North Midlton Conn. 1845" in four lines. Barrel is marked with the initials "J.H.," at left to the rear of the sight, both barrel bands are stamped on top with the number "1" and number "40" on the left side. No other visible marks. A piece of wood has been neatly replaced from the rear band back to the left stock cheek, approximately 10-1/4". The wood grades good with the metal grading antique very good. The ramrod appears to be a replacement. **$700**

Jenks, Navy

Serial no. 417, .54 caliber, 24-1/4" round barrel, strong rifling with minor pitting. Sharp metal markings include, "U.S.N./JCB/P/1843" on breech's top, which has an oval loading aperture, 50-60% original barrel browning, attractive mustard-brown patina on the brass furniture, the case colors on the lock and hammer turned to a blue patina. Very thin stock crack between the lockplate and top tang, nothing is loose, light handling marks to an old oil refinish and two worn inspector's cartouches. Very-good overall condition. **$1,400**

Browned 24-1/2", .54 caliber, barrel marked at breech, "W. Jenks//USN/RC/ P/1846." Casehardened mule ear lock marked, "Wm. Jenks" and "NP Ames/ Springfield/Mass." Brass furniture and walnut stock of standard pattern, faint inspector's cartouche opposite lock, fine to excellent condition. Barrel retains 90% brown finish, light spotting, wear at muzzle, and area of wear and light pitting behind lever barrel band. Lock retains 80% faded casehardening colors. Stock with scattered light blemishes and one deep dent to right side of buttstock. **$3,163**

Joslyn, Model 1862

Serial no. 1849, .52 rimfire caliber, 22" round barrel, good bore, hook-type latch on the breechblock and brass furniture. Dark-plum patina on iron, small patches of light corrosion, metal markings are clear. The brass is dark, stock has been sanded, inlet for a band spring at the tip that is missing. The tip has a 1" crack, thin crack between the breechblock and sling bar, good overall condition. **$1,300**

This piece is 100% original and complete, barrel retains 60-70% barrel blue thinning and turning plum color. Lock exhibits 25-35% case color, as does the base plate under the sling ring bar. Brass barrel band and buttplate have delicate age patina, stock has very strong edges and some expected handling bruises, near mint cartouche "VP" in rectangle, serial in 2,500 range. **$2,450**

Joslyn, Model 1864

Serial no. 15759, good condition, .52 rimfire caliber, 22" round barrel, good-plus bore. The barrel has a dark patina with even light surface corrosion; the lock case colors have gone dark with a large patch of very light surface corrosion. Firing pin hood has a piece missing at the bottom. Sanded stock with an old refinish in oil, no visible cartouche, buttplate heel marked "U.S." There is a 1" long crack behind the upper tang and the name, "BREADON," has been stamped numerous times into the butt. **$700**

Excellent stock with sharp edges and vivid, near mint "FDL" cartouches, dried linseed oil on the butt stock, barrel retains 75% factory blue turning plum mixed with light areas of surface rust. The lock has faint traces of case color, the bar under the sling ring bar has much vivid case color. The bore is as dark and filthy as a West Virginia coal mine. The action is crisp as new, serial is 6,xxx range and matched. Attic brown condition with a whole lot of original factory finish mixed with the age, 100% original and complete except for the bar ring. **$1,950**

Maynard, 2nd Model

Serial no. 17971, .50 caliber. Standard military configuration, good condition. Barrel with smooth mottled patina retaining generous traces of thin blue finish. Frame shows scattered minor pitting. Stock has scattered minor blemishes, series of small dents to right side, hairline cracks to lower-left side and with abrasion marks removing the cartouches. **$575**

Serial no. 22381, .50 caliber, 20" round barrel, perfect bright bore. Carbine shows 98% blue on barrel, 98% case colors, most quite bright, about 50% blue on buttplate with balance flaked, no metal pitting, all markings sharp. Buttstock shows only a few slight blemishes with raised grain still evident, two sharp inspector's cartouches, "G.W.S." and "J.M." **$3,250**

Serial no. 25145, .50 caliber, 20" round barrel, fair bore, manufactured in 1865, remains of two cartouches on stock's left side. The metal is now gray and dark brown with pitting, missing chip from stock's toe, also shows refinish. **$300**

Merrill, 1st Type

Serial no. 6676, .54 caliber, 22-1/8" round barrel, dark bore, brass furniture, including patchbox. Hammer nose and nipple are chipped, iron dark with scattered pitting, the stock with cracks (not broken) at the wrist with the grain, fair plus condition. **$800**

Palmer, Bolt Action

.50-rimfire caliber, 20" round barrel, bright, excellent condition bore, outstanding carbine (probably never issued). Sharp inspector's marks, "M.M." on the stock and barrel, sharp manufacturer's marking on barrel and lock. Bright case colors remain on the lock and barrel band. The case colors are just a little duller on the trigger guard, buttplate, and sling ring with well over 90% remaining. The buttplate has slight heel corrosion, the barrel and action retain 99% original blue that has a little dried grease and a small area of light rust at the muzzle. Sharp-edged stock with raised grain evident, the

forend has three small nicks, and a couple of shallow scratches have been
sanded on the buttstock. **$3,100**

Sharps & Hankins, Model 1862, Army

Serial no. 2487, .52 rimfire, 24" round barrel, fair bore, saddle ring, brass
buttplate. Dark patina on all metal, scattered fine pitting, missing safety lever.
Stock with two short grain cracks at the frame, epoxy filler at the broken
lower tang, about-good overall condition. **$750**

Sharps & Hankins, Model 1862, Navy

Serial no. 11933, .52 rimfire, 24" leather covered round barrel, very good bore,
manufactured circa 1864, carbine retains almost all the leather covering
on barrel. Muzzle right side missing small piece from 1/2" crack. Leather
separated where action enters leather covering. Some case color is visible
on action and hammer, all markings crisp. The stock has had some added
shellac, overall this carbine is nearly fine. **$1,350**

Serial no. 3270, .52 rimfire caliber, 24" barrel, very good bore, missing leather
barrel cover, iron has gray patina with faint pitting, clear factory markings.
The brass buttplate is stamped, "PHIL" on the heel (Philadelphia Navy Yard?).
The walnut buttstock has the base only for the swivel and shows several small
circular dings the size of a nail head. The lever catch needs adjustment.
.... **$350**

Serial no. 8237, .52 rimfire, 24" round barrel, good bore, leather barrel covering
has a couple of small holes near the muzzle, and is torn at one of the rear
screws, otherwise it is in good condition with most of the surface intact.
Second model with floating firing pin, one of the early ones without an
inspector's stamp on the metal. The frame is gray with scattered pitting on
the right side, the walnut buttstock shows only a few light handling marks,
very-good overall condition. **$750**

Sharps, Model 1853, Slanting Breech

Serial no. 21649, .577 caliber, 25" round barrel, good bore. This carbine was never equipped with a sling ring bar, although the frame has a factory-plugged hole for one. The caliber is relatively unusual in a Sharps. There are no foreign proof marks or government marks, barrel has matching serial no. Standard markings except small factory stamped number "319" on the top tang in addition to the serial no. All markings are clear with iron having a dark patina and the front half of the barrel showing pinprick pitting. Oil-finished walnut stocks show extensive handling marks with the brass patchbox, buttplate, and barrel band having a light patina. Good-plus condition. **$1,900**

"John Brown Model," .52 caliber, serial no. 119xx, good condition barrel with brown patina and original bright finish. Long-range leaf ladder site with slide missing. Saddle sling bar and ring are original with brass barrel mounting band, intact pellet primer. Breech retaining pin has ear broken, wood is in very good condition, normal handling marks, initial "LRD" carved in left stock flat. Brass patch box is original with letters "MD" carved on mounting brass and door. **$4,695**

Sharps, New Model 1859

Serial no. 31535, .52 caliber, 21-5/8" barrel, very good bore, early model with brass patchbox, buttplate, and barrel band. Iron has smooth gray patina, only minor scattered faint pitting. Lawrence patent sight shows quite a bit of blue. Brass has been cleaned in the past, metal markings are good. The stocks show moderate wear with what appears to be an arsenal-style toe repair, overall condition is very good. **$3,500**

Overall good to very-good condition, 100% original and complete, shows nice honest signs of wartime use, classic saddle wear line on butt stock's left side. The metal is overall clean steel color with good markings including the "New Model 1859" stamp on the barrel (all metal markings are deep and legible), barrel has 1,000-yard rear sight and the serial no. is in the 58,000 range. The wood shows handling and bruises, yet has attractive deep-brown walnut color. The cartouche is barely visible under the sling ring bar. The bore is very good with deep rifling. **$1,650**

Sharps, New Model 1863

Serial no. 98876, .52 caliber, 22" barrel, fair bore. Missing the cover and feed arm for the pellet primer mechanism, sling bar removed, stock base ground flush. Dark patina on frame and lock with light pitting on the block's top and hammer nose. Barrel has mottled gray patina, stocks without patchbox have a nail repair to a wrist splinter and a crack at the rear of the forend. Good overall. **$800**

Overall very-good condition, 100% original & complete (serial C4, 9xx range). The metal is uniformly smooth, brown age patina with good strong markings. Bore rifling is deep and sharp, faint silvery case color along the edge of the lock and lever. The rear sight is the standard 700-yard carbine sight. The stock has the faintest light crack in the forearm, standard 1863 with no patchbox in the butt stock. There are two visible cartouches under the sling ring bar, a great-looking gun with character. **$1,795**

Smith

Mass Arms, serial no. 10681, .50 caliber, 21-5/8" octagon to round barrel, fair bore. Manufactured between 1861-1865, has the barrel bands and no sling ring. No military markings show on the wood or metal. The rear tang screw, hammer and percussion nipple are missing. Overall condition is fair. .. **$650**

100% blue on the barrel and strong case colors with a lot of purple on the frame. A fine walnut stock with a couple of small use or storage dings and a good cartouche, mint bore, serial no. 5524. ....**$3,350**

Serial no. 3221, honest issued example with strong bore and solid markings, wood has a splinter here and there, but no major damage. No visible cartouche, which is normal for this weapon. **$1,250**

Spencer

Serial no. 30307, .52 caliber rimfire, 22" round barrel, good bore. Barrel's breech shows vise marks, the metal with a dark patina and fine pitting on the frame and front portion of the barrel, the frame address partially illegible on the top line. The original stocks show normal handling marks, a 5" grain crack in the buttstock at the magazine tube, traces of two cartouches, and has had a little extra oil rubbed on through the years, good overall condition. **$1,500**

Serial no. 8308, .50 caliber, 19" barrel, folding rear sight, casehardened frame, saddle ring, walnut stocks with inspector's cartouche, sling mounts, excellent condition. Retains approximately 85-90% finish overall, with scattered wear throughout. Wood has a few minor marks present. **$3,450**

Serial no. 39533, .52 rimfire caliber, 22" round barrel, fair bore. Metal is a dark gray with even pitting, the stocks have several thin age cracks and show normal handling marks on an old refinish, several screws are replacements. Fair to good condition. **$900**

This carbine has original blue finish on the barrel, a lot of blue in the area around the rear sight, and it tapers to light blue to plum around the front sight. The barrel metal is very smooth with no pitting. There are light case colors on the frame on the saddle ring side. There are light case colors on the block and buttplate, crisp action, the bore is very fine. The walnut stock is fine, with two clear cartouches, serial no. 54236. ....**$4,600**

Spencer, Model 1865

Serial no. 426, .56-50 caliber, 22" barrel, strong three-groove rifling with a little scattered pitting. Made without the Stabler cutoff, metal has a plum patina, a little scattered faint pitting on the barrel, several small barrel breech dings, lettering is clear on the metal. The stocks show relatively few light handling marks, retains most of the original finish, has a 2-1/2" grain crack in the

*.52 caliber, Spencer 7-shot repeater carbine, **$11,000-$20,000**.*

*Activating the lever on a Spencer ejected the spent casing
and loaded the next round.*

forend (easily glued), and has two very-good to fine inspector's cartouches. Also with the carbine is a Civil War snap hook and swivel for the carbine shoulder sling. Fine condition. **$1,350**

Serial no. 7329, .50 rimfire, 20" barrel, made without a Stabler cutoff. Dark-gray patina on the barrel, mottled-gray frame, frame has areas of fine pitting and scattered faint barrel pitting. The buttstock has a 2" grain crack at the magazine tube, otherwise the stock shows light wear and handling marks. Good overall condition. **$850**

Starr

.54 caliber, 30% blue on barrel, all markings are clear. Smooth metal is plum brown where it is not blue, no pitting. The walnut stock is in very-good condition with the usual usage marks, no cartouches, serial no. 19786. Very crisp action and a very-good bore. The brass has a smooth, uncleaned patina. **$2,295**

Serial no. 18175, .54 caliber, 21" barrel, dark bore, overall plum-brown patina and patches of light to moderate pitting on the action and breech end of the barrel. The brass barrel band and buttplate have tarnished to ochre. The buttstock and forearm have an added varnish finish over mild handling marks, good condition Starr. **$950**

Triplett & Scott

Serial no. 1719, .50 rimfire caliber, 22" round barrel, good bore. The rear sight leaf is broken, as is the spring on the cartridge stop. The top swivel is missing from the heel of the buttplate, as is one small screw at the front of the frame. Smooth dark-gray metal with sharp markings, minor faint muzzle pitting, light buttplate pitting, several small breech dents. Clear metal markings with "KENTUCKY" marked on left side of breech. Forend has a large piece of replaced wood, the buttstock has a replacement strip of wood over part of the magazine tube and two line cracks. Overall condition is good. **$700**

Outstanding example of long barrel version (30" barrel). Barrel exhibits 95% vivid blue as does the receiver. Frame has 40% case color that is starting to fade. Left side of receiver marked, "Kentucky." Wood is excellent, faintest hairline stress crack on the left side of the wrist, but the right side (the display side) has no visible crack at all. Since 90% of these guns have bad fractures at the wrist (caused by the design flaw of running the magazine tube too close to the sides of the wrist) finding one with nice wood is a great bonus. Very fine to excellent. **$2,850**

Musketoon, U.S., Model 1816

.69 caliber, smooth bore, excellent mechanics, still in the original flintlock configuration. Musket has been arsenal-altered to musketoon length with a 38" barrel with top muzzle mounted bayonet lug. Barrel retains 60-70% bright "armory brown" lacquer finish. Crisp eagle head/"P" proof with deep condemnation mark at breech. Superb lock with crisp horizontal eagle head over "Springfield" in the lock's center. Fine brown-lacquered finish iron furniture with both sling swivels and button tipped ramrod. Excellent oil-finished stock with super edges around the lock, flats, and barrel and ramrod channels. This musket was obviously arsenal shortened, because the double band and spring were set back the proscribed distance as was the bayonet lug and ramrod. Fine, overall condition. **$2,750**

Imports

Austrian, Froewurth

Commonly called the "Froewurth" carbine. Short, .71 caliber percussion conversion carbine, George Schuyler imported 10,000 in 1861. Fine, smooth metal with a blue hue. Austrian proofs along the barrel channel. Smooth lock with huge percussion hammer. Iron ramrod and trigger guard with extended pistol grip. Fine bore and mechanics. Excellent stock has been tongue oiled. Double iron ring hooks at left flat for sling belt. **$650**

British, Model 1856 Enfield

.577 Caliber percussion carbine manufactured by Barnett of London. Typical of the cavalry carbines so coveted by the Confederate cavalry, 20" round barrel with flip up three-leaf rear sight and captive swivel ramrod. Clear proofs at left breech. Barrel and lock are both a smooth, plum patina. Crisply marked lock, "Crown/Tower" to the rear of the hammer and "Barnett/London" under the bolster. No British military marks which is typical of imported Civil War arms. Good bore and mechanics. Brass furniture is a deep umber patina. Fine oil-finished stock with sharp edges around lock and flats and along the ramrod and barrel channel. Sling ring and bar at the flats.............. **$1,995**

Confederate imported Tower Enfield percussion carbine. Crisp overall, with all original parts, clear markings, 1859 dated lock, strong action. Bright metal and solid wood. **$2,650**

P-1856 .577 Caliber British-produced percussion carbine. No British military markings. Metal is a bright smooth plum overall. Crisp Birmingham proofs at breech and "Barnett" markings on the lock. Good bore, excellent mechanics, fine stock, missing yoke on swivel ramrod, otherwise complete **$1,895**

British, Greene

Serial no. 1602, .54 caliber, 18" barrel, nearly new bore. Great example, probably unissued/unfired. All metal and wood markings are sharp. Case colors faded on lock and breech to a mottled, dark patina with the colors on the primer door a little more prominent, 80% dark barrel blue remaining. Stock has repaired crack between lockplate and the breech with much raised grain, shows no wear and only minor handling marks, barrel has one small ding. Metal has several British inspectors' markings and a broad arrow with release marking and "S." Stock is stamped with a 5/16" high numeral "1" in front of the patchbox and on the left side near the heel is stamped in 1/8" high letters "U.S." These stock markings appear to be of the period and are evidence of the Union purchase of British Green carbines during the Civil War. ... **$3,000**

Muskets and Rifles

Undoubtedly the most popular and longest-collected item of Civil War memorabilia has been the very tool used to decide the war's outcome, the muzzle-loading long arm. Immediately following the war, a booming business emerged wherein dealers readily supplied souvenir muskets, rifles, and other weapons to a public fascinated by war. No longer regarded as the implements of carnage, these firearms were regarded as historic relics. Holding the ancient Springfield or Enfield rifle, the sense of purpose and honor seemed to transmit from the old walnut and iron into the collector's sense of self. The weapon of war became a relic worthy of devotion. Soon, collectors covered their walls with weapons and continued to look for variations and rarities.

This hobby has continued uninterrupted since those early days when a collector could actually approach veterans of the war. The search continues for rarities, oddities, and variations. Simultaneously, research has dug deep into armory records, military archives, and personal collections of correspondence to piece together new interpretations and statistics about firearm production, deployment, and usage.

A person should not feel that there are not quality weapons out there to be had. The opposite is true. Actually, now more than ever, there are well-researched and documented pieces available. Furthermore, long-held traditions and suppositions about questionable arms have been either proven or dispelled. Guns that were once attributed as being Confederate or arsenal-adapted into one form or another have been revealed as something else. In the best case, simply misidentified. In the worst, clear misrepresentations with the intent to deceive. The collector of today is more informed and better equipped to assemble quality collections and to avoid the many costly pitfalls that often entrapped earlier collectors.

Like all areas of Civil War collecting, and maybe even more so because of the prices involved, if you intend to collect long arms, decide *how* you are going to collect before making your initial purchase. For example: Do you simply desire a representative weapon from both sides? If so, a Model 1861 Rifled Musket and a Model 1853 Enfield might suffice. But, perhaps you want to collect weapons used by a certain regiment? Through three years of service, several units may have carried a variety of weapons ranging from Potsdam imports to Austrian Lorenz rifles to .58-caliber rifled muskets. This sort of approach will provide for a limited variety and also help develop a feel for the arming of one particular regiment.

Collecting long arms can be addictive. Perhaps you will begin collecting by buying a nice Trenton-marked Model 1861 at a show. Pretty soon, you might think, "Hmm, it might be fun to collect one of each of the Model 1861 contractors." After time, and several thousand dollars spent, your habit might blossom into, "Now that I have those, I will need to have a representative of all the U.S. martial .69-caliber muskets." Before you know it, you have branched out into "breechloaders of the sharpshooters" and you are mortgaging your house to buy a Henry repeater! There are too many weapons out there, and you simply can't buy them all.

Collecting Hints

Pros:

- Muskets are great visual aids for learning or teaching about the Civil War. The Civil War soldier's existence came down to the weapon he carried. Collecting long arms places your hands on the very tools that made history.

- Firearms tend to hold their value, making them a tangible hedge against inflation.

- Civil War long arms are in plentiful supply, so it is fairly easy to enter the hobby.

Cons:

- Guns draw attention, both welcome and unwelcome. They are a prime target of thieves.

- Muskets and rifles are cumbersome to display and collect. As your collection grows, you will find that wall space fills quickly.

- You must answer the question, "Do I restore a weapon to the way it appeared when issued, or keep it in the condition as I found it?"

- Because of the quantity and variety of weapons available, unless you are independently wealthy, you will be faced with a limited collection.

> **Availability ★★★**
>
> **Price ★★★**
>
> **Reproduction Alert ★★**

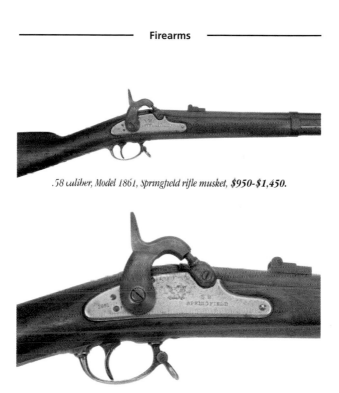

.58 caliber, Model 1861, Springfield rifle musket, $950-$1,450.

The "humpback" hammer is a carry-over from the Maynard Primer system used on the Model 1855 rifled musket.

*.58 caliber, Richmond, Confederate 3-band rifled musket, **$18,000-$25,000**.*

The Richmond rifled musket is distinguished by the humpback hammer, a lockplate that was designed (but not cut) for the Maynard Primer system, and brass furniture.

Confederate Muskets and Rifles

Rifled Musket, Model 1861

Pristine Confederate "High-Hump" 1861-rifled musket, one of the first made
in Richmond using parts and machinery captured at Harpers Ferry Arsenal.
Beautiful specimen, all matching, complete with the original Confederate
linen sling, initials "WHH" carved deeply in stock. Weapon from the family of
William H. Hutcherson who served in Company D, 38th Virginia Infantry—
Picketts Division, present at the infamous charge at Gettysburg. Comes with
full documentation and family affidavit. **$27,500**

Rifled Musket, Richmond

An 1863 example, barrel has a clearly visible "VP" and eagle, but the date is not
visible. The rear sight is the proper "stepped" 1855-1861-style held in place by
an old copper disc rivet. The front band's "U" stamping is classic Confederate
workmanship stamped at an angle on the wrong edge of the band. The
middle and lower band have the "U"s hit off center as well. The stock has
strong edges, and the lock inlet is absolutely Richmond done, with no
provision for the Maynard tape "arm" as found on the 1855 muskets, and no
cartouche mark. Straight ramrod channel, not milled for the swelled ramrod
on the U.S. guns. Classic Richmond brass buttplate with rich undisturbed
patina and color that melds with the butt, Federal steel nose cap. The patina
and wear are uniform and wonderful overall, never improved or gunsmithed.
.... **$11,500**

Rifled Musket, Richmond Armory, Type III

.58 caliber, lockplate dated "1863" and marked "C.S./ RICHMOND, VA," barrel
shortened to 38" and has a good bore. Breech dated 1864 and marked with
"V/ P/(eagle head)." Gray patina on all iron, minor light pitting, vise marks
on barrel breech, clear markings on lock and barrel proofs, barrel date
legible. Stock has a nice older refinish, a few light handling marks, and a
small forend cap chip. The brass buttplate and forend cap have an ochre
patina, good-plus condition with ramrod. **$1,600**

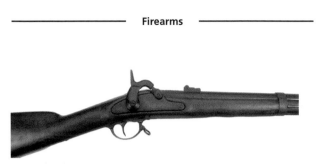

.58 caliber, 3-band William Muir contract rifled musket, $1,150-$1,700.

The Federally-contracted 3-band, .58-caliber rifled muskets featured 3-leaf rear sites.

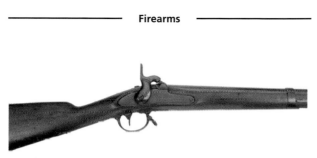

.69 caliber, Model 1842, Harpers Ferry, 3 band musket, ***$950-$1,450.***

The Model 1842 musket (unlike the rifled musket) had no rear site.

Confederate, dated 1863, replaced nose cap and ramrod, stock has dings and bruises, metal overall very good, clear markings. **$5,850**

Rifle, Fayetteville

Manufactured on machinery captured at the Harpers Ferry Arsenal. Rare transitional model with features including an iron nose cap, filled in muzzle slot (for the saber bayonet, discontinued in early 1863), and the stamped inspector marking of "P.B." (Philip Burkhart, Master Armorer). Rear sight altered during the time of actual use to a simple V-notch type; ramrod not the typical Fayetteville pattern, same color as the rest of the weapon, and likely used with it; sling swivels are modern additions. Weapon is a pleasing deep-brown patina overall with brass bands and buttplate (stamped "C.S.A."). Clear lockplate markings of Confederate eagle, "Fayetteville" and "C.S.A." as well as date of 1863. Rich, deep-colored walnut stock is free of defects such as cracks or deep gouges. **$16,500**

.58-caliber percussion Confederate manufactured long arm dated "1863" at lock and barrel flat. Crisp markings include the proofs at left breech and lock, "1863" to the hammer's rear and an eagle/"CSA" and "Fayetteville" in the center and right of the lock. Barrel and lock are a smooth, deep, plum patina with only some light salt and peppering around the bolster. Lock has no hump and the distinctive S-shaped Fayetteville hammer, rear sight removed, simple military-style post sight dovetailed to the barrel. Bayonet lug has been removed from right of muzzle, but this may be a factory alteration, because this rifle falls right on the cusp of the Confederate authorities' decision to go from an unwieldy saber bayonet to an easier-to-produce socket style. Good bore, fine mechanics, transitional-style iron stock cap, fine brass furniture with deep, deep umber patina. Crisp "CSA" on tang of buttplate. Ramrod is Confederate- produced, champagne-glass-shaped rod. Fine stock with very crisp edges around the lock and both the barrel channels and ramrod channel. Sharp "PB" inspector's cartouche at the left flat. **$19,500**

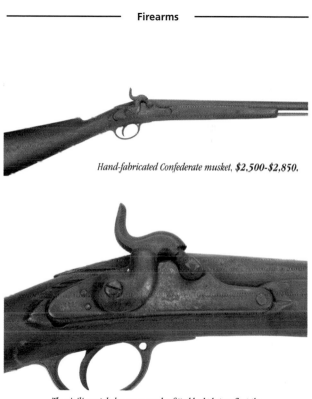

Hand-fabricated Confederate musket, $2,500-$2,850.

The civilian-style hammer and refitted lockplate reflect the Confederacy's need for expedient weaponry.

Rifle, Read and Watson

Recovered from the Hanging Rock Battlefield in Virginia, early studies believed that these arms were made by J.B. Barrett of Wytheville, Virginia, from parts captured at Harpers Ferry. Authorities on these arms recently discovered that they were alterations of Hall rifles and carbines belonging to the Virginia militia and that the work was performed by N.T. Read and John T. Watson of Danville, Virginia. Arm is classed as a Type 1. The rifle is 48-1/2" overall with a 32-5/8" long barrel of .54 caliber. Rifle is half-stocked in walnut with a single spring retained barrel band and a single iron ramrod ferrule beneath the barrel. The barrel band and spring are missing. All of the iron is dark and evenly pitted. Stock has old repairs to a wrist break and shows erosion at the buttplate. It has had some oil added since its recovery from the field. The ramrod is a replacement. The stock has fourteen notches carved behind the trigger guard and the left side is carved in 5/8" high letters "B. Mc. C." over a 3/4" high "A." It is believed that these initials may be those of one of several related individuals by the name of McClung who participated in the battle with the 14th, 16th, 17th, 22nd, and 23rd Virginia Cavalry. Includes a copy of the book *Civil War Tales* by Gary C. Walker, that has a chapter on this rifle written by Col. William Terry Slusher who found this rifle as a seven-year-old boy. This chapter includes the names of several of the McClungs and the cavalry units with which they served, and also has a picture of Col. Slusher holding this rifle. Few Confederate arms have such interesting provenance.
.... **$3,500**

Rifle, L. G. Sturdivant

.58 caliber, serial no. 109. Less than 300 produced by Lewis G. Sturdivant of Talladega, Alabama. In March 1862, he had a contract for 2,000 Mississippi Type Rifles. Overall in very good condition with a forend repair and buttstock repair both look to be period and done at the factory. Stocks very cheaply made, lock marked, "Robbins, Kendall & Lawrence, U.S. Windsor, Vt., 1848."
.... **$5,500**

U.S. Muskets and Rifles

Musket, Model 1808

No serial no., .69 caliber, 42-5/8" round barrel, fair bore, manufactured in 181?. A contract musket by Rudolph and Charles Leonard, shows traces of the eagle with the U.S. in circle. The last digit of the date is illegible. The hammer is the correct Harpers Ferry-type with a straight hammer spur. No other marks appear on metal or wood. The metal is a gray-brown with darker spotting and pitting near the breech and lock area. The frizzen has been re-faced and a few screws appear to be older replacements. The wood shows a well-done repair forward of the trigger guard. Missing ramrod, and overall fair to good condition. **$1,100**

Musket, Model 1816, Conversion

.69-caliber smoothbore, 37" shortened barrel is almost flush with the front band that has been altered by removing the front strap. Lockplate has clear standard Harpers Ferry markings and is dated 1837. The percussion conversion was done by the addition of a new bolster with a clean-out screw and is almost identical to one done by M.A. Baker of Fayetteville, North Carolina, shown in *Confederate Longarms And Pistols,* by Hill and Anthony. Barrel's bottom is struck with Roman numbers "LLXXXXIII." The new percussion bolster, barrel, lockplate, hammer and trigger are all marked with a 5 over 74, with sideplate marked only 74. The metal has been cleaned in the past and is now mostly a smooth gray with light pitting on the breech's top. The stock's right side has carved "XV," refinished wood with glued joint under rear band, ramrod modern replacement, good condition. **$350**

.69 caliber, 42" barrel, smooth bore, clearly marked, "Spring/Field/1839," the barrel date is illegible and the stock cartouche is faint. Arsenal-style cone conversion, all metal has dark patina, scattered fine pitting with the breech heavily pitted, missing hammer screw, replacement ramrod, overall fair condition. **$600**

.69 caliber, Model 1816, conversion flint to percussion Springfield musket, $850-$1,250.

The brass inset on the lockplate is all that remains of the flintlock flashpan which was cut off at the time of conversion.

100% original and complete, lock marked, "US/P.& E.W. Blake," and, "New Haven/1826." The stock's left side bears two cartouches as well as a deep "OHIO" stamp. There is a small hairline crack over the word "OHIO." The conversion is the standard cone-style with the nipple being threaded directly into the barrel. The metal has a deep-brown patina overall with areas of pitting around the nipple. The stock is nice and shows normal expected wear, with a little burnout near the nipple. It is mechanically perfect and totally complete including the ramrod. **$695**

Converted to percussion ignition, .69 caliber, 42" barrel, smooth bore. Lock marked "Harpers/Ferry/1828," no breech date, but proof marks are good, side of breech marked "S.M. Co." and the conversion uses a crude drum and nipple. The metal is dark with scattered areas of light pitting, the stock is refinished with an old repair to a large crack from the wrist through the lock recess. The front swivel is missing, but the original ramrod is present, overall fair-plus condition. **$400**

Rifled Musket, Model 1816, Conversion

.69-caliber rifled weapon, "1857" dated lock and breech, fine overall condition, clear "NJ" surcharge on left breech, complete with both sling swivels and coned button tip ramrod, fine oil-finished stock with clear cartouches at left flat. **$1,950**

100% original and complete, lock marked, "US/P.& E.W. Blake," and, "New Haven/1826." The stock's left side bears two cartouches as well as a deep "OHIO" stamp. There is a small hairline crack over the word "OHIO." The conversion is the standard cone-style with the nipple being threaded directly into the barrel. The metal has a deep-brown patina overall with areas of pitting around the nipple. The stock is nice and shows normal expected wear, with a little burnout near the nipple. It is mechanically perfect and totally complete including the ramrod. **$695**

Rifle, Model 1817, Conversion

No serial no., .54 caliber, 33" octagon to round barrel. This rifle is marked on the lockplate, "S. Cogswell Troy." The barrel is marked "SNY" (State New York) and "AWP" who was most-likely the barrel maker. "AWP" is also stamped under the barrel and can only be seen when the barrel is removed from the stock. The only reference found for an AWP was Allen W. Page, listed as working in New York City in 1801. The under rib, rod pipes, trigger guard, oval patchbox and buttplate are of brass. The percussion conversion was done with a drum and nipple threaded into the barrel. Part of the removable brass pan remains, as do the holes for the frizzen and spring. The walnut stock has a cheekrest and is also stamped "SNY" behind and below the rear lock bolt. No U.S. marks or stamps appear on the rifle, suggesting it was a state and not a U.S. contract rifle. In appearance, the gun appears to be the Model 1803, but the oval patchbox and removable brass pan suggest a later model. The iron ramrod has no brass tip. The stock is single wedge fastened and shows a recent oil-type finish applied. The barrel flats measure 11-3/4" transitioning to round with a single wedding band. Overall rifle length is 49", gun has both 1803 and 1814 features, grade is fair. **$900**

Rifle, Model 1819, Conversion

Superb, top-quality example of the percussion conversion of the M1819 Hall Rifle. The Hall was one of the most advanced weapons of the period, being a breech-loading flintlock, and then a breech-loading percussion weapon. This one retains 98% original lacquer brown finish on the barrel, has nearly mint stock, and is mechanically like new. **$3,450**

Musket, Model 1822, Conversion

Whitney contract percussion conversion musket with 42" .75-caliber barrel with tang dated "1828." Lock with Belgian alteration to percussion. Lockplate marked "U.S./P/ & E.W. Blake" and "New Haven/1828." Stock and furniture of standard pattern. Gray metal has been cleaned and shows scattered areas of light pitting and some heavy pitting at the breech. Sound wood with scattered dents, scratches, and bruises. **$460**

69 caliber, Model 1816, Remington-Maynard, conversion rifled musket,
$1,850-$2,500.

With the door swung open, one can see the workings
of the Maynard (tape) Primer system.

Musket, Model 1840, Conversion

Overall very good (near "fine") condition example of the scarce Model 1840
Springfield (only 30,000 produced), that is 100% original and complete,
and has matched dates on the lock and barrel. The metal is all-clean steel
color with strong markings. The lock is marked "Springfield 1841" as well as
"US" and having an eagle. The barrel is stamped with a "VP" and eagle and
the tang bears a matching date of "1841." The percussion conversion is the
standard nipple threaded directly into the barrel. The stock is beautiful with a
rich-brown antique walnut patina, and good lines. Two inspector's cartouches
are faintly visible on the stock's left side. The lock action is as crisp as new.
Ramrod is original and proper, having the trumpet-shaped head. **$1,195**

Rifle, Model 1841

Colt factory alterations performed late in 1861 by reboring to .58 caliber, fitting
Colt-style folding-leaf rear sight, and having trumpet-head ramrod without
brass tip. Barrels were serial numbered by Colt with matching saber bayonet
and Colt adapter ring. This gun is serial no. 8350, metal is in excellent
condition with sharp markings overall with an 1853 lock date. Brass furniture
is in excellent condition, with buttplate having "US" and "42" stamped.
Walnut stock has two original cartouches on stock flat with a Colt factory
cartouche on butt. Bore is very good, an excellent example. **$3,950**

.54-caliber percussion weapon in good to very good condition overall. Two-leaf
flip-up carbine rear sight appears to have been put on during the period of
use. Moderate pitting around the breech, but clear, "JPC/ P," proofs at the
left. Barrel and lock have been cleaned to bright steel. Crisp lock marked,
"Windsor VT./1849," to the hammer's rear and "Robbins/&/ Lawrence/US"
in the center. Fine bore, excellent mechanics, bright, golden brass furniture
including the large, distinctive Mississippi patchbox. Retains both sling
swivels, and has an original Austrian Lorenz ramrod as a replacement for the
original rod. Fine, oil-finished stock with two clear cartouches at the left flat.
....**$2,100**

E. Whitney contract, unmarked 33" barrel in .58 caliber. Lock marked "E. Whitney" and at tail "N. Haven." Brass furniture, walnut stock, condition: very good. Gray metal showing scattered light pitting with heavier pitting at breech, missing rear sight, excellent wood. **$863**

Harpers Ferry Percussion Rifle, standard model with 33" .54-caliber barrel, Harpers Ferry lock dated 1850 and brass furniture. Condition is poor, gray metal showing areas of pitting, bayonet lug and sights missing, wood shows heavy use and cleaning. **$460**

Model 1842

.69 caliber, 42" barrel, Harpers Ferry lockplate dated "1842," last digit on breech date is illegible. Dark gray patina on all metal, fine pitting on the buttplate and breech. The stock has been sanded and has a 3" long crack at the front band. Good-plus condition with original ramrod. **$500**

.69 caliber, 42" round barrel, excellent bore, Springfield Armory lock and tang both dated "1853," the heel of the buttplate with a rack number "3A3/3." Sharp markings on all metal, which is still in the white, showing tarnish and a little very light rust that should clean without a trace. The stock has been sanded and has no cartouche, shows several dings and dents, and an incipient chip behind the lockplate. With an original ramrod and matching condition bayonet. Overall very-good-plus condition. **$1,200**

.69-caliber, 42" round barrel, marked on the breech's side, "W.G. & Co.," and on top of the breech, "V/P/(palmetto tree)." Lockplate marked vertically behind hammer, "Columbia/S.C. 1852," and in front of the hammer is the palmetto tree encircled by, "Palmetto Armory S*C." Buttplate heel is marked, "SC." All iron has a gray patina with pitting on the breech and bolster and only minor pitting elsewhere. Brass bands have a light-ochre patina. All of the metal markings are clear. Stock is in fine condition with sharp edges and some raised grain evident, relatively few light handling marks, but has probably had a little extra oil wiped on. Original ramrod is about 1" short. ...**$4,750**

42" round barrel .69-caliber, this musket was made by Springfield Armory and has an "1848" dated barrel and lock. The musket probably was never issued with the stock having sharp edges, raised grain, crisp "R.C." inspector's cartouche and New Jersey surcharge. The stock has a small nail hole behind the middle band and shows several fine scratches and small dings. Metal has a dark-brown patina with very light surface roughness, will probably clean with very little fine pitting remaining. Barrel date lightly struck, all other metal markings good, has correct ramrod. **$1,625**

Musket by Springfield Armory, .69-caliber, 42" long barrel, lock and barrel dated 1851, the lock and breech markings are good, no markings on bands. Most metal is gray with light pitting, the stock has been refinished and has a hole in the butt and two forend cracks, replacement ramrod, fair-plus condition, the musket is covered in grime and needs a good cleaning. **$350**

Rifled Musket, Model 1842
.69 caliber, lockplate marked, "Springfield," and dated 1855. The 42" rifled barrel fitted with a long-range sight, dark bore. Good metal markings, no visible stock cartouche. The ramrod is a replacement and the front band spring is missing the tip. The gun is covered in grime, after cleaning this should grade good-plus to very-good condition. **$1,000**

Rifle, Model 1853, Sharps, Sporting
Serial no. 8375, .44 caliber. The 25-3/4" octagon barrel has a dark bore, a legible Hartford address, a fixed-leaf rear sight, and added markings on the breech's side, *40-.90-420.* The rifle has double set triggers and plain walnut stocks with a pewter forend tip and an iron patchbox. Missing lever spring and the tip of the takedown lever. All of the metal has a dark patina with extensive fine pitting, a little heavier around the breech. The stocks are sound, but have several short grain cracks and show wear with the pewter forend tip missing a small piece. This old Texas Sharps is in fair condition and has great character. **$1,100**

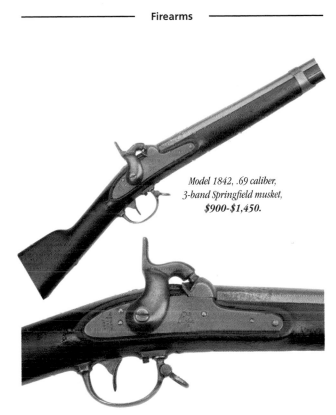

*Model 1842, .69 caliber,
3-band Springfield musket,
$900-$1,450.*

*The Model 1842 was the first Federally-contracted infantry
musket to be made with a percussion ignition.*

Rifle, Model 1855, Colt Revolving

Serial no. 3449, .56 caliber, 31-1/8" round barrel, good bore, fitted with a lug for a saber bayonet. Dark patina on all metal, patches of light pitting, the cylinder battered with several broken nipples. The fore stock has a large piece missing at the left side of the loading lever, the butt has a 3" crack with the grain at the top tang. The ramrod is a replacement, fair to good overall condition. **$2,750**

Root Military by Colt, serial no. 131, .56 caliber, unmarked 31-9/16" barrel. Lower tang with sling swivel mount, walnut half-stock forend and varnished walnut buttstock, poor to fair condition. Metal has been cleaned to gray metal showing areas of light pitting. Fore stock replaced, refinished buttstock shows dents, scratches, small hairline cracks and pinned wrist repair, action not functioning. **$1,150**

Rifled Musket, Model 1855

.58-caliber, 40" barrel, fair bore, "1858"-dated on lock and breech, the lock cleaned in the past and the "HARPERS" a little weak, all other metal markings are clear. Gray patina on all the metal with scattered areas of fine pitting. The stock has an old refinish and shows very few light handling markings with two legible oval inspector's cartouches and a clearly stamped set of inspector's initials on the wood and metal "W.C.K." Made by Harpers Ferry Armory. Good-plus condition with an original ramrod and matching socket bayonet. **$2,400**

Maynard-primed, percussion-rifled musket with 40", .58-caliber barrel with standard proofs at breech, dated 1860 and additionally stamped, "W. Raurs/ N.Y." Harpers Ferry lock dated 1860, stock and furniture of standard pattern. Comes with brown leather sling, condition is good, gray metal showing areas of light pitting, wood with scattered dents and bruises, and slivered losses at forend. **$805**

Rifle, New Model 1859, Sharps

Serial no. 36794, .52 caliber, 36" round barrel with bayonet lug on the bottom, good bore. Breech-loading rifle, Lawrence patent rear sight, single trigger, iron patchbox, frame and lock case colors have turned gray with large areas of pinprick pitting, all markings are very good. Barrel has a smooth dark patina with no visible markings. The head of one frame screw is marred and the primer feed arm is missing. The buttstock has a 3/8" high letter "H" stamped into the left hand side and has a legible "W.W." cartouche. The stocks show normal handling marks on an old oil refinish with a 1/2" age crack behind the lock, overall good-plus condition. **$3,000**

Serial no. 40570, .52 cal, 30" barrel has bottom lug for saber bayonet, bore is bright and appears to be unfired. The rifle shows no wear and has only minor storage blemishes. All metal markings are sharp, 95% vivid case colors remain with most of the loss due to fading on the lever and bands, 99% original barrel blue, minor scattered age spotting, some of which should clean. The wood has sharp edges with raised grain, a very small ding at the front of the comb and other minor small handling marks. An outstanding Sharps Rifle.
....**$10,000**

Rifle, Henry

Fine Henry repeating rifle number 8718, exceptionally nice brass and wood (a few tiny patches of filler in buttstock), very crisp action. Clear barrel markings, very nice bore, minor surface pitting. Original cleaning rod in butt and has original sling. Rear sight ladder is replacement, as is upper bracket of sling (not the barrel attachment). **$15,000**

Serial no. 9561, .44 caliber, 24" barrel, sling swivels, varnished walnut stock, fair condition. Barrel cleaned and showing patches of light pitting. Front sight blade altered, frame cleaned and showing scratches, dents, and dovetailed for rear sights, action needs adjustment. Wood has numerous deep dents and bruises. **$8,625**

Rifle, Spencer

Very-fine walnut stock with two very clear cartouches. The metal on the barrel is very smooth with a little blue around the rear sight, the rest is a soft plum-brown patina. The bore is bright with strong grooves, very crisp action. The markings on the barrel are, "SPENCER REPEATING/RIFLE CO. BOSTON MASS/PAT'D.MARCH 1860." A fine untouched Spencer Rifle with serial no. 24026. .... **$4,100**

NRA "very good" Spencer 3-band infantry rifle. Totally honest and 100% original and complete. All metal surfaces are uniformly discolored with a mixture of steel color mixed with light brown aged patina. The stock is a pretty deep walnut-brown with good edges, and excellent wood to metal fit. Decent bore, has complete rear sight, swivel in butt, etc. The firm name on the frame's top is clear and legible. **$2,850**

Rifle, Model 1861, Navy

Serial 34247, .69 caliber, 34" round barrel, bright bore with sharp rifling and minor fine pitting. Made by Whitney, dated "1863" on the breech and lock, double-stamped inspector's initials "F.C.W." on left side of breech. The lock has the first-style large eagle-shield-flag stamping, and all metal markings are excellent. All of the iron still has the arsenal bright finish, shows light tarnish. Stock has been lightly sanded and shows a few light scratches and small dents, the inspector's cartouche, "FCW," is still legible. Very-good to fine condition, with original ramrod. **$2,000**

Rifle, Model 1861, Sharps & Hankins, Navy

.52 caliber breech-loading U.S. Naval long arm. Barrel is bright steel with bottom mounted bayonet lug. Frame and tang retain traces of the original blued finish. Fine bore, excellent mechanics. Crisp markings, complete with both sling swivels. Very good oil-finished buttstock and forend. Comes with a fine brass-hilted, 1861-dated Collins' saber bayonet, serial no. 495. Very scarce rifle with a rare bayonet. **$3,950**

Serial no. 240, .52 rimfire, barrel has been cut to 27-15/16" in length and ends just in front of the forend, which appears to be original length, bore is dark. The barrel has dovetailed front and rear sights with the original sight dovetail filled by a blank. The safety device is missing and the lever catch is broken. Dark patina on all metal, scattered fine pitting, frame markings are legible, stocks show normal handling marks on an old refinish with several age cracks at the butt. About good overall condition. **$400**

Rifled Musket, Model 1861

Rifled musket by William Mason of Taunton, New Jersey, .58 caliber, 40" barrel, fine bore may clean to excellent, 1863-dated lock, 1862-dated breech. Gray patina on all the metal, a patch of fine pitting on the lock and pinprick pitting on the breech near the nipple. All metal markings are sharp, the stock never marked with an inspector's cartouche, as this was likely delivered to the State of New Jersey. The stock has a few small storage dings, all edges are sharp and some raised grain is still evident. The buttplate and tip of the comb have the rack number "20" and in front of the trigger guard is a small shallow hole made for some obscure purpose. Fine-plus condition, original ramrod, fine socket bayonet in a later scabbard. **$1,000**

1863-dated, .58 caliber by Trenton, an historical Gettysburg-related item. The name "J. Hodge" is neatly carved in wood opposite lock. Hodge served in Company H, 142nd Pennsylvania Infantry and saw action at Fredericksburg and Gettysburg, dying in November 1863. Weapon is missing ramrod and rear sight, and is a very honest brown patina overall. **$1,750**

Unfired example of Colt Special Model 1861 Musket with matched dates of 1863 on lock and barrel. With the exception of some light surface pits in a couple small areas on top of the barrel, the weapon is nearly mint. Stock has crisp edges and raised grain. Metal is bright and shiny, all markings are crisp and appear like new, barrel is surcharged "NJ" for New Jersey, and the stock has the "NJ" cartouche. Rear sight has all the blue on it, bore is mint. ... **$3,950**

Lock marked "Wm Muir & Co./Windsor Locks, Ct.," and dated 1863. The rear sight has a base only and the 40" barrel has been bored smooth to .60 caliber. The rifle is covered in grime, but the exterior should clean to fine or better, most metal is gray and covered in light rust. Stock has two very good inspector's cartouches, "H.J.," and, "E.C.B.," has good edges and shows fewer than normal light handling marks. Gun has original ramrod showing pitting, a poor condition original leather sling, and a very-good condition original bayonet. **$550**

Rifled musket by Springfield Armory, .58 caliber, 40" barrel, dark bore, 1862-dated lock and breech. Gray patina on all metal with extensive fine pitting, lock markings are good, breech markings are faint. The stock shows light handling marks, but not much wear with two very good cartouches. Good-plus with incorrect reproduction ramrod and a very good original bayonet.

.... **$850**

Rifled Musket, Special Model 1861

Lamson, Goodnow & Yale Of Windsor, Vermont, .58 caliber, 40" round barrel, very good bore, 1863-dated lockplate and breech, lock marked, "L.G.&Y./Windsor." Almost illegible "VT" marking, all the metal has a light gray patina with some tarnish, faint pitting near the nipple. The eagles on the lockplate and bolster are faint. The stock has good edges, no cartouche, has had a little oil added through the years. Buttstock has a 1" high cross scratched into it near the buttplate, otherwise the wood shows only light handling marks. Overall condition is very good with original ramrod that is 1/4" short.

.... **$1,100**

Special contract musket by Colt, 28" barrel dated 1862 and bearing surcharge, "NJ," for New Jersey, very-good condition, barrel and stock shortened. Gray metal has light pitting, wood with scattered dents and bruises, forend cap missing. **$460**

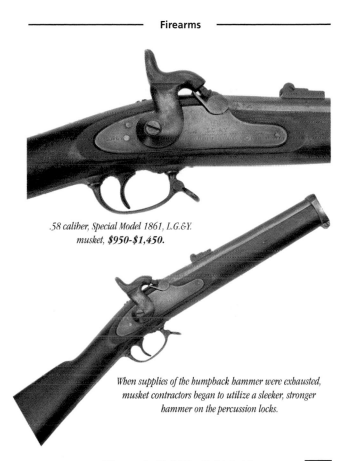

.58 caliber, Special Model 1861, L.G.&Y. musket, $950-$1,450.

When supplies of the humpback hammer were exhausted, musket contractors began to utilize a sleeker, stronger hammer on the percussion locks.

Rifle, Model 1863, Remington

No serial no., .58 caliber, 33" round 7-groove barrel, fine bore, manufactured
  in 1863. This "Zouave" retains most blue with case color grading 90% on
  lockplate and hammer with some fading to gray. All marks are correct with
  lock and barrel dated 1863. The barrel inspector is, "M.S.L.," with the stock
  cartouches for, "H.D.J.," and "R.H." The wood shows a light sanding with both
  cartouches very readable and the brass has been cleaned. **$2,000**

Manufactured by Remington, Ilion, New York. .58 caliber. Total quantity made
  was 12,501. Lockplate and hammer retain case-hardening with excellent
  markings. Barrel has 98% of its original deep blue finish. Brass nose cap,
  barrel bands, patchbox, buttplate and trigger guard have nice mellow patina.
  All have inspector marks. Wood is in excellent condition with minor handling
  marks and two sharp cartouches. Small sliver missing at barrel tang (looks
  original from factory). Bore is very good with minor pitting. **$4,795**

Rifle, New Model 1863, Sharps

Serial no. C33300, .52 caliber, 30" barrel, good bore, adapted for a socket
  bayonet, has iron patchbox, 20% fading case colors remain on frame, 50%
  case colors remain on lock, balance faded to gray. All metal markings are
  clear, 95% dull blue on barrel, small patch of faint pitting, 50% bright blue on
  pellet primer cover with more on some screw heads. Forend shows no wear,
  legible, "A.W.M.," inspection stamp. Buttstock shows light handling marks,
  two very good, "F.W.R.," cartouches with most of the oil finish remaining. The
  buttplate and patchbox have turned silver/gray while the bands have some
  faint case color. A great three-band rifle in fine-plus condition. **$3,350**

Rifled Musket, Model 1863, Double

.58 caliber, 41-1/8" barrel, excellent bore, metal is still in the white, has not
  been cleaned, shows a little tarnish, fine rust, and grime that should clean
  without a trace. Sharp markings on metal, stock sanded and stripped of

.58 caliber, Model 1861, Norwich contract 3-band rifle musket, $1,100-$1,500.

Markings on the lockplate often indicate what contractor made the particular weapon.

finish, shows handling dings and dents, two legible, "ADK," cartouches, correct ramrod and bayonet, very-good overall condition. **$2,000**

Rifled Musket, Model 1863, Type I

No serial no., .58 caliber, 40" round barrel, good bore, manufactured in 1863, correct two-leaf sight and barrel, lock dated 1863. No marks show on wood, all metal is gray with brown spotting and appears to have had an old cleaning. Split barrel bands with no retaining springs. Overall condition is good with an incorrect ramrod. **$700**

Made by Springfield Armory, .58 caliber, 40" round barrel, excellent bore, 1863-dated on lock and breech. All metal is bright including exterior of the lockplate with an old layer of dried grease or lacquer, all metal markings are sharp, no pitting. The stock has good edges, two clear inspector's cartouches, "W.T.T.," and, "E.S.A.," only normal light handling scratches and a shallow imprint of a vise jaw forward of the lock. With the original tulip-head ramrod, tompion, and an issue leather sling in sound condition. The buttplate has the initials "W.S." neatly formed with small punch dots, the sling has a partially legible name scratched into the surface. Fine-plus condition. **$2,400**

This has been altered to two-band style with a 32" long barrel, fine bore, lock dated 1864, all metal markings are clear. The barrel is gray with light surface rust, the stock has been refinished with a legible, "E.S.A.," cartouche and a partially legible second cartouche, small chips, and dings. Stock has a rack number stamped onto an aluminum washer on the left side opposite the lock, tulip-head ramrod, very good. **$350**

Rifled Musket, Model 1863, Type II

.58 caliber, 40" barrel, very good bore, lockplate marked, 1864-dated "US/ SPRINGFIELD," the breech with an 1864 date and "V/P(eagle head)" proof marks. Light gray patina on all the iron, sharp markings, a couple of patches of very faint nipple pitting on the muzzle, the hammer with some mottled case colors remaining. Stock shows relatively few light handling marks and a paint splatter on an old refinish with two legible inspector's cartouches. Overall condition is very good, very nice looking Civil War musket, complete with correct ramrod. **$1,500**

.58 caliber, 40" barrel, bright bore, strong rifling with a couple of rings. 1864-dated lock and breech, sharp markings. The stock has a small piece of wood replaced at the toe, nicely refinished, legible, "E S A ," cartouche, and an only partially legible second cartouche. The bands and band springs are incorrect, the ramrod has been repaired. The buttplate has an extra hole, good-looking musket with clean gray barrel and lock, only minor marks on the wood. **$600**

Rifle, New Model 1865, Sharps

Serial no. C30287, .52 caliber, 30" barrel, very good bore. This rifle has a single trigger and an iron patchbox, clear markings on lock and frame, legible barrel markings. The frame and lock are mottled-gray with patches of faint pitting. The barrel has a dark patina with light corrosion, some original blue visible in protected areas and at the muzzle where the bayonet was affixed. The forend has a surface chip at the rear, the butt has one legible cartouche and a trace of the second. Both stocks show very few light handling marks and have had a little oil added through the years. The nipple is a replacement, good-plus overall with correct unmarked socket bayonet that has remnants of nickel plating. **$2,500**

Rifle, Greene

.54 caliber percussion, under hammer, bolt-action weapon. The first bolt-action long arm that the U.S. military adopted. Doomed by its component ammunition and a silly, unworkable underhammer. The arm still had some very forward-looking ideas with a streamlined look and breech-loading bolt and gas seals. Brightly blued barrel retains 90-95% original finish. Bottom two bands retain 90-95% brilliant charcoal blue. Top band was held and

sweat probably rubbed most of the blue off. Hammer retains 70-80% vivid case color hardening, excellent oval bore and mechanics, fine solid stock with typical storage dings on butt. Complete except for a replacement ramrod.
.... **$2,650**

Rifle, C.B. Holden

Serial no. 142, .44 rimfire caliber, 24" octagon barrel, good bore. Less than 200 of these open frame rifles were made from 1862 to as late as the early 1870s. Barrel shorter than standard length, but appears to have been made this way. Barrel is marked on top, "HOLDEN'S PATENT/APRIL 1862." All of the metal has dark gray patina, the walnut stocks show normal handling marks on an old refinish and have a 2" long grain crack on the left side of the forend. This rifle (with a unique action) was made by a former employee of Frank Wesson. Good-plus condition. **$300**

Rifle, Joslyn

Produced by Springfield, serial no. 863, .50-.60-.450 Joslyn rimfire caliber, 35-1/2" barrel, fair bore, manufactured in 1864. This Joslyn breech-loading rifle has dark freckling overall, which has turned to moderate pitting with the heaviest pitting on the breechpiece, hammer, and lockplate. The stock has an added oil finish over many small handling marks and blemishes. Included with the rifle are a modern leather sling and a non-matching socket type bayonet. Fine overall condition. **$550**

Rifle, Maynard, First Model

No serial no., .50 caliber, 26" round barrel, octagonal at the breech, poor bore. This breech-loading rifle has the Maynard tape primer, factory barrel sights, factory long-leaf tang sight, iron patchbox. Made without a sling swivel, but one has been added by notching the stock under the lower tang. The frame case colors have turned to dark mottled patina, the barrel is a dark blue/black, scattered light pitting and rust freckling. The hammer will not engage, we suspect the action is gummed up with dirt and grease. The stock shows relatively few handling marks, and has a few small paint spots. Many of these were southern state purchases, this is likely one of them. Came from an old Texas collection, very-good overall condition. **$4,200**

Rifled Musket, P.S. Justice

Overall very good condition being 100% original, complete, and mechanically perfect. Metal is all clean steel color and free from rust or pitting except for some moderate barrel pitting between the front and middle bands. Lock is nice, "P.S. Justice PHILAd," marking. Barrel has same stamp and is .69 caliber, rifled. Stock has great color and good edges showing just honest handling age and use. Early "stepped" 1855-1861-style rear sight, and double curve-style trigger guard. These guns were made from refurbished 1816 parts and issued almost exclusively to Pennsylvania troops during the Civil War, very nice example, with a good look. There are numerous variations on these Justice rifles and muskets, this is one of the more scarce and desirable with the brass furniture (most are found with iron in this pattern). **$1,595**

Rifle, Whitney-Enfield

Very rare Whitney "Enfield" pattern musket, circa 1861, that has the odd .69-barrel with pewter nose cap, and is marked "E. Whitney" on lock. Has very nice wood and a totally attic-brown patina overall. One of the models rejected by the U.S. Government for "good and serviceable arms" that Whitney promptly sold on the open market, many of which ended up in the hands of Southern troops. This one is missing the hammer screw and has some initials carved in the buttstock. **$975**

> **"Several of the officers in the regiment refused, or affirmed that they would refuse to accept the flintlock musket or go until better guns were procured."**
>
> —*Cyrus F. Jenkins, 13th Georgia Infantry*

Import Muskets and Rifles

Musket, Model 1809, Conversion

German Potsdam Model 1809 converted to percussion. This is approximately .70 caliber. The lockplate is marked, "DANZIG 1835," and has a crown over the Danzig name. The wood is in very good condition, with some buttstock markings. All brass fittings are present as well as the sling swivels. The barrel has some pitting near the end, but not too bad. There are markings on the barrel with the rear sight present. The ramrod is present as well, the mechanics work fine. **$650**

Rifled Musket, Model 1815, Conversion

.69-caliber rifled percussion conversion of a French standard military long arm, 42-1/2" round barrel with French proofs and date, "1820." Good bore with shallow rifling, iron ramrod cupped for the new pointed projectile. No sights except for the standard brass blade on the top band. Bayonet lug mounted under the muzzle. Barrel was brown lacquered and still retains 20-25% of this fragile finish. Lock is blank with a blackish patina. Large, proofed percussion hammer. Rifle retains both iron sling swivels. Fine iron furniture with 20-25% original armory brown finish as well. Fine oil-finished stock with one or two drying cracks at the lock mortise. **$950**

Musket, Model 1816, Conversion

No serial no., .71 caliber, 41" smoothbore barrel, dark bore. This Mutzig-made musket has a massive bolster conversion with slightly shortened barrel. All metal has a dark-brown patina with pitting around the breech. The stock has a dished-out comb and many small handling marks under an added finish. It is likely that this musket was imported during the Civil War. Fair overall condition. **$300**

Musket, Model 1842, Conversion

.71-caliber smoothbore French military Musket with right barrel with crisp proofs and "Mdle 1848" at the tang and "1844" manufacture date at the bolster. Bright smooth back action lock marked, "Mre Rle/de St. Etienne."

Complete, bright iron furniture with original sling swivels and ramrod. Excellent stock with sharp French manufacturing marks at the right butt. Smooth bore, excellent mechanics. **$1,350**

Rifled Musket, Model 1816, Conversion

Maybe a Model 1816 French pattern. It is roughly the same as the U.S. 1816 conversions. Very good to fine condition, metal surfaces are smooth steel with light-brown patina. The barrel is marked "1818." The lock has a tiny proof mark incorporating a cipher, script "R," and numeral "17." This has a long-range rear sight (elevation slide missing). The stock has good edges and shows only honest use (no abuse). Carved into the back of the buttstock is "M.S." Stamped into the buttstock are "AR 1840," "NR," and two other script cartouches. This comes with a modern U.S. 1816 pattern ramrod. **$750**

Musket, Model 1842

Classic back-action lock French 42, 3-band infantry musket in overall very good condition being 100% original and complete (except for the missing ramrod), with great color, nice stock, and great patina. **$650**

Rifled Musket, Model 1842, Conversion

Austrian Model 1842, .69 caliber, 42-1/2" barrel is smooth bored and has a long-range rear site, metal cleaned to bright with scattered fine pitting. The refinished stock shows relatively few handling marks. Good condition with replacement ramrod. **$800**

Musket, Model 1848, Conversion

.71-caliber smoothbore French military musket. Thousands of these were imported during our Civil War. Bright barrel with crisp proofs and "Mdle 1848" at the tang and "1844" manufacture date at the bolster. Bright smooth back action lock marked, "Mre Rle/de St. Etienne." Complete, bright iron furniture with original sling swivels and ramrod. Excellent stock with sharp French manufacturing marks at the right butt. Bright, smooth bore and excellent mechanics. **$1,350**

Rifled Musket, Model 1849

Austrian Jaeger with no serial no., .71 caliber, 33" octagon to round barrel, fair
   bore. Manufactured circa 1850. A large caliber rifle/musket showing no marks
   other than the number 70 punched into the trigger guard and lock bolt plate.
   All furniture is brass with steel sling swivels, ramrod and barrel band. The
   barrel is also fastened to the breech stock with a rear wedge. The cheekrest
   is for a right-hand shooter. The sight is a two-leaf affair with one fixed blade
   and a flip-up leaf with three apertures marked 3, 4, and 5. A side-mounted
   bayonet lug is mounted on the barrel 2-7/8" from the muzzle. The antique
   condition is good for this Civil War era import. 25,000 were purchased by the
   U.S. War Department in 1862-1863. .... **$325**

Rifled Musket, Model 1853, Enfield

.577 caliber, 39" barrel, rifled bore is dark, lockplate is marked with a crown
   and "1862/TOWER." The gun is dirty, should clean to good plus. Complete
   with correct ramrod and a U.S. socket bayonet that does not fit. **$800**

.577-caliber British manufactured weapon, bored smooth. Fine dark patina on
   metal, light to moderate pitting around bolster. Clear proofs and "24-24"
   caliber markings. Crown and "Tower/1862" crisply marked on the lock. No
   British military markings, so this is most probably one that was brought in to
   the U.S. during our Civil War. Complete with sling swivels, ramrod, and brass-
   chained nipple protector. Mellow brass trigger guard, buttplate, and stock cap.
   Complete except for the rifled bore. **$1,050**

Extremely rare .577 Confederate Sinclair-Hamilton import three-band Enfield
   Rifle complete with sling, bayonet, tompion, and nipple protector with
   chain. Sinclair, Hamilton and Company imported Enfield muskets through
   Wilmington, North Carolina, for the Confederacy. The musket is marked
   "SH" over "C" behind the trigger guard. The markings have been cleaned
   out with a needle to make them more visible. This musket is out of a central
   North Carolina estate. The metal has a smooth brown uncleaned patina with

.577 caliber, Enfield 3-band rifled musket,
$950-$1,500.

*Part of the equipment issued with the English-produced Enfield rifled muskets
included a nipple protector on a chain*

lockplate markings of "1861 Tower." The wood is pretty with normal small marks and dings from use. The stock has the soldier's initials "O.P.L." and name "Betty" carved into the left-hand side. **$2,850**

Tower-marked 1853 Enfield Pattern Musket, .577 caliber, 39" barrel, dark bore. Manufactured in 1862. This musket is dark brown overall with light pinprick pitting throughout. The socket bayonet has rusted tight to the muzzle. The stock has been sanded and is dry without any wood finish at present. Fair condition overall. **$750**

Rifled Musket, Model 1854, Austrian Lorenz

.54-caliber percussion Austrian arm, really typical Confederate-style Lorenz with the original caliber, simple block post rear sight, and raised cheekrest. Rifle is in outstanding condition, overall a smooth, dark black patina. Crisp proofs and date on barrel flat, "859" match those on the lock, every part is numbered and inspected alike. Excellent bore and mechanics, original sling swivels. The ramrod is brass tipped and appears period, but it is not one usually associated with Lorenz rifles. The stock is superb, like new and inspected everywhere. **$1,650**

.58-caliber percussion Austrian military rifle has cleaned metal, a good bore and mechanics. Repro leaf-style rear sight, missing ramrod, but otherwise complete. **$750**

Rifle, Model 1856, Enfield

P-56, 1861 tower with sharp barrel proof marks. Lock marked, "Tower 1861." Barrel has nice plum patina with only very minor breech pitting, original chain and nipple protector. Wood is in very good condition, but appears to have been lightly cleaned. Rear sling swivel is missing screw, bore is average. **$2,495**

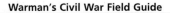

.68 caliber, Potsdam import musket, $750-$1,100.

*The nipple was fixzed directly in the flashpan cutout
on the converted Potsdam muskets.*

Rifled Musket, Model 1858

Looks very much like an Austrian Lorenz, but this 1858 Bavarian has interesting patent breech. Metal is smooth with overall light-brown patina. The stock is the reddish blonde wood just like on the Lorenz. Good edges, various parts are marked with "1675" assembly or inventory number. Interestingly, this has a U.S. Springfield two-leaf rear sight that has been with this gun. This is complete with the tulip-tipped ramrod drilled with a hole for cleaning rag. Overall very good condition, only defect is a piece of wood knocked out behind the tang, it has been reglued in place. Front sight has had a taller silver blade added presumably by a shooter. **$595**

Rifle, Model 1858, Enfield

.577 caliber manufactured between 1857-1860. Barrel retains 98% original blue with sharp markings. All metal parts have sharp markings, bore is very good. Walnut wood stock is in very good condition with minor handling marks, stock and barrel both marked "VII." This rifle was probably one of the arms purchased early in the war by Major Huse and shipped to the south.
.... **$3,995**

Overall "very good" condition and 100% original and complete with the exception of the bayonet lug that was removed long ago. The steel parts are all gun-metal gray color with strong markings. The lock is stamped "1861 Tower" and has a crown. The barrel has the British "25-25" marking indicating manufacture for shipment to North America in .577 caliber. The wood is a deep-brown English walnut with excellent lines and free from any major nicks or bruises. This gun is 100% steel mounted including the buttplate, trigger guard, and nose cap. It has the 1,000-yard long-range rear sight firmly in place, and still retains its original ramrod. Both sling swivels are present. **$950**

Revolvers and Pistols

Though not the source of a great number of wounds or deaths during the Civil War, the revolver or pistol held a mystique for soldiers on both sides. Issued only to mounted troops, thousands of foot soldiers purchased handguns to carry in addition to their government-supplied weapons. In most cases, the only time they withdrew their handgun, though, was for a cleaning or posing in a warlike stance for the photographer.

The Union purchased 373,077 handguns during the Civil War, more than a fourth of which came from Colt. Total Confederate purchases were probably near half of that number. Assuming there were 500,000 government purchases of handguns, this can only be considered a fraction of the weapons carried by soldiers, as period sales of handguns doubled the sales to government agencies.

This is all good news for the collector. Because it takes a good deal of effort to totally destroy a revolver, many have survived. A Civil War collector looking for representative handguns can easily acquire Colt and a Remington New Model Army for a couple of thousand dollars. Be careful though, it is easy to become distracted by the variety of revolvers out there! A Civil War memorabilia collector can become a gun collector in the blink of an eye.

Gang mould for .44 caliber, Colt Model 1860 Army revolver,
$400-$475

Collecting Hints

Pros:
- Many revolvers from the Civil War period have survived. There is an ample supply available for both beginning and advanced collectors.

- Revolvers and pistols do not take up much space.

- The "wow" factor is high. Most people recognize the lethalness of a handgun, and when they see weapons used during the Civil War, there is a sense of connecting with the past.

- High-end pieces tend to be very stable investments. This is not true for less-desirable makes and conditions of revolvers.

- Reproductions of common arms were produced with reenactors and shooters in mind. Therefore, the reproductions tend to be appropriately marked.

- Plenty of references are available for both beginners and advanced collectors.

Cons:
- Revolvers are probably the most frequently stolen Civil War relics.

- Rare models are often faked or pieced together from parts. High-end purchases should be left to advanced, extremely knowledgeable collectors.

- Though there are plenty of representative pieces available, handguns that have a provenance proving actual use in the Civil War are rather scarce and, therefore, much more expensive. Provenance can add hundreds or thousands of dollars to the price of the most mediocre weapon.

Availability ★★★

Price ★★★

Reproduction Alert ★★

Excavated, boot pistol, $85-$95.

Pistols, Confederate

Fayetteville Conversion

Single-shot percussion pistol started as a flintlock, but with the capture of
the Fayetteville Arsenal in April of 1861, the state of North Carolina began
converting flintlocks to the percussion system as rapidly as possible. While
there were plenty of volunteers to fill the cavalry ranks, the government
was unable to arm them. Military Secretary Warren Winslow was pushing
the conversions as fast as possible, writing to the commander at Fayetteville
on July 24, 1861, "You will please hasten as much as possible the work of
changing the flint and steel muskets. As fast as the carbines are ready, send
them to Raleigh and also other cavalry weapons." The next day he wrote,
"send us the carbines as rapidly as done, but I tremble to think it will take
five or six weeks to do them. What shall we do?" Two days later, on July
27, the Confederate Government took over the arsenal as the demand for
guns continued to grow. By the middle of October, the armory was still
doing conversions, according to the *Richmond Examiner,* "a large force
is now engaged in altering old flintlock guns to percussion, making very
efficient weapons," referring to Fayetteville. Finally, in November, altered
pistols were beginning to trickle out and by the middle of January 1862,
564 had been shipped to the 2nd North Carolina Cavalry. The last 529
of the Fayetteville percussion pistol alterations had been completed and
shipped to the 3rd North Carolina Cavalry by March of 1862. Fayetteville
converted a total of 1,093 U.S. Model 1836 pistols from flint to percussion,
all of which were shipped to the 2nd or 3rd North Carolina Cavalry. The
Fayetteville Conversions are quite distinct, having a drum-type bolster with
cleanout screw threaded into the barrel. The new percussion hammer is
easily recognizable, smaller, but having the same "S" shape as the Fayetteville
rifles. This pistol is an untouched example of the 2nd and 3rd cavalry's
armament. The lock is marked, "A. Waters Milbury. MS 1839," in three lines
with a prominent "F" stamped to the right. The drum bolster with cleanout

screw and the Fayetteville hammer clearly identify this as one of the 1,093 alterations issued to the 2nd and 3rd North Carolina Cavalry. The Rebel who carried it carved "SLH" into the left side of the stock and an "A" just below. The only cavalryman in the 2nd or 3rd Company A with the initials "SH" is Solomon Haney. Haney enlisted in June of 1861 at 41 years of age. Despite his age, he served until late 1864. ....**$2,800**

Revolvers, Confederate
Griswold and Gunnison

When the war broke out in 1861, Griswold began making pikes for the Georgia Government. Arvin Gunnison had begun the manufacture of pistols in New Orleans, Louisiana. When the city fell to the Yankees in the spring of 1862, Arvin and his machinery moved to Griswoldville. He joined up with his old friend Sam Griswold, and together they made handgun history. From July of 1862, until November 22, 1864, when the factory was destroyed by Yankee cavalry, Griswold and Gunnison produced more than 3,600 revolvers on the Colt's pattern. This 1st model is marked with the serial number 766 on the frame, barrel lug and cylinder. The loading lever is secondarily marked, "8." The cryptic "G" appears on the underside of the barrel and "II" on the back of the lug. This revolver is also well marked internally. The cryptic "G" appears on the cylinder back, and "GG" on the back strap, back of frame, and trigger guard. The secondary number "16" appears on the trigger guard, back of frame, back strap, hammer, trigger and even the grips. All screws are original as well. The wedge is probably a period replacement, as it is unmarked. The gun is in very good condition inside and out. The metal has a nice smooth, untouched ashen patina. Both the barrel and cylinder show good twist lines. The cylinder even retains its safety stops. The grips are excellent with the exception of the bottom of the butt. It has been dinged up and its owner carved in the initials "HR." The brass is smooth and uncleaned as well. The action is smooth, strong and tight. **$29,500**

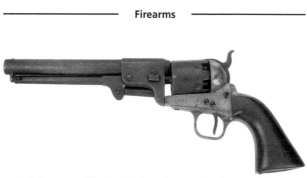

*Confederate, Griswold, .36 caliber, brass-frame revolver, **$22,000-$30,000**.*

The Griswold factory produced at least 3,600 revolvers based on Colt's Model 1851 "Navy." The brass frame is the distinguishing characteristic.

Pistols, U.S.

Allen & Tuber, Bar Hammer

Percussion firing system, very fine condition, only 400 produced from 1837
to the Civil War period, serial number 260, marked "Patented 1837, Allen's
Patent." **$475**

Allen & Wheelock

Action works, single shot, 32 rimfire, fine condition. Only 1,000 produced, serial
number 898. .... **$425**

Model 1836

.54 caliber, smoothbore, single shot US martial pistol converted to percussion
by applying a drum bolster and a civilian "mule ear" hammer. Smooth
yellowish-plum barrel with crisp, "NWP/P" proofs at the breech. Lock crisply
marked, "US/R. Johnson/Middn Conn/1838." Smooth bore, fine mechanics.
Iron furniture is a smooth, dove gray, captive ramrod. Excellent stock
with fine oil-finished stock. Clear oval cartouche at the left flat. Barrel has
standard Federal inspectors' initials underneath. **$750**

Remington-Elliot, Derringer

4-barrel pepperbox-style derringer, hard rubber grips, overall very-good
condition. Marked on left side, "Manufactured By E. Remington & Sons Ilion
NY," and on the right side, "Elliot's Patent May 29 1860-Oct. 11, 1861."
.... **$365**

Revolvers, U.S.

Adams Patent Percussion Pocket by Massachusetts Arms Co.,

Serial no. 4991, .31 caliber, 3-1/4" barrel. Checkered walnut grips, condition:
fair to good. Grey metal showing areas of light pitting. Some nipples
damaged, one missing. Trigger return spring broke, grips with light wear.
.... **$345**

Allen & Thurber, Pepperbox

6-barrel, .31 caliber, nice medium-size pepperbox with straight bar hammer on top of the frame which is stamped "Allen's Patent 1845." This measures roughly 7" in overall length. The barrels are fluted and are marked, "Allen Thurber & Co. Worcester." The frame has some delicate scroll engraving, as does the separately affixed nipple shield. Overall is in very-good condition, with gray steel surfaces and lightly worn walnut bag-style grips. There is light pitting in spots on the barrel and frame. **$295**

Allen & Wheelock, "Providence Police"

Made late 1850s thru early 1860s with only 700 produced, 5-shot cylinder, .36 caliber, nice grips, action works, very-fine condition. **$595**

Bacon, Pocket

5-shot, 4" barrel, and fluted cylinder. Metal is light brown patina, smooth with some extremely fine texture pitting on small surfaces only. Mechanically tight and perfect, very nice grips, markings on top of barrel, "Bacon Mfg Co.," very hard to read. **$395**

Colt, First Model Dragoon

Serial no. 4966, .44 caliber, 7-1/2" barrel fitted with open rear sight. Walnut grips, condition: fair. Metal has been cleaned and shows areas of light pitting and scattered scratches. Cylinder with no markings remaining except light serial number. Loading lever replaced, grips showing wear, dents, and repairs with copper pins and replaced pieces. **$2,300**

Colt, Third Model Dragoon

Serial no. 16459, .44 caliber, 7-1/2" barrel, poor bore. Matching numbers except for cylinder and replaced wedge. The revolver has been cleaned, iron is gray with scattered light pitting, brass polished, one-piece walnut grip has old refinish and is worn at the butt. Barrel address is legible, frame patent marking is gone, good overall condition. **$1,900**

Model 1849 Colt Pocket Revolver

Manufactured 1856, .31 caliber, "W.W.S.," William W. Squire, 1st New Jersey Infantry, Company A. Inscription on butt and front of back strap, next to hammer. Gun has a nice even patina overall with sharp markings and showing 85% of cylinder scene. All numbers match, brass has approximately 40% of original silver finish. Walnut grips are in excellent shape with 85% original factory varnish. Squire enlisted as a private and was later promoted to sergeant and further served in the Quartermasters and Commissary Departments. His official records reflect that he was, "in some hard fought battles and proved his patriotism and courage." The 1st New Jersey was a hard fighting unit that engaged C.S.A. troops at many battles including Antietam, Gettysburg, and the Appomattox campaign. Records included. **$4,750**

All matched serial numbers, 100% original and complete, mechanically good with some finicky response in the handspring. The 5" barrel has rich traces of finish mixed with plum patina. Cylinder is gray mixed with splotches of light pitting and retains 50% of the cylinder scene. Frame is gray steel, grips are excellent, in the 318,xxx serial range, overall very-good condition. **$550**

Colt, Model 1851 Navy

.36 caliber, serial 144821, 7-1/2" barrel; deep untouched plum-brown patina overall; indexes fine, all matching numbers, light cylinder scene; grips show honest use and wear; minor chip on corner of left grip; great barrel marking. **$1,125**

Colt, Model 1851 Navy, Third Model

Serial no. 67436, .36 caliber, 4 1/4" barrel with New York markings. Varnished walnut grips. Metal has been cleaned and showing areas of minor pitting. Right side of barrel lug with series of small dents at wedge. Replaced loading lever pitted overall. Cylinder retains 80-85% of scene. Trigger guard/grip straps retain 15-20% silver-plated finish, grips with 60-70% varnish and showing scattered dents and scratches. Overall condition: good. **$748**

Serial no. 50359, .36 caliber, New York-marked barrel fitted with non-factory German silver blade and open rear sights. Walnut grips, barrel has light gray patina and retaining generous traces of blue finish on underside. Cylinder has good scene partially obscured by several series of dents. Four chambers retaining original charges, grips show wear, small chips at forward toes, possibly replaced. Good to very-good condition. **$1,035**

Colt, Model 1851 Navy, Fourth Model
Serial no. 104990, .36 caliber, 7-1/2" octagon barrel, manufactured 1861. This 51 Navy has all matching numbers and retains traces of protected barrel blue and case color on the loading lever. The cylinder has six safety pins and shows a naval scene that is 75% complete. A mechanically very tight Navy that grades good to very good. **$1,400**

Colt, Model 1860 Army
A nice brown, uncleaned patina on all the metal. Barrel markings, "ADDRESS COL. SAML. COLT NEW- YORK U.S. AMERICA." The cylinder scene is 95%. The walnut grips are very good and is cartouched. The serial number is 63880, and the revolver is all matching except for the wedge. The gun was made in 1862. Shows use, but not abused. **$2,100**

Serial no. 79890, .44 caliber, 8" New York marked barrel. Frame marked, "Colts/ Patent." Oil-finished grips, both with inspector's cartouche. Good to very-good condition. Grey metal has been cleaned and shows scattered areas of pitting, mainly to cylinder. Most cylinder scene remains, but shows wear. Left grip with series of fine notches and illegible inscription. Right side with chipping at butt and series of dents to butt. **$1,265**

Serial no. 66357, .44 caliber, 8" barrel with New York address. Condition is poor. Mottled-gray metal shows areas of pitting. Cylinder heavily cleaned and frozen. Bruised and heavily worn grips replaced. **$345**

Colt 1851, .36 caliber, Navy revolver,
$750-$1,400.

The quality of the engraved scene on
the cylinder will greatly affect the
value of a Colt Navy.

Colt, Model 1862 Police

.36 caliber, iron back strap, all matching number 376 (early 1861). A smooth, gray gun with fine walnut stock, clear markings and tight as new. Hangs now and then (weak hand spring). Tip of loading lever has been repaired by professional gunsmith. **$1,350**

Serial no. 28194, .36 caliber, 6-1/2" barrel, fair bore. All matching numbers including the wedge. The New York barrel address is clear, frame marking is legible. All the iron is a mottled gray with large areas of faint to fine pitting. The original walnut grip has a repaired crack on the left side with four notches carved near the back strap. This 1864-manufactured Colt looks like it saw plenty of service in the Civil War, fair condition. **$500**

L. Whitney, Navy

100% original, complete, very tight, mechanically perfect, and well marked. The grips on this revolver are nearly perfect with a crisp cartouche, "SB" (probably Samuel T. Bugbee, armory sub-inspector) on the left grip. The metal is overall plum-brown with traces of blue on the underside of the barrel and lower flats. The cylinder has 60% original scene clearly visible (rare as Whitney scenes are incredibly delicate and almost always worn away), and traces of finish on the cylinder. The top of the barrel is marked, "E. Whitney/N.Haven". There are various sub-inspectors' marks such as letter "D" twice on the barrel and once on the frame, an "S" on the loading lever, and a "DB" on the cylinder. The serial is in the 19,000 range. It shows honest age, but no abuse whatsoever. **$2,250**

Manhattan Arms Co.

Serial number 43227, all numbers match, 6-1/2" barrel. The grips are original and the markings are fine. The cylinder scene is 100%, and the words on the cylinder are excellent. Indexes properly sometimes, and other times it needs a little help. There is a little minor pitting on each side of the frame, but not bad. **$650**

Manhattan Arms Co., Navy

Serial no. 3499, .36 caliber, 4" barrel, cylinder with oval panels of military scenes. Varnished walnut grips, very-good condition. Metal with dark-gray patina and areas of light pitting. Cylinder scenes show moderate wear, grips with small dents and scratches. **$633**

Massachusetts Arms, American Adams Pocket

.31 caliber, five-shot, long barrel, pocket revolver in superb condition. Barrel and frame retain 95% high luster factory blue, checkered grips are near mint, action is tight, cylinder has had some touch up on the blue there and is mixed with plum original blue and touch up on the cylinder. Serial is 1,800 range, reference shows that of the 4,500 pocket models made only 100 had round barrels in 4-1/4". **$1,250**

Moore's Patent, Belt

Brooklyn, New York, single-action belt revolver, also known as the "Seven Shooter." .32-caliber rimfire with 6" octagon barrel. Seven-shot cylinder, removable ejector rod mounted under barrel. Barrel and cylinder swing to right for loading. Brass frame and handle with decorative broad scroll engraving with traces of silver plating remaining. Some blue left on barrel and cylinder. Walnut grips with square butt. A couple of chips on the toe of the left grip are present. Barrel marking is, "D. MOORE PATENT SEPT. 18, 1860" and there is some pitting where the pistol laid on the obverse side, serial number is 107. .... **$625**

Moore's Patent, Teat-fire

Very nice example of this 1860s hideaway revolver. Overall very-good condition with delicate age patina, and nice engraving, excellent grips. This fired an unusual teat-fire cartridge. **$295**

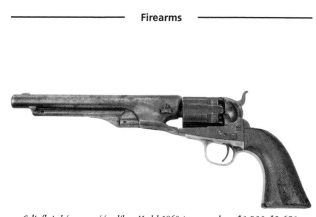

*Colt, fluted 4-screw, .44 caliber, Model 1860 Army revolver, **$1,900-$2,650.***

*Example of an 1860 Colt Army revolver, with less bluing
and case hardening will sell for **$1,200-$1,800.***

Remington Beals, Navy

.36 caliber, very-good condition aside from the fact that there is no original finish on this gun, making it closer to fine condition. It is 100% original and complete, and exactly as it was shipped from the factory. All of the edges are sharp, as is the barrel address. The grips are outstanding with virtually no wear or dents. The metal has a uniform light-brown age patina that is quite appealing. It is mechanically perfect, and as tight as a drum. The serial is in the 10,000 range that would indicate manufacture in late 1861 or early 1862 (roughly 14,000 were produced in total). **$1,395**

Remington, New Model Army

Serial no. 78271, .44 caliber, 8" octagon barrel, fair bore. Standard model purchased by the Union during the Civil War, has sub-inspector's initials on the metal with the inspector's cartouche visible on the left grip. The barrel and frame are a light gray, the cylinder is probably a replacement with a dark-gray patina. The barrel address is partially legible, the metal has large areas of faint pitting with a few patches of fine pitting. The grips have a repaired crack on the left side with a large chip missing at the toe on the same side. The grips have been refinished with the cartouche legible, good condition. **$500**

Serial no. 28332, .44 caliber, early example with German silver-cone front sight. Retains 45% blue, traces of case colors and has clear government inspector's cartouche. **$1,425**

Very crisp action, 60-70% original blue on the barrel frame and cylinder, grips have 95% original varnish, no cartouche. Serial number is 80613. The gun has fancy initials, "W.D.", on the trigger guard. On the inside of the grips is the name, "W. Dunn." **$2,000**

Remington, New Model Navy

Overall very-good condition, 24,000 serial range with all numbers matching, 100% original and complete. The metal is overall smooth, with a deep-brown patina, totally uniform in color and very pretty. Barrel marking is clear three-line new model marking, edges are sharp with only light wear. Good grips with some toe chipping. Front sight is early style cone, and the cylinder is early Beals-style without safety notches between the nipples. **$875**

Serial no. 23920, .38-centerfire caliber. Standard configuration with factory conversion. Walnut grips, mottled-gray metal with areas of light pitting and series of small dents to barrel lug. Ejector rod missing, trigger return, spring fatigued. Grips showing dents and bruises, series of notches to left butt and chipping at toes, fair condition. **$345**

Rogers & Spencer, Army

.44 caliber, extremely nice example in excellent condition, 100% original, mechanically perfect, tight, solid, and all matched serials in the 1900 range except for the loading lever, which is marked with a number "39." This gun has roughly 75% to 80% original factory blue. The frame has 90% blue, the barrel has some wear to the finish in the center portion of the top five flats. The cylinder retains roughly 50% blue, the hammer and loading lever have generous amounts of case coloring. The grips are super with sharp edges, vivid cartouche "RPB" and a few light bangs on the bottom of the grip.
.... **$1,450**

Smith & Wesson Model No. 1, 2nd Issue

Serial no. 83055, .22 rimfire, 3-1/8" barrel, very good bore, fine nickel-plated revolver which retains 98% of its nickel finish with only a few very small peen marks above the trigger on the right side of the frame. Fine case colors on the hammer. The rosewood grips are also fine and are stamped on the interior with the serial number (83055). Revolver is housed in original revolver lid motif gutta-percha case that has one small chip on the lid's outside edge and two small chips in the interior shell holder. Interior maroon velveteen lining is in very good condition with some minor fading of the color. A fine cased Smith and a rare accessory. **$3,500**

7-shot, .22-caliber pocketsize revolver. This one is very good with much silver plate, on the brass frame, fine rosewood grips, nice steel barrel free from pitting, and good strong markings. Cylinder bears the 1855, 1859, and 1860 patent dates. The revolver still cocks and functions perfectly, except the cylinder does not fully lock in place when cocked, and just needs a tiny spring in the cylinder stop device on the top of the frame, 79,000 serial range.
.... **$265**

Smith & Wesson, Model 2, Old Army
Brass framed, serial no. 15, fine condition, action works. **$1,200**

Serial no. 46726, .32 rimfire long, 6" octagonal with rib barrel, poor bore, manufactured from 1861-1874, 3-pin, retains thinning original blue on the frame behind the cylinder. The balance is gray-brown with scattered pitting and dark spotting. The rosewood grips show considerable finish with no chips or cracks. Good condition, the frame latch spring needs attention and the hinge is loose. **$370**

Springfield Arms, Pocket
.22 caliber, virtually identical to the Smith & Wesson No. I, this brass frame example made by Springfield Arms Co., circa 1863, is in overall very-good condition, being all original and mechanically perfect except for a small catch on the loading gate. **$225**

Starr Arms Co., 1858 Army, Double Action
Serial no. 5720, .44 caliber, 6" round barrel, fair to good bore. A Starr Army with a gray-brown metal surface and several dings, mostly on the left side of the barrel. Several areas show file marks and scattered light pitting. Small inspector's "W" is visible on left of barrel and on the cylinder under the serial number. Cartouches show weakly on both grip panels, but the initials cannot be determined with any certainty, good condition. **$650**

Starr Arms Co., 1863 Army, Single Action

.44 caliber, serial no. 27809, 8" barrel, fine action with crisp markings, Civil War inspector cartouches on both grips, 35% original blue, no pitting. Fine example of this handsome and well-balanced revolver. **$1,425**

Serial no. 39611, .44 caliber, 8" barrel, very good bore. Matching serial numbers, good markings, legible cartouche on right side of stock, partially legible cartouche on left side. Most of the metal has a dark-gray patina with some faint pitting, the frame has quite a bit of old black paint and traces elsewhere, the bottom of the butt with scratched, "USN." Very-good condition. **$850**

Serial no. 84378, .44 caliber, standard civilian model, mottled gray metal showing areas of light pitting. Barrel with period non-factory modification comprising a band at muzzle with fitting to retain loading lever. No markings visible, but serial number. Grip strap drilled for shoulder stock. Grips show wear and small chips. Good to very-good condition. **$374**

Whitney, Navy, 2nd Model, 6th Type

.36 caliber, has loading lever with Colt-style catch and five groove rifling in barrel. Serial number in the 30,000 range, all edges and markings are strong, and the metal has a nice, deep plum color (done with "cold blue" or similar coloring agent), which looks very nice. The grips are excellent, the action is as tight and crisp as new, and the gun is 100% original and complete except for a replacement wing-screw, which secures the loading lever and cylinder pin. Overall good to very-good condition. **$850**

Import Pistols
France, Pinfire

Civil War-era, double-barrel 12mm French import pinfire vest pistol. The pistol has a smooth, brown aged patina and still works perfectly. This one comes complete with an unfired original 12mm pinfire cartridge. **$275**

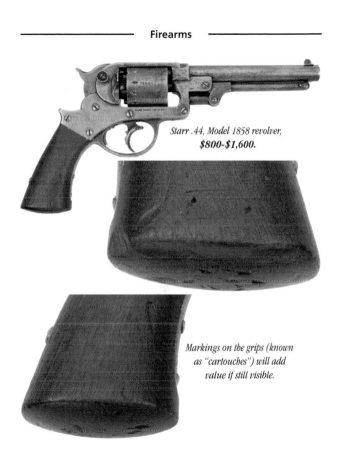

Starr .44, Model 1858 revolver,
$800-$1,600.

Markings on the grips (known as "cartouches") will add value if still visible.

Import Revolvers

England, Kerr

.44 caliber, single-action, serial number 11075, fine condition overall with a smooth steel-gray patina. Traces of original blue under the barrel and in the frame's recesses. Excellent bore and mechanics. Crisp markings, "London Armoury," on the frame and, "LAC," on the barrel. Belonged to Captain Cushman of a New York Infantry Regiment. Excellent diamond checkered grips, complete with lanyard loop and ring. **$2,500**

France, LeFaucheaux, 7mm

Import, nice grips, with ejector rod, very fine condition, 7mm pinfire, 6-shot cylinder, marked "LeFaucheaux." **$275**

Nice grips, with ejector rod, very fine condition, 6-shot engraved cylinder, marked, "LeFaucheaux." **$275**

France, LeFaucheaux, 12mm

Holster 6-shot cylinder, Holster in fine condition as is the revolver. Comes with six pinfire cartridges and a glass display case. **$695**

Serial no. 19920, 12mm caliber, 6-1/4" barrel. The frame and barrel are marked, "INV on E. Lefaucheaux/Brevet SGDG (Paris)." The cylinder has a name neatly engraved in small punch dots, "Lieut. J.S. Abraham 164 Reg. T.N.Y." The hinge on the loading gate is broken. All of the metal has a gray patina, minor fine pitting, very good walnut grips. The revolver is in a modern walnut case with six pinfire cartridges. **$1,300**

Serial no. 5197, 12mm caliber, 6" barrel, good bore. Appears to be identical to the Model 1854, but does not have a spur on the trigger guard. The only markings on the revolver are, "LF 5197," on the right side of the barrel lug. Missing the handspring, dark patina on metal with very fine pitting, refinished grips in good condition. **$175**

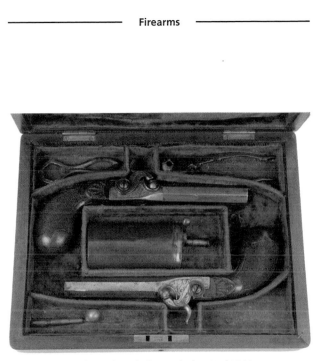

*Cased set, Belgian dueling pistols, **$1,300-$1,700**.*

CHAPTER 8

FLAGS AND MUSICAL EQUIPMENT

Early in the war, each regiment was mustered with a band. The belief was that playing martial tunes would elevate the soldiers to tasks they normally would not consider. Furthermore, each infantry company assigned a drummer and fifer. In addition to eliciting a military spirit, these two individuals performed the important business of communicating a commander's desire to the company by playing particular "calls" on their instruments. By mid-1862, regimental bands were, for the most part, eliminated. At the same time, the bugle began to replace the drum and fife as the preferred method of communicating calls on the battlefield.

In addition to the musicians, a regiment also assigned men to function as the color guard. In the field, each regiment carried a stand of colors consisting of the national flag and the regimental flag. A color guard of four men—two to carry the colors and two to act as guards—were given the task of safeguarding the regiment's flags. These banners were as treasured and protected *after* the war as they were during the war, so very few have ended up in private hands. The vast majority of regimental flags that have survived reside in museums or other public collections.

Regimental colors, though, are not the only variety of flag that existed during the Civil War, and therefore, the prospect of collecting flags does become better. In addition to headquarter flags,

KP photo/Wisconsin Veterans Museum collection

These three sheet music pouches were Union issued. The top two pouches are made of black leather and were owned by George Winn while serving with the 5th Wisconsin Volunteer Infantry Band. Both are valued at $500.
The bottom black leather pouch was used by George T. Spaulding to carry music books while serving with the 3rd Wisconsin Infantry band through 1962.
Value: $675.

recruiting flags, garrison flags, and other miscellaneous military-associated flags, there are all the civilian expressions of patriotism that were created in many different sizes and shapes. Usually, a person who specializes in collecting flags looks for them in a variety of forms and sizes. At the outbreak of the Civil War, the United States flag had 33 stars. Though the arrangement of the stars varied greatly, the most common arrangement was of five horizontal lines of stars, from top to bottom in these numbers: 7-7-5-7-7.

Nevertheless, the ultimate trophy in this area of collecting is a regimental banner. Because of the extremely fragile nature, flags that haven't been stored properly over the years should be handled and stabilized only by a professional textile conservator. Should you happen to stumble onto a rolled or folded banner that has been forgotten since the 1800s, resist the urge to open it yourself. You will be amazed at how fast a silk flag can turn to crumbs and dust if not handled properly. On the other hand, the variety of small, personal flags that were made on wool, cotton, or linen bunting will withstand light handling, but still, it would be best to have a conservator evaluate any flag before displaying it.

A final thought in regard to flag collecting: Flags possess the ability to evoke strong emotional responses from viewers. After all, that is the very reason of a flag's existence. The political and social environment may have changed since the Civil War, but one can be surprised how soon old emotions of our ancestors are drug to the surface.

Collecting Hints

Pros:

- Original Civil War flags are extremely impressive when on display.

- It is extremely difficult to create an appropriately aged reproduction Civil War flag.

- Brass musical instruments (and some wood) can still be played today.

- The folk art crossover of a painted drum or Civil War era instrument is large, lending credibility to interior decorating with martial items.

Regulation Civil War snare drum, $1,000-$1,250.

Cons:

- Original Civil War flags carried or utilized by the military of either side are exceedingly rare to find in private hands. When they do become available, the cost can be prohibitive.

- Proper storage for flags will require special, rolled storage in a humidity-monitored environment. Silk flags are especially sensitive to their environment and will literally crumble if not cared for properly.

- To actually display a flag without contributing to its decay, the lowest of light levels should be used. Dark viewing isn't real conducive to enjoying the pride awarded by ownership.

- Much controversy surrounds the ownership and repatriation of flags, particularly those once flown over Confederate soldiers. Several museums have been involved in litigation over ownership. It is only a matter of time before private collectors are impacted.

- Little has been published on musical instruments to aid the collector. The most wanting area for quality research is almost the most popular area collected: military drums.

- Other than regimentally-marked drums or fifes, it is very difficult to ascertain whether an instrument was actually used by soldiers or is simply a civilian item of the era.

Availability ★
Price ★★★★★
Reproduction Alert ★★

Flags and Guidons

Flag, Confederate

Texas, "Lone Star" flag, 24" x 39", made of hand-sewn flag bunting. Would
have been appropriate as an infantry flanker flag, a main unit battle flag,
or equally as a cavalry flag, as many were rectangular, rather than of the
swallow-tail design. Double-sided with large white linen or cotton star hand
sewn to each side of the blue canton. Narrow hoist binding of white sailcloth
with hand-sewn grommet top and bottom. White/red stripe section is a single
piece, the red being dyed brilliantly giving an irregular rough edge between
red & white. Overall clean, excellent, with several small holes scattered, yet
having a very clean, solid appearance. White stripe is actually a pale beige.
.... **$4,750**

Flag that flew over the Capitol of the Confederacy—"I certify that this is a piece
of the large flag taken from the State House in Richmond, Virginia, on the
morning of April 3, 1865, by a detachment of General Witzell's Command the
day of the evacuation of the Confederate Capitol. It has been in my possession
until this date, Chicago, Illinois, March 8, 1886. John O. Foster, late delegate,
U.S. Christians Commission." One can only imagine this soldier's excitement
at tearing down and cutting up the Confederate flag that flew over the capitol
of the Confederacy. Two large swatches approx. 2" x 3". Accompanied by a
small swatch from the Fort Sumter white Flag of Truce, Charleston Harbor,
1862. .... **$2,500**

Original and rare, 33-1/4" on the hoist and 67" on the fly, eleven stars appliquéd
on both sides, as well as four "moons," representing the four slave states
that had not seceded as of June to November 1861. Likely from Tennessee,
Kentucky, or Missouri, according to a 1998 evaluation by H. Michael Madaus.
Fonda Thomsen, Textile Preservation Associates, performed a full textile
authentication evaluation in 1998. .... **$15,000**

*This Confederate battle flag is hand-sewn with wool bunting and white silk trim. Either a cavalry or artillery guidon, the flag is 27" tall and 36" wide. **$12,000-$14,500***

KP photo/Wisconsin Veterans Museum collection

This hand-sewn, pieced construction Confederate flag has nine stars and is 14-1/2" tall and 20" wide. It was captured by the 1st Wisconsin Infantry at the Battle of Falling Waters, July 2, 1861. ***$10,000-$13,000***

1st National

1st National pattern flag, very early 11-star example (1861). All-wool bunting construction with hand-sewn polished cotton stars, large field size 51" on the hoist by 130" on the fly. Associated history with the area surrounding Galveston, Texas. Exceptional with very little damage—but does have a few weak seams and some minor use-associated wear, retains vivid, strong colors, hoist has whipped eyelets. **$16,000**

Very rare and attractive Confederate 1st National Flag made by famed sailmaker James A. Cameron of Memphis, Tennessee, one of the most trusted and sought-after sail and taurpin makers. In the summer of 1861 he was commissioned to make this richly colored Confederate flag for a Nashville volunteer regiment. Although records are unclear which regiment or company it was, Mr. Cameron was a talented craftsman, and it is certain that his skills were well known throughout Tennessee. Cotton sailcloth flag is in excellent condition. In addition, James A. Cameron signed his masterpiece by embroidering "JAC" into the hoist. Only a few Confederate flags are actually identified by their maker. This Confederate 1st National flag has 13 stars in the blue canton. Accompanied by Howard Madaus' authentication. Size: 60" x 84" framed. **$45,000**

Regimental

Very rare and historical Regimental Battle Flag of the famous Palmetto Sharpshooters, South Carolina Volunteers. They surrendered this flag to Michigan troops in 1865. The men of the Palmetto Sharpshooters marched at the front of Bratton's Brigade during the Surrender Ceremony at Appomattox and laid down their arms and surrendered their Confederate regimental battle flag, ironically, in front of the same Michigan regiment which they had fought a bloody battlefield duel with during the Battle of Gaines Mill. Of the 1,400 men and officers that served in the Palmetto Sharpshooters since its formation in 1862, until it surrendered at Appomattox with Lee in 1865, the overwhelming majority were volunteers. Over 470 men lost their lives

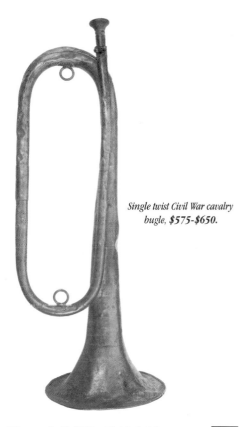

Single twist Civil War cavalry bugle, $575-$650.

fighting under this flag, most of which laid down their lives on the battlefield. It is interesting to note, however, that during the Surrender at Appomattox, the Palmetto Sharpshooters was the largest single Confederate regiment to be surrendered, with 356 men and 29 officers who stacked their weapons and surrendered this flag [recently purchased from Lieutenant John P. Anderson's descendants (27th Michigan), accompanied by Howard Madaus' letter of authenticity]. One of the finest and most historical battle flags to come on the market. It is a Richmond Depot issue, Army of Northern Virginia Battle flag with bold fresh color. It has several bullet holes, size 48" x 48". .. **$250,000**

A unique Confederate 1st National flag with eleven stars in the blue canton and interesting salmon-colored bars made of silk indicating that it was likely made in the Western Theater. The star arrangement is unique to Confederate 1st National, as originally there were 13 stars, but two were removed during 1861 in conjunction with Missouri and Kentucky refusing to "officially" secede. This flag was discovered in Louisville, Kentucky, with an oral tradition of having been made for a Kentucky regiment. Superb with unique star design within the canton, accompanied by Howard Madaus' authentication, size: 84" x 38". **$35,000**

Flag, U.S.

A large, regimental-size Civil War flag with 36 stars. Nevada was the 36th state to join the Union on October 31, 1864, authorized by Congress for statehood, so they could vote for President Lincoln's, "Emancipation of Slaves being the 13th Amendment to the United States Constitution." A superb flag of red, white, and blue wool bunting with bright fresh color. The five-point cotton stars measure 6" across. A few minor rips and tears as one might expect on a flag of this size that was flown during the Civil War, 90" x 138". **$3,500**

Painted and stenciled 36-star flag from November 1864. Polished cotton, excellent condition, no tears. Framable size, approximately 36" x 20-1/2", nice, aged look, colors have faded slightly, banner on parade flag. **$725**

KP photo/Wisconsin Veterans Museum collection

*Generally, a mounted unit carried a "guidon" (a smaller version of a national flag) to denote its command. Often, a guidon is cut in a "swallow tail" design. This banner was carried by a unit that began the war as an infantry regiment and was later equipped as cavalry. Value: **$4,500.***

KP photo/Wisconsin Veterans Museum collection

A Union Army regiment carried a "stand" of colors that usually consisted of the national flag and a regimental banner. Most often, the regimental banner consisted of the state seal with the regiment's name included. Value: $5,500.

Naval

Civil War U.S. Naval Commodore's silk flag with stars from Pensacola Naval Yard, 1861. This very large remnant is part of the silk Naval Flag lowered by Commodore James Armstrong, Commandant of the Pensacola Naval Yard when it was captured by Confederate forces on January 12, 1861. The flag was found in an old chest in 2000, folded up in a canvas bag with a hand-written history (complete history of flag, Commodore Armstrong and how it was found, comes with this remnant). The remains are the red and white stripes, measuring 32" x 28", the blue canton area was cut out of the original 6' x 9-1/2' flag by the Florida and Alabama militia units that captured the Naval Yard. There are four gold stars with a blue circle around them (found in the folds of the flag) on each corner. This remnant was professionally framed using non-acid materials to preserve this unique piece of American Naval history. The flag has been passed down through the Armstrong family after Commodore Armstrong "liberated" it from its Confederate captors, just before he was released to return to Washington. Also includes a carte de visite of Commodore Armstrong taken in 1862 upon his retirement. **$2,330**

Regimental

Flag of 23rd New Jersey Infantry, all-wool bunting construction with polished cotton stars. The 9' x 15' headquarters flag of the unit, as sent home by its Quartermaster, Lieutenant Abel H. Nichols (name on hoist). Retains great, vivid original color and shows just a few field repairs. Hoist is tattered in some places, as is bunting. All hand-sewn stars and brass grommet construction in the style of the Philadelphia Depot. Originally constructed with 34 stars; has two additional ones sewn on (pretty obvious, and definitely of the era) indicating use into 1863. This unit served from September 13, 1862, until June 27, 1863, and saw heavy action in the 1st Brigade, 1st Division, 6th Corps, Army of the Potomac, suffering 90 casualties, primarily at Fredericksburg and Chancellorsville, very historic item, with sterling provenance. **$2,000**

KP photo/Wisconsin Veterans Museum collection

Carrying a regiment's "National colors" was a mark of distinction. The flag served as a rallying point as well as badge of honor for each unit. Each Union infantry regiment would have carried a National color. In many cases, a regiment's battle honors would be recorded on the white stripes of the flag. Value: $5,000.

Guidon, Confederate
1st National
Cavalry guidon. **$12,200**

Guidon, U.S.
Regimental
Beautiful hand-painted gold stars, 35-star silk cavalry guidon carried by the 8th
Ohio Cavalry throughout the battlefields of Virginia. The 8th Ohio Cavalry
was organized March 28, 1864, from the veterans and recruits of the 44th
Ohio Infantry. The newly outfitted regiment proceeded to West Virginia to
join General Averell's raid on Lynchburg, Virginia where they met with heavy
resistance from the Confederates. This cavalry guidon floated proudly above
the regiment as it fought throughout West Virginia and the Shenandoah
Valley. U.S. Cavalry guidons are rare, especially in superb condition.
Beautifully made of silk with hand-painted gold stars. Red stripes have
slightly bled over the white, yet in remarkable condition and silk in fresh
condition, size 42" x 28". Howard Madaus' letter of authenticity. ... **$25,000**

Musical Equipment

Bugle
8th Wisconsin Light Artillery
Bugle is in near perfect condition and free from any major dents or damage,
it is 100% regulation Union army having a single twist, copper body, brass
bands and mouthpiece, and the reinforced bell. Family legend on this bugle is
that it was given to Lieutenant Stiles, 8th Wisconsin Light Artillery, after being
captured from Confederate troops at the Battle of Lookout Mountain.
.... **$2,450**

Cavalry

Very pretty "Turner Ashby" Yeager hunting horn configuration cavalry bugle. Bugle is out of the personal collection of Mark Elrod, author of, *A Pictorial History of Civil War Bands and Band Instruments.* Bugle comes with full-page letter from Mark authenticating the bugle. **$850**

It is 16" l with a 4-1/4" reinforced bell with a floating rim, there are double loops 12" l and 6" h, has a few dings. **$685**

10" brass bugle and mouthpiece, right side of bell crumpled and straightened, otherwise very nice condition. **$400**

A very attractive bugle, made of brass and copper, seamed the entire length, as is typical of all Civil War-era instruments, the brass and copper have a soft uncleaned patina, marked "Potter's Aldershot/ I.P." **$995**

Concertina

Could easily date from the 1830, 14" l x 4-1/2" w. Edges of box frame almost entirely inlayed with lighter wood in rococo sprays and scrolls, plus line borders, 26 circular mother-of-pearl valve caps, 23 keys also capped with mother-of-pearl, four keys need new caps. Bellows faced with pretty colored print paper, does not seem to leak, finish lightly worn/rubbed. **$335**

Cornet

All-brass cornet with nice aged patina, three valves, no visible maker's markings, no breaks in the seams. **$995**

Civil War-era-rotary cornet in excellent condition, there are no dents, and only a few very minor dings, no missing parts. Small patch on the bow near bell, valves work great and are lightning fast. Cornet is made of nickel silver, also known as German silver, comes with two shanks. One puts it in B-flat, the other in A-flat. Bell is engraved "yon & Healy Chicago." Horn was made somewhere between 1860 and 1880. .... **$2,095**

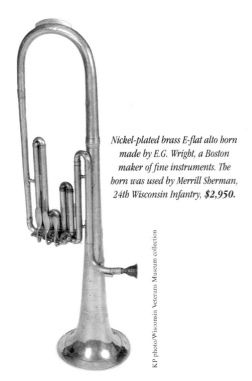

*Nickel-plated brass E-flat alto horn made by E.G. Wright, a Boston maker of fine instruments. The horn was used by Merrill Sherman, 24th Wisconsin Infantry, **$2,950.***

KP photo/Wisconsin Veterans Museum collection

Drum

23rd Connecticut Volunteer Infantry

Exquisite United States eagle drum made by Horstmann Brothers of Pennsylvania and presented to Drummer Boy James W. Skidmore of the 23rd Connecticut Volunteers. Beautiful drum is in excellent condition. Hand-painted in bold patriotic colors and detailed flourishes around each head with the Horstmann Bros. label still evident through the peephole. Presentation on a solid silver plaque attached to the top rim reads, "Presented to Julius W. Skidmore, The Drummer Boy aged 15 years of the 23rd C.V., Aug 25, 1863." The drum was ceremoniously given to Pvt. Skidmore by the citizens of Bridgeport, Connecticut in appreciation for his bravery in the line of battle. **$25,000**

2nd Ohio Volunteer Infantry

Drum was made by, and still retains the label of, "George Kilbourn, Drum Maker, Albany, New York." Accompanying this instrument is the original museum tag from the Civil War Centennial display where it was last publicly shown. The tag is a 40-year old cardboard label which reads, "Carried by A.S. Reeder 2nd Regt. O.V.S. Civil War 1861-65." The drum has damage to the heads; a nice brass tack design on the shell, and it comes with the original drum sling and one broken drumstick. It is dirty and grungy and the ropes are old replacements from the 1960s. **$1,608**

7th Mississippi Infantry

Homemade with a tin shell and crude wooden hoops put together with iron rivets. The vellum drumheads are in perfect condition and the regimental designation is hand-painted in large red letters on either side of the drum, "Co. E- 7th Miss-CSA." The 7th Mississippi Infantry was raised in Franklin County, Mississippi, in May 1861, where it was known as the Franklin Beauregards. Drum's history is clear. It was discovered in 1967 by the original owner of the Old Country Store Museum in Jackson, Tennessee, who acquired

KP photo/Wisconsin Veterans Museum collection

Snare drum and single drumstick. Drum is 16-1/2" in diameter and 14-1/2" tall with Maryland State Seal painted on the side. The drumstick was found on Rowley Farm near Williamsburg, VA. The farmhouse was used as a Confederate Hospital for several years. Because this item can easily be associated with the Confederacy, the value jumps from about $3,500 to around $15,000.

KP photo/Wisconsin Veterans Museum collection

This snare drum was used by Silas D. Taylor, 3rd Regiment, Wisconsin Voluntary. The band of the 3rd Wisconsin was broken up in 1862 in accord with the decision to eliminate regimental bands by the Federal Army, $5,500.

it from a family near Corinth, Mississippi. Leather harness shoulder strap still attached, and the original red paint has faded to a medium brown, size 21" around x 8" d. **$27,500**

Drumsticks

Good condition showing use and age, and one stick has a small crack, made of ebony. **$49**

Fife

23rd Ohio Infantry, fine regulation maple fife with brass end ferrules in excellent condition. Includes note from a previous owner detailing that it was purchased from a family estate sale, and was carried by Alfred Paton (aka Patton) of the 23rd Ohio Volunteer Infantry. The note details family stories about Alfred, including his being wounded and carried from the field at Cedar Creek by his brother. **$159**

16-1/2" overall. Standard fife with the turned and border decorated brass ferrules at the end, excellent condition. **$210**

"Nought is heard but the sound of the drum, and the shrill note of the fife accompanied by the regular tread of hundreds of soldiers, as they pass through, or leave this city for Manassas Gap, Harpers Ferry, Norfolk, or Yorktown."

—*Dr. Robert Hunter Peel*
Surgeon, 19th Mississippi Regiment

KP photo/Wisconsin Veterans Museum collection

Large bass drum was used by Silas D. Taylor, 3rd Regiment, Wisconsin. The maple rings still have remnants of red paint, ***$3,100.***

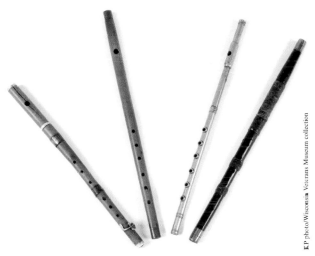

AP photo/Wisconsin Veterans Museum collection

Four Union fifes. From left to right: wood fife with six finger stops and brass key (14-1/2" long), **$250;** *wooden fife with six finger holes used by James W. Goram, Co. G, United States Sharpshooters (16-1/2" long),* **$1,200;** *Nickel-plated brass flute with six finger holes (16-1/4" long),* **$225;** *wooden fife with one brass ring on each end (17" long)* **$200.**

CHAPTER 9

MEDICAL INSTRUMENTS

These items probably won't come cheap. Solid, identified, surgeon sets easily run in excess of $5,000. An engraved surgeon's sword will go for at least $2,500. Understandably, a lot of your competition will come from twenty-first-century doctors and surgeons. They may be in a better financial position to acquire these top-end collectibles.

Even if your funds don't abound, you can still succeed by acquiring knowledge. In all the different aspects of Civil War relics and memorabilia, medical items are perhaps the most misunderstood and misrepresented items. In most cases, this is not a result of trying to take advantage of an unknowing customer, but simply because the dealer doesn't know the hobby. It is a very intricate hobby requiring a deep study to understand the nuances of what makes a particular item "of the period" or not. Time and money invested in acquiring and studying many books will be the second best thing to having lots of money to just, "learn as you buy."

Collecting Hints

Pros:
- Nineteenth-century medical tools have been popular for many years. Therefore there are several excellent references available to aid in collection development.

- The survivability rate is rather high for medical tools.

Cons:
- Many surgical sets and tools are represented as being Civil War, when in fact, they are simple late nineteenth-century items. In most cases, these misrepresentations are not so much intentional as they are wishful. Medical collecting is highly specialized, and most folks simply don't have a general understanding of its nuances.

- Though many items may indeed date to the Civil War, or even pre-date it, this does not mean that the items were actually used in the treatment of war-related injuries. To be sure of actual Civil War surgeon-used items, one must limit themselves to pieces with solid provenance. This severely limits the number of collectible items and greatly increases the cost involved.

- As a subject, medical items are not for everyone. You may be greeted with less than enthusiastic responses when showing off your collection to the squeamish.

- Collecting medical items can be its own specialty. The key is to look beyond the obvious. For example, while it is fairly easy to recognize a surgeon's set on a table, you will have to look deeper for other medical-related items.

Availability ★★★★
Price ★★★
Reproduction Alert ★

*Civil War-period, medical 2-blade bleeder, **$125-$150.***

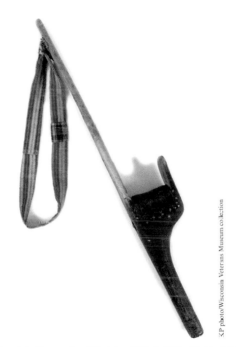

XP photo/Wisconsin Veterans Museum collection

Prosthetic leg originally worn by soldier injured Feb. 7, 1865 at Hatcher's Run. The soldier had his right leg amputated below the knee at a hospital in Baltimore, Maryland, $1,150.

Civil War-Era Instruments

This list of instruments typically found in or associated with Civil War-era surgical sets and their values, are based on sales catalogs, Internet auctions, and private sales (add 20% for handles made of real ivory and not bone)—*Compiled by Dr. Michael Echols, Ft. Myers, Florida.*

Excellent= no rust, no cracked handles, no problems

Good= about average, but serviceable

Marked= maker name on instrument

Prices are given "EX" and "G" grades.

	EX	G
Amputation Knife, large, unplated, composite handle with crosshatching.	$80-$120	$70
Artery Forceps, unplated, olive-tipforceps for holding and tying off arteries.	$60-$65	$35
Amputation Catlin, large, double-sided blade, composite handle with crosshatching.	$80-$120	$70
Blade Director, to direct knife blade.	$18-$20	$10
Bistoury Knives, unplated, curved blade with blunt tip or curved blade and sharp point.	$40-$45	$25
Bone Hammer and Chisel, hammer.	$55-$75	$40
Bullet Forceps, long shank, serrated tips, marked.	$190-$230	$150
Chain Saw, both handles, unmarked, no rust on chain.	$180-$200	$100

	EX	G
End Cutting Bone Forceps, marked.	$140-$150	$75
Gemrig Amputation Saw, early, marked.	$200-$250	$100
Gemrig Bow Saw, amputation saw for large military set, marked.	$300-$350	$200
Gnawing Bone Forceps, round tip, marked.	$125-$150	$60
Hernstein Amputation Saw, military, marked.	$250-$300	$150
Hey Saw, skull-trepanning saw, marked.	$75-$120	$90
Metacarpal Saw, for small bones, marked, composite crosshatched handle.	$110-$120	$75
Sequestrum Forceps, for bone fragments, holding tissue, shallow bullets, short shanked, marked.	$80-$85	$50
Side-Cutting Forceps, for bone, unplated, marked.	$170-$180	$75
Stethoscope, uncommon during Civil War; marked, early elastic band.	$400-$500	$200
Tenaculum, for artery traction during suturing, marked, composite crosshatched handle.	$50-$60	$35
Tissue Forceps, to clamp off artery or holding tissue, unplated, unmarked.	$40-$50	$20
Tourniquet, petit brass screw frame, fabric strap, marked.	$270	$200

	EX	G
Tourniquet Strap, belt type for field use.	$170	$100
Trepanning Bone File, for smoothing edge and elevating tissues of skull, marked.	$75	$55
Trepanning Trephine, for boring hole in skull, unmarked.	$150	$90

KP photo/Wisconsin Veterans Museum collection

This is the surgeon's kit used by Dr. James T. Reeve, 10th and 21st Wisconsin Infantry. It consists of a mahogany veneer case with the top is padded in red velvet and shaped to fit instruments. The bottom has a second compartment that lifts out and both are padded and shaped to hold the bone-handled instruments. Identified medical sets can fetch from $3,000 to $5,000, depending on who carried it and what it contains.

Civil War-Era Surgical Sets

Civil War surgical sets, which were made or used during the war, generally come in three variations: civilian, U.S. Army Medical Department, or U. S. Army Hospital Department. Civilian sets that existed prior to the war may have been used during the war. The prices shown here are for sets made during, or specifically for, the military during the Civil War.

As a general rule, military sets usually have double sliding latches and no keys. Civilian sets usually have only a central key (note: for extensive information on identifying Civil War surgical sets, see Dr. Michael Echols' Web site, Pre-1870 American Surgical Sets, at: www.braceface.com/medical).

Values vary greatly due to condition, maker, presence of correct and original instruments, maker or military markings, inscriptions on the case brass plaque, and proven ownership by a Civil War surgeon. The prices included in this visual directory are derived from sales catalogs, Internet auctions, and private sales.

Gemrig Bone Surgery Set

Specialized surgical set issued to military surgeons for bone resection or removal. J. H. Gemrig was a supplier of military and civilian surgical sets both before and during the war, excellent condition. ....**$3,500-$4,000**

Gemrig Capital Military Set

Instruments for field surgery, amputation, trepanning, urology, minor surgery, bullet removal; type issued to Union Army surgeons, excellent condition.
....**$4,500-$5,500**

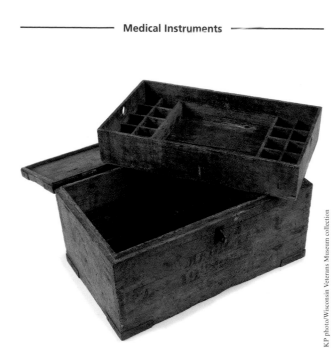

KP photo/Wisconsin Veterans Museum collection

Wooden medicine chest used by Surgeon Ezra M. Rogers, 12th Wis. Inf. The wooden lid has hand-cut dovetail joints, iron bands on corners, two iron strap hinges secured with screws and a handle for carrying. The interior of chest has lift-out section with 20 holes for medicine bottles. The lower section is also divided to hold 24 bottles. Because the surgeon who owned the chest is identified, the value increases from about $1,100 to $1,850.

KP photo/Wisconsin Veterans Museum collection

Surgeon's kit used by Assistant Surgeon Theophilus R. Vankirk, 209th Pennsylvania Infantry. The mahogany case is padded in red velvet and shaped to fit instruments. A second compartment lifts out and is also padded and shaped to hold the gutta-percha-handled instruments. ***$4,500.***

Kern Trepanning Set

Civilian set for skull surgery. H. Kern was a supplier of military and civilian surgical sets before and during the war, in excellent condition.
....**$1,800-$2,800**

Hernstein Military Amputation Set

Strictly for field amputation, marked instruments for U.S. Army Hospital Department. H. Hernstein was a supplier of military and civilian surgical sets both before and during the war, excellent condition. ....**$3,500-$4,500**

Kolbe Military Set

Intended for major bone surgery, trepanning, amputation, a specialized set for bone resection or removal. Marked for U.S. Army Medical Department. Date of manufacture determined by label address of maker. D. Kolbe was a supplier of military and civilian surgical sets both before and during the war, excellent condition. ....**$5,000-$6,000**

Shepard & Dudley Civilian Set,

For amputation and trepanning, made during the war years and typical of civilian contract surgeon sets. Documented set in various catalogs as having been produced ca. 1862. Shepard and Dudley supplied civilian surgical sets before and during the war, excellent condition. ....**$3,500-$4,200**

Wade and Ford Civilian Set

Documented/inscribed brass plaque shows it was owned by a Civil War Union Navy surgeon, purchased in 1861. Pictured in Smith's Manual of Surgery. For amputation, trepanning, urology, minor surgery, and eye surgery. Wade & Ford supplied military and civilian surgical sets both before and during the war, excellent condition. ....**$5,000-$6,000**

Containers

Bottle, Medicine

USA Hospital Department bottle recovered at Point of Rocks, Maryland, in excellent condition with no cracks or chips, small flaw on bottle neck made during manufacture, measures 9-1/2" x 3-1/2". **$895**

Original and near perfect Jacob Dunton bottle marked, "Ext. Cinch. Arom. Fl/US Army Medical Supplies/ Jacob Dunton, Philadelphia," original glass stopper, 2" x 2" x 5". Excellent label is intact. The interior is stained from the original contents. **$850**

Box, Pill

Mint condition, circular cardboard container exactly the size & shape of a pistol percussion cap tin. Deep blue lid with gold lettering, "Dr. Chilton Manufactured by Comstock & Brother New York/ One Dollar/Per Box/Fever and Ague Cure." **$49**

Canteen, Medical

This one carried quinine, and is identical to one in Sylvia's *Civil War Canteens*. The only difference is this one has the design painted on the cover, not the metal body, standard M1858 smooth-sided canteen with coarse medium-brown original cover, no holes. Painted in faded white, on one side is the large word, "QUININE," with shell-like decorations above and below. Lacks sling, lip of spout trimmed off for unknown reason. **$675**

This tin canteen has the basic shape of the Model 1858 canteen, but is 13" d, has no sling loops, and has a spout at the top edge of one face with a metal screw top. Though screw tops are very unusual on Civil War canteens, this one is marked with a patent date of, "Oct. 27, 1857." The canteen has scattered surface rust and is dented. It comes with a well-worn carry bag/cover made of multicolored carpet. **$100**

Chest, Medical

A large walnut Medical Chest with Brass end-handles, measuring 12" x 8" x
7" (closed) and containing 26 period medicine bottles, some with contents.
Interior is fitted for various-sized bottles from very small to very large, and is
full. The case and bottles are all in excellent condition. **$722**

Container, Medicine

Original Edward Squibb, "Stronger Ether for Anesthesia," one-pound tin with
original labels, extremely rare, excellent condition, labels are clearly readable
and original. **$1,000**

Saddle Bags, Medical

"Crow-foot" strap design, black leather, even the straps and roller-buckles. The
leather was hardened and brittle, but has been treated with a museum leather
restorative and is now supple as original. One strap is broken, but all there.
There is an assortment of medicine bottles (some still with contents), two tin
containers, one wood container and a number of the original paper-wrapped
and string-tied dry medications (some never opened). A leather instrument
roll contains an amputation saw and knife with interchangeable handle,
complete urethral catheter, small bullet forceps, assorted suturing needles,
suturing material, old cotton, etc. **$2,500**

"Sick call does not number more than 30 men and my work is
done before breakfast. The papers are a little wearisome, but
all in all the work is not hard..."

—*Dr. Cyrus Bacon, Jr., Assistant Surgeon, U. S. Army*

Medical Instruments and Devices

Amputation Set

A beautiful and 90% complete Civil War-era set in a fitted rosewood case with brass hardware, 12" l x 4-1/2" w x 2-3/4" t. Case and hardware, in excellent condition. The green velvet lining has some minor damage. Instruments include the following: Petit Tourniquet with brass screw and original linen strap; 6-1/2" scalpel marked, "Spangenbere," ivory handle; 5-3/4" scalpel marked, "Coxeter London," ivory handle; 6-1/2" knife marked, "Coxeter London," ivory handle; 6" tenaculum marked, "Tiemann," ivory handle; 8-3/4" amputation knife blade marked, "Rose & Sellers," has some pitting and nick in blade; 8" amputation knife blade marked, "Rose & Sellers," some pitting and nick in blade; 10-3/4" amputation saw blade, unmarked, some pitting; 9-1/2" amputation saw blade, unmarked, light pitting; rosewood handle measuring 3-1/2" l and marked, "Dodel S.F. Cal. pat sept 5 99" and two tools that fit into the handle both marked, "Dodel;" 5-3/4" long forceps marked "35095"; 5-1/2" hollow funnel-shaped probe; 5-3/4" scalpel guide; extra and unused tourniquet strap, "J. Satlee" surgeon's silk. The Dodel instrument and the forceps are later additions to this set, but were with it when it was found. Missing handle for amputation saw blades and knives, and an instrument that was housed between the two saw blades in the upper compartment, appears to be bone nippers that are gone. Use of ivory handles by Tiemann and other manufacturers ended in 1865. Case is definitely Civil War period, as are the amputation saw blades and knives. A beautiful and attractive cased amputation set worthy of display in any venue. **$1,250**

Absolutely wonderful surgical kit. Set is housed in a beautiful mahogany-veneered box with red velvet lining, and each instrument is nicely marked, "H.G. Kern/Phila." The set is nearly complete, but does lack the rongeur, one small scalpel, and a bone scraper. It has a fine, large amputation saw, a fine smaller saw, which resembles a hacksaw in terms of its design (this one rests in a hidden spot under the larger saw), the original tourniquet with strap, three large amputation knives, and the small hooked tool that supports blood vessels during cutting. Inside the case is still present a typed note which reads "Amputation set used by Dr. A. W. McClure during the Civil War." Dr. McClure is listed as the surgeon of the 4th Iowa Cavalry. He received his commission on October 20, 1861, and served with the regiment until April 1863. During this time frame the 4th was attached to the Army of Southwest Missouri and the Department of Missouri, and saw action at such battles as Talbot's Ferry, Little Red River, White River, Jones Lane, Helena, Marianna, and St. Francis River. Very attractive, appealing set, wonderful Civil War history. **$2,950**

Authentic U.S.A. Hospital Department-marked, four-tier major amputation set by Brinkerhoff, N.Y. This outstanding set is 99% complete, excellent condition. Most of the major pieces are marked and all are matching. The maker's label is present in two places. **$6,900**

By George Tiemann, near-mint condition, missing three small scalpels, two small tweezers, all major pieces intact, in excellent condition. Wooden box with tray in excellent condition. **$5,800**

Scales, Apothecary

Cased set of scales with weights of the type used during the Civil War. The case is green with a patriotic eagle embossed on the top. The scales are made of brass, case is 3" x 5-7/8", fine condition. **$250**

Civil War-era, eagle-marked, cased set of apothecary scales. The scales are complete and still work perfectly. **$250**

Surgical Set

Three-tier USA Hospital Department-marked surgical/ amputation set that is military issue, as evidenced by inscribed plate on front. Maker is Tiennken, New York. Over 30 original instruments, most marked. All major instruments matching, few minor pieces missing. **$5,900**

Outstanding item in near-perfect condition, leather book- shaped device measures 7.5" x 4" x 1-1/2" thick when closed, and roughly double that length and width when open. It is designed to hold 48 vials of medicine, of which 43 are still present (a few with contents). The body is made of tooled leather with impressed gilt scrolls and designs like on the cover of an expensive book. Inside are two areas or compartments with two dozen leather loops in each, the loops holding the glass vials in place. The vials are covered by a pair of leather flaps lined in red velvet. The cover of this miniature pannier is equipped with a German silver lock that consists of a rotating pin on the body and a key-slot hasp on the closing flap, superb condition.
.... **$225**

Cased set contains 20 tools including tourniquet, pliers, trepanning tool, three saws, nine scalpels and knives, silk thread, needles, probes, etc., all but a few with checkered ebony handles and some with "W.F. Ford," and, "Caswell Hazard," marks, rosewood veneer case with brass oval-engraved, "J.R. Roberts, M.D." 6" x 13-3/8" x 4" case. **$2,090**

Great example of a roll-up case circa 1850-60, maybe even run in via the blockade to Rebel forces. Family history notes that it belonged to Benjamin T. Green of Lincoln County, North Carolina. Green served as surgeon of the 14th North Carolina Infantry from April 1864 until captured and imprisoned at the Old Capital Prison in Washington, D.C. until paroled on April 19, 1865. Great Russian red leatherette with iron locking clasp, and full of surgical instruments by Rogers, an English tool maker. Some handles of the folding instruments are fancy, artistic patterned faux tortoise shell. **$950**

Very attractive 1860 "S. Maw & Son-London Master Surgeon's Kit," consists of master amputation saw, tourniquet, and an array of knives, probes, tweezers, and pliers. The case itself is red velvet lined, and in nice solid condition.
.... **$2,250**

Tool, Bleeder

This scarificator was a device made and used in the 19th century for bleeding. This one is made of solid brass with 12 steel blades that pop out and cut. It is in very good condition, works perfectly. It cocks in the center position, which shows the blades extended, upon doing some research, this must have been made around 1830. .... **$332**

Brass handle, iron bleeders marked, "Joseph Rodgers/ No 6/Norfolk St/Sheffield." All three blades are intact and freely swing out. **$125**

This brass scarificator, or "bleeder," was used by medical personnel to open wounds to permit cleaner blood-flow and reduce the chance of infection. Item is in superb original condition, never cleaned or polished. It functions as well as when it was made, and the five blades are still razor-sharp. The cock and release mechanism is extremely crisp. **$154**

Tool, Dental Elevator

Civil War-era elevator in excellent condition. Has a wood handle and an unplated steel shaft. The angulated tip has a serrated edge, measures 4-3/4" l. **$91**

Tool, Electric Magneto

Patented in 1855, "Davis & Kidder's Patent Magneto-Electric Machine For Nervous Diseases," so states the illustrated label/ instructions inside the lid. A fine, working piece of handsome machinery that puts out a strong pulsing electric charge designed to apply to the diseased body parts. It was so popular in its time that it was copied extensively in this country and in Europe. Comes in a fine mahogany case with hinged lid 10" x 4-1/2" x 4-1/2". Has brass corner reinforcements. Inside, there is a large horseshoe magnet, a spinning coil, and heavy brass framework and gears. Front has a handle to turn. Two probes at end of wires come from each end. Handle of probes are housed inside, all original and working. Case finish is excellent with some wear. Label stained and 95% intact. **$445**

Tool, Pill Roller

A physician would first combine the powdered dry mixture and then add a binding agent. He next dampened the batch and spread a wad onto the brass, channeled base. He would then place the moveable top over the mass and move it back and forth on its brass railed track. The medicine would thereby be divided and rolled into spherical pills. The roller consists of a solid walnut base 4-5/8" x 11-7/8", and a top piece also of walnut, which moves over the base. Top piece is 13-1/2" long and 7/8" thick. Both top and bottom have a channeled brass plate, which rides over each other, forming the pills. Excellent condition, showing some use. **$395**

Tool, Saw

Blade 12-1/2" l, with teeth on one side and a cutting edge on the other. Blade has a nice dark patina to it, but is not badly pitted or rusted, not missing any teeth, some very small nicks in the knife's edge. Has a nice solid handle, and a hole bored in the end (this was probably for a lanyard). Nice mellow patina to the wood, never cleaned. **$178**

Tool, Syringe

This hard rubber syringe bears the Goodyear 1851 patent mark. **$75**

This type of syringe was used by doctors to irrigate wounds. The hard rubber is complete with both leather washers intact, overall length is 5-3/4" l (closed), barrel tube is 3/4" d, unmarked, no chips or cracks. **$235**

Tools, Surgical

Included in this lot is a standard size (small) scalpel and a small hook-like instrument both signed "Helmold Phila", with ivory handles. **$85**

GEN. TOM THUMB AND LADY

Carte de visite of Tom Thumb, $55-$65.

CHAPTER 10

PHOTOGRAPHS

Image collecting is a great way to pursue all sorts of Civil War interests including: swords, firearms, uniforms, particular regiments and famous personages. While it is relatively inexpensive to assemble a collection of interesting carte de visites, collecting the "hard" images—ambrotypes, tintypes, and even daguerreotypes—of soldiers, runs into some serious money. It is best to develop a focus for your collection. Perhaps you are interested in collecting only identified images, images of soldiers from a particular state, soldiers of a particular branch of service, or even images in which weapons are displayed. By narrowing the field from the beginning, you will be able to assemble a meaningful collection.

Be cautious about buying every cheap image you see—you will soon be overwhelmed. Soldiers by the tens of thousands sat for their likenesses. Many received six copies or more of their cartes de visite and tintypes. That means there are hundreds of thousands of images out there. All of them are not going to be strong in content. Try to resist placing that bid or buying that straggler when you see it. You may very well need the cash you spent when that absolutely stellar image does come up for sale.

So what exactly makes an image "stellar?" There are several factors, and it can almost become formulaic. First is the view itself. A full-length view is more desirable than a bust shot because more of the soldier's uniform is visible. A weapon of any sort will immediately increase an image's value, as will any visible accoutrements. If the soldier is wearing a corps badge, that will also add a few dollars to the price. Outdoor shots, just by their rarity, tend to sell for more than a comparable indoor shot. Finally, for many collectors, it is all about identification—do you know the name that goes with the face in the photo? If so, research can begin tracing the soldier's unit and history of service.

An area not mentioned, but widely collected, is famous faces—the generals, politicians, and public speakers of the day. Many photographic enterprises printed quantities of images of the likenesses of people like President Lincoln, General Grant, and even a wide selection of Confederate leaders. The public read about these people everyday, and they wanted to see how the heroes and enemies looked. These likenesses were collected much as a young person today will collect bubble gum cards of their sports heroes. When the historic images of these folks are available with the sitter's signature, the price will jump dramatically.

The *carte de visite*, another use of collodian, was invented by the famous French photographer Andre Disderi in 1854. Their similarity to a visiting card and their relatively easy production, made them hugely successful. People not only wanted to have their own cartes de visite, they wanted cartes of famous personalities from royalty to actors, which they put in albums alongside of their family portraits. When a person sat for their likeness in carte de visite form, they generally received six images. Because a negative existed, reprints were easily made as well. This lent itself ideally to selling and collecting images of famous personages.

If you do decide to collect Civil War photography, do make time to learn proper handling and storage methods. Even though the images have survived for more than 100 years, they are fragile documents. Simply handling them with bare fingers can speed their deterioration. Humidity is also a villain to historic photographs. Nothing is as sad as seeing an image disappear as the emulsion flakes off a tintype or ambrotype. Purchase and study a basic guide to care and handling of historic paper and photographs. The image you save will be available for future students of the war.

Collecting Hints

Pros:
- The human connection with the Civil War has the strongest potential through studying images.

- The crossover to other areas of Civil War collecting is strong. For example, a weapons' collector may want to embellish his displays with a few images of soldiers holding weapons similar to those in his collection. Or, an historian of uniforms will rely on photographic evidence to support their research conclusions.

- Though there are some current photographers working in the style of 19th century artists, very few do it with the intent to produce forgeries. A few spectacular images have hit the market that turned out to be newly produced photographs of reenactors, although this is still the exception to the rule.

- Image collecting is relatively inexpensive. A decent cdv of a Union soldier still can be purchased for $50.

Carte de visite, General Meade, $85-$100.

Carte de visite, unidentified Union infantry officer, $90-$105.

Cons:
- As with most arenas of the Civil War hobby, anything Confederate is going to be expensive. Images are no exception.

- Internet auctions have become a dumping ground for images. Prices paid are not in line with the rest of the hobby. Also, many spurious and questionable images are sold via the Internet.

- One type of forgery has emerged in image collecting, and it involves using a laser color copier to produce copies of albumens and then gluing them to old cdv stock. In years past, this same sort of forgery was perpetrated by soaking off mundane images from desirably marked cards and replacing the image with a soldier. Many of these cdvs are out there, so study each image before you buy.

> **Availability ★★★★**
> **Price ★★★**
> **Reproduction Alert ★★**

Cartes de Visite

Confederate, Generals

General Ambrose Powell Hill, lieutenant general, Confederate States of America, Hill was one of the South's most famous fighting generals. He was also a graduate of the West Point class of 1847. Hill was killed by two Union 6th Corps soldiers on April 2, 1865, while riding to rally his men. Excellent view of Hill, minor foxing and soiling, "C. D. Fredricks, New York" backmark with a tax stamp. **$350**

General Fitzhugh Lee, bust view, fine ink inscription on front "Fitz Lee Cav Div," great backmark "Vannerson & Jones Richmond, Va." Image is yellowed, has a small hole below the image, small pinhole at top and bottom. ... **$150**

Carte de visite, Jefferson Davis, ***$75-$125.***

Gen. Mitchell, bust view cdv., ***$80-$90.***

General John Hunt Morgan, image of the Confederate cavalry general and wife, Mattie Ready Morgan. This is an Anthony-backmarked photograph and has, "John Morgan & Lady," in old brown ink on front below image. ... **$350**

General Nathan Bedford Forest
Nice, clear image in good condition with some foxing. The tax stamp is dated 1865 in pen, published by, "E. & H.T. Anthony." **$330**

Superb E. & H. Anthony view of Forrest printed immediately after the war. This so-called "common" view of Forrest is still the mainstay for the average collector who cannot obtain or afford photos of Forrest with extremely rare southern backmarks. This particular view is exceptionally clean and crisp, with no damage anywhere on the card. Sharp, mid-chest-up image with a hand-cancelled, two-cent federal tax stamp. **$1,350**

Unusual and scarce postwar cdv of an engraving of Forrest. This view probably dates from late 1865 to early 1866, though it may have been published earlier by one of the five photographic entities, which bore the Bingham name in Memphis. This view is imprinted on the front with the name, "Bingham Bros. Memphis, Tenn." Some soiling around the cameo oval, along with handwriting in red at bottom of card, otherwise clear and historic. **$325**

General P.G.T. Beauregard, vignette bust view retouched photo, shows Pierre G.T. Beauregard in prewar U.S. uniform. J Gurney NY backmark. **$75**

General Robert E. Lee
Previously unpublished, signed cdv of General Robert E. Lee. **$7,400**

Rare, fantasy view of General Lee with his right hand on the headstone of General Stonewall Jackson. Front mark of "Geo. O. Ennis, Richmond, Va." Essentially a mint card representing the bond between two of the greatest C.S.A. generals. George O. Ennis is a known Confederate photographer and is listed in the *Catalogue of Civil War Photographers*. **$995**

Large, wartime shot in his Confederate uniform, in nice condition, but is chipped just slightly on two corners. **$275**

General Sterling Price, bust portrait from a retouched negative showing prewar uniform. Notated in period hand front and back as "Price" and "Gen Price." **$69**

General T.J. "Stonewall" Jackson

Clear image, no backmark, excellent condition. **$75**

Classic early war bust portrait (mass produced variety) of old Stonewall wearing prewar U.S. uniform, corners of card lightly trimmed. **$45**

Mexican War era-bust shot, in nice condition with strong sharp corners, slightly faded from light exposure. **$150**

Bust view in Confederate uniform, photo, unfortunately, has faded and is somewhat light. For this reason, the price is much, much more reasonable than it would otherwise be for this rare cdv, has no backmark. **$195**

President Jefferson Davis

Handsome portrait of the President of the Confederacy, negative slightly re-touched, but good clarity and photo contrast. Shows him in a fine suit of clothes circa 1861. .... **$49**

Photo has some yellowing from age, but is complete and sound, has a rare "Webster & Bro. Louisville" photographer's mark. On the back is written "Jefferson Davis Pres. Confederacy—Mrs. Hart's mother and Jeff Davis were intimate friends—1861." **$275**

1865 cartoon depicting Confederate President Jefferson Davis, and his ill-fated attempt to escape Union forces by dressing in women's clothes. Shown here escorted by a Union soldier to a prison cell at Fort Monroe. **$130**

Confederate, Other

Captain John C. Underwood, 9th Tennessee Cavalry Battalion, armed Confederate Captain prisoner-of-war John C. Underwood. He was a prisoner of war at Fort Warren, Boston Harbor, during 1863-1865. Very unusual pleated Confederate uniform, as well as two-piece belt buckle. Underwood is holding a sword, obviously a photographer's prop. Image is in very-fine condition. This image was part of the large album of confederate prisoner of war images that included many officers from the Confederate ironclad Atlanta. **$1,500**

Colonel Edward Dillon, 2nd Mississippi Cavalry, formed in the Spring of 1863 from soldiers originally destined for the 47th Mississippi Infantry. They fought in Mississippi and Georgia and probably served under Forrest at one time. A number were captured at Selma, Alabama, in 1865. A strong, sharp postwar image in his colonel's uniform. **$500**

First Assistant Engineer William Thomas Morrill, served aboard the Rebel ironclad Atlanta. Image taken while a prisoner of war at Fort Warren, Boston Harbor, black, Boston backmark. Signed in period ink on front. **$1,500**

Lieutenant William Anderson, absolutely wonderful cdv of Quantrill Raider William Anderson (also known as "Bloody Bill"). Noted for riding into battle with a necklace of Union scalps around his horse's neck and encouraging his men to scalp and mutilate their corpses. Image taken in death, no photographer's backmark. Anderson had been shot twice in the back of the head. Very-fine condition! **$3,500**

Officer, Armed, full standing view crisply contrasted with fine clarity. Officer is short of stature wearing regulation C.S. cap, frock coat with vivid galloons on sleeves, sword belt with two-piece interlocking buckle, and holding his foot officer's sword directly in front of him. Edges have been trimmed to round the top and bottom, some edge scuffs on the extreme right not touching the subject at all. **$575**

Union, Generals

General Abner Doubleday, fought at Gettysburg, but most famous for the false attribution that he had founded the game of baseball. A beautiful 1863 cdv in fine condition, Brady imprint. **$750**

General Abram Duryee, wounded 5 times during the war (twice during the 2nd Bull Run campaign, and three more times during the South Mountain and Sharpsburg battles), Duryee was the Colonel of the "Duryee's Zouaves" (5th New York Infantry). This is an outstanding image, with superb contrast and clarity. Anthony by Brady backmark. **$275**

General Alexander C.M. Pennington, very boldly signed image of Alexander C. M. Pennington as Colonel of the 3rd New Jersey Cavalry (the famous "Butterflies") and brevet Brigadier General. Pennington was an 1860 graduate of West Point and a very famous artillery officer during the early part of the war. He was an extremely active commander of Battery M, 2nd U. S. Artillery until his promotion to Colonel of the 3rd New Jersey Cavalry. He was given a brevet promotion for his gallantry in supporting Custer's Brigade at Gettysburg. Faint hint of shoulder board can be seen on what appears to be a civilian coat. Tax stamp, New York backmark. **$1,100**

General Alpheus Williams, a rare bust pose of a young looking Alpheus Williams in a brigadier's frock with straps. The backmark reads "Photographed by AR Henwood 46th Regt PV Gen Williams Division 12th Army Corps." Bottom edge of carte is irregularly trimmed. **$190**

General Alvin Gillem, not only a great civil war general, but his postwar career as Colonel of the 1st U. S. Cavalry included duty during the Modoc War. Very minor corner crease on lower left-hand bottom of image that affects nothing and is difficult to notice. Merritt's National Portrait Gallery, Nashville, Tennessee, backmark. Also a period ink id. of "Brig Genl Gillem" on verso.
.... **$495**

General Ambrose Burnside, one-time commander of the Army of the Potomac, Burnside was also Governor of Rhode Island after the war, very-fine condition, Anthony by Brady backmark. **$185**

General Andrew Jackson Smith, appointed to be the first colonel of the 7th U. S. Cavalry in 1866, a command he held until he resigned it in 1869. Smith had an excellent civil war service record, receiving three brevet promotions for Pleasant Hill, Louisiana; Tupelo, Mississippi; and Nashville, Tennessee. Fine condition with soiling, no backmark. **$200**

General E.R.S. Canby, sharp clarity and content, excellent mount, blue tax stamp on verso. Anthony backmark. Canby had a long, successful career in the army, only to have it cut short by the treachery of Captain Jack and the Modoc Indians in April 1873. He is the only General officer to be killed by Indians. **$450**

General Edwin Sumner, standing outside of his headquarters near Yorktown in May 1862. Brady's Album Gallery image, No. 408, outstanding contrast and clarity, minor clipped corners. **$295**

General Ely S. Parker, image taken by Gutenkunst, Philadelphia. Previously framed, you can still see a slight discoloration caused by the mat around the image. Signed with both his military rank, and his Indian Nation name of "Do-ne-ho-ga-wa" (translated as "Open Door"). **$3,200**

General Franz Sigel, superb condition, image of the famous German general dated 1862, Anthony by Brady backmark, M.B. Brady frontmark. Sigel was soundly defeated by the cadets from VMI at the battle of New Market in 1864. .... **$275**

General George Gordon Meade
General Meade is famous for commanding Union forces at the Battle of Gettysburg. Image displayed in a paper holder possibly out of a period photo album. Photo is shorter than normal, probably cut to fit the holder. **$85**

General George H. Thomas

Superb, period, ink signed image of "The Rock of Chickamauga." Thomas is one of the most famous western union generals, and his signed cartes de visite are highly sought after. **$1,250**

Truly pristine, mint, magnificent seated portrait of "The Rock of Chickamauga" boldly autographed in brown ink on the bottom front of the mount. The image has impeccable contrast and depth showing him in Major General's frock and straps. The autograph is likewise bold and strong and dark: "Geo H. Thomas/Maj. Gen'l. USV." **$1,595**

General George McClellan, bust-shot view shows his general straps on the double-breasted frock coat. No backmark. **$65**

General Gordon Granger

Handsome bust portrait bearing Brandy/Anthony imprint showing this famed Western Campaign general in his Major General's coat and straps. **$24**

Colonel of the 2nd Michigan cavalry in the early part of the war, Granger had a fine record while in the army, and at the end of the war he was appointed to be the Colonel of the 25th U.S. Infantry. This superb image has an Anthony by Brady backmark, and is in exceptional condition. **$195**

General Governor K. Warren, at Gettysburg he handled the 2nd Corps after Hancock was wounded. Brady, Washington backmark, minor corner clips, superb contrast and clarity. **$195**

General Green B. Raum, beautifully signed cdv of Illinois General Green B. Raum, signed while a Colonel commanding the "2 Brig 3rd Div 15th AC." Fine condition with minor wear and foxing. **$595**

General Henry Slocum, rare image bearing the backmark of "Goldin Wash DC." This shows Slocum seated (knees up) wearing his regulation major general's frock coat w/shoulder straps. Excellent near-mint image. **$125**

General James A. Garfield

Clarity and crispness are outstanding. Every wrinkle in his uniform is evident and you can actually count whiskers. There is minor wear to top left corner as you look at the image, no photographer's mark. **$495**

Very sharp view of assassinated President James A. Garfield, taken during the war when he was a Union Army General. Outstanding contrast and clarity. "J. W. Campbell, Army Photographer, 20th Army Corps, Army of the Cumberland" backmark, trimmed. **$295**

General James B. Ricketts, great standing view by Brady of Ricketts in Brigadier's uniform coat and straps. Nicely notated on back in brown ink "Ricketts commanding division 6th Corps Army of Potomac." **$95**

General James Birdseye McPherson

McPherson has the unlucky distinction of being the only Union Army commander to be killed in the Civil War. This 1863 image is in fine condition, with very minor foxing on albumen and mount. Photographers imprint on bottom front of carte reads "Maj. Gen. J. B. McPherson. Entered according to Act of Congress, A.D. 1863, by Barr & Young, in the Clerk's Office of the District Court of the U.S. for the So. District of Ohio." Also imprinted "Barr & Young" on verso of image. **$300**

Nice view of the only Union Army commander to be killed during the war. Minor foxing as shown, "J. Carbutt, 131 Lake St., Chicago" backmark, orange tax stamp. **$175**

General James M. Shackelford, began the war as colonel of the 25th Kentucky Infantry, he then raised to the 8th Kentucky Cavalry, the unit credited for capturing the Rebel General John Hunt Morgan during his famous raid. A beautiful image with wonderful contrast and clarity. Period ink writing on the back reads "Brig. Gen. Shackelford Morgan's Capturer." Schleier, Nashville, backmark. **$375**

General James S. Jackson, Jackson began the Civil War as colonel of the 3rd Kentucky Cavalry and was promoted to Brigadier General in July, 1862. At the battle of Perryville on October 8, 1862, Jackson and both his brigade commanders were killed on the field. Image is in fine condition with one bottom (right) corner clip and very minor soiling to Jackson's. Broadbent, Philadelphia backmark. **$295**

General James Shield, the only man to represent three different states in the U. S. Senate. Shields almost fought a duel with future president A. Lincoln (Lincoln wrote an insulting article about him) and he also was a Mexican War General of Illinois Volunteers. Appointed a brigadier general by his now close friend Lincoln in 1861. He resigned his commission in 1863. Superb condition, Fredricks' backmark. **$495**

General James Wadsworth

Absolutely superb war date image of Wadsworth with his sword. "At the Wilderness on May 6, 1864, while leading his men in an attempt to repel an assault, he was shot off his horse, a bullet entering the back of his head and lodging in his brain." Very minor wear to image, striking contrast **$325**

Absolutely superb war date image of Wadsworth with his sword, standing outside. Very minor wear to image, good contrast, Anthony by Brady backmark. **$250**

General John G. Foster, very nice knees-up standing view with Brady/Anthony imprint showing the general standing in his regulation Brigadier's frock and straps and holding his kepi. **$89**

General John MacArthur, albumen measures 5.5" x 4". Minor stain on thin paper mount as shown, otherwise very good condition. Good contrast and clarity. Facsimile signature near bottom of mount. Authentic period albumen, not a modern reproduction. **$195**

General Kit Carson and Edwin Perrin, a rare image of Carson in his Army frock coat with Edwin Perrin, taken in Albuquerque, January 1862. Perrin was a government expediter, sent to New Mexico by the Secretary of War to help arm New Mexican troops for conflict in the Southwestern theater. Imprint of Anthony. Rich tones, very slightly clipped corners. **$3,000**

General Nathan Augustus Monroe Dudley, Nathan Augustus Monroe Dudley joined the 10th U.S. Infantry in 1855 and served until his retirement as Colonel of the 1st U.S. Cavalry in 1889. Dudley became the colonel of the 30th Mass. Infantry and earned brevets for Baton Rouge and Port Hudson during the war. As lieutenant colonel of the 9th Cavalry, Dudley refused to send troops to keep the peace during the famous "Lincoln County War." No backmark, but superb period ink identification along the edges of the image. Small pin holes in upper corners. **$450**

General Oliver Otis Howard
Excellent view of this famous Gettysburg commander. Colonel of the 3rd Maine Infantry, Howard was quickly promoted to Brigadier General. He lost his right arm at the battle of the Seven Pines. Howard was given the thanks of Congress for his actions during the battle of Gettysburg. "Gutekunst, Phila." backmark. Minor ink stain and very minor soiling. **$195**

Spectacular signed view of Union General Oliver Otis Howard. Clear and crisp 1/2 view, signed boldly by Howard in the top background of the albumen. Minor trim to bottom of the card, Anthony backmark. **$950**

General Ormsby Mitchell, a clear from life standing view circa 1862 showing Ormsby Mitchell with his large full head of hair wearing a brigadier's frock with straps, buff general's sash, sword belt, sword, and holding his forage cap. A very obscure view taken by Hoag & Quick in Cincinnati, Ohio, and bearing their backmark. **$95**

General Philip H. Sheridan

A super crisp image of the Union's famous cavalry commander. Minor wear at very bottom of the mount, not affecting the image, no backmark. **$375**

Uniformed steel engraved portrait of Union Cavalry General "Little Phil" Sheridan. "New York Photographic Co." Broadway backmark. **$110**

General Richard Oglesby, colonel of the 8th Illinois Infantry, he distinguished himself at Forts Henry and Donelson. Promoted to general, he was so severely wounded at Corinth he was out of action for over a year. Elected governor of Illinois in 1864, he also served as a senator. Excellent half-view with minor wear, Decatur, Illinois, backmark. **$225**

General Robert Anderson

Absolutely pristine image (richly contrasted and incredibly clear) showing Major Robert Anderson, the hero of Fort Sumter, seated in the uniform of a major general. He has his frock coat with shoulder straps, a cape draped over his left shoulder, a pair of reading glasses in his right hand, a book in his left hand, and his kepi with "US" in wreath insignia on the table next to him. Best of all the bottom front of this rich card is boldly autographed in brown ink "Robert Anderson" making this a truly historic piece of photo history. The left and right sides of the card have been slightly trimmed, not affecting the photo or signature at all. **$1,150**

"Hero of Fort Sumter." 3/4-view, in uniform with hat, backmarked, "J. Gurney & Son, New York." **$185**

General Robert Cameron, lieutenant colonel of the 19th Indiana Infantry (Iron Brigade) before becoming the colonel of the 34th Indiana Infantry (Zouaves). Tax stamp, New Orleans backmark. **$650**

General Robert S. Foster, born in Vernon, Jennings County, Indiana on January 27, 1834, where he received a common school education. Joining the Union army at the outbreak of the war he fought to the close, being advanced from rank to rank until, on March 31, 1865, he received the brevet of major general of volunteers for gallant conduct in the field. He resigned September 25, 1865, and was offered a lieutenant-colonelcy in the regular army, but declined and took up his residence in Indianapolis. Anthony backmark, blue two-cent cancelled tax stamp. **$275**

General Rufus Saxton

Rare Gurney view of Rufus Saxton, Medal of Honor winner. **$225**

Saxton was awarded the Medal of Honor for defending Harpers Ferry in 1862. Great period ink identification on front. Minor wear and foxing. Anthony by Brady backmark. **$145**

General Thomas L. Crittenden

Crisp and sharply contrasted view of the General who is full length seated and close to the camera. His hair is long and pulled behind his ears. Beard is full and covers only the mustache and chin areas leaving gaunt cheeks showing. His major general's frock has huge, ultra rich grade shoulder straps with 2 stars in each. He sports a sword belt, gauntlets, and holds his 1850 pattern staff sword in his left hand. **$325**

Minor foxing and wear. "Schwing & Rudd, Photographers, Army of the Cumberland" backmark. **$195**

General U.S. Grant

A wonderful waist-up seated photo of a pensive looking Grant posed with his eyes cast downward. He is wearing the coat and shoulder straps of a major general (2 stars). The clarity, contrast and condition are all superb. Boldly autographed on the front is Grant's distinctive signature "U.S. Grant/Maj. Gen. USA" executed in deep-brown ink. The photo bears an imprint, "T.F. Saltsman, Nashville," which would date this photo to late 1862 or 1863. .... **$2,500**

Fine "from life" bust view in uniform with three stars on shoulder straps. Short hair, well-trimmed beard, Brady copyright printed on bottom front with date of 1865. .... **$150**

General William Averell, colonel of the 3rd Pennsylvania Cavalry. "His 2nd Cavalry Division won the first claimed victory of the Federal horse over the Confederates at Kelly's Ford, Virginia, in March 1863-an action said to be the turning point of cavalry fighting in the Eastern theater." Has rubber stamped numbers "13166" near bottom verso. R. W. Addis backmark. **$185**

General William F. Bartlett
Rare image of amputee 4-time wounded General W. F. Bartlett, not long after his release from Libby Prison. Taken by Black & Case in Boston in March of 1865. Wonderful photographer's proof stamp on verso, minor corner clips. Images of Bartlett as a General are extremely rare, as he received his commission towards the end of the war (June 1864) and spent most of the time in prison.
.... **$495**

Signed image of Bartlett, taken as colonel of the 57th Massachusetts Infantry. Boldly ink signed on verso. Excellent view of this general wearing a sling for his wounded arm, Pittsfield, MA backmark, very-fine condition. **$1,250**

General William Hazen, long outstanding career in the U.S. Army spanned over 30 years. Wounded severely by Indians in 1859, Hazen was appointed colonel of the 41st Ohio Infantry in late 1861. Superb contrast and clarity, no backmark. **$375**

General William Tecumseh Sherman
Superb signed Civil War-date Brady image, light sepia-tone. This is a head-and-shoulders portrait of the general wearing his dress uniform. Signed at the lower margin, "W.T. Sherman, General." Verso is printed, "Brady's Nation Photographic Portrait Galleries, No. 627 Pennsylvania Avenue, Washington, D.C." Image is in mint condition. **$2,500**

Rich and deeply contrasted waist-up seated pose of Sherman giving the camera his best "stare." Wears frock and straps of major general. Excellent image with some damage to the cardstock along the right edge and bottom right corner, canceled revenue stamp on the reverse. **$69**

Sherman as he looked in 1862, taken by "Peplow & Butch" in Memphis, though there is no backmark. It shows "Uncle Billy" in a bust portrait wearing the coat and straps of a major general. His hair is shorter than normal and not combed. His beard is a little messy and his eyes are younger not the hardened eyes in the more common later images. **$135**

General Winfield Scott Hancock, almost three-dimensional, this is a very nice Hancock image. The contrast and clarity are almost perfect. As to condition, it is very-fine overall, with minor wear to the Brady mount (a small amount of softness to the bottom corners). The albumen has a minute amount of chipping near the bottom in two areas. Also two small rubbed areas. Someone long ago wrote "Hancock" in pencil above his head in the background, this appears to have been erased, leaving a very, very faint background smudge. **$395**

Generals Stoneman and Naglee, outdoor view of Generals Stoneman and Naglee sitting on chairs in front of a tent with four staff officers and enlisted man. Among the staff officers are two future generals: Brevet Generals Andrew J. Alexander and Edwin V. Sumner Jr. A dog is visible in front of the group lying on the ground. Other tents, men, and horses are just visible in left background. Backmark is, "Brady's Album Gallery. No. 438. Generals Stoneman And Nagle and Staff, Richmond, June, 1862." Nice period-ink identifications on image. **$625**

President Abraham Lincoln and Family
Mass produced cdv-lithograph of Lincoln and his family seated around a table in a fine family setting, circa 1864. .... **$39**

President Abraham Lincoln, published in 1862 by E. Anthony from a "Photographic Negative in Brady's National Portrait Gallery." Period ink identification on verso, minor back stains. The rich tones and clarity of this image are what separate it from the normal Lincoln images available. **$1,500**

President Andrew Johnson, crisp, near full-seated view in the famous Brady chair. Excellent with one tiny scuff at the top of image. Beautifully inscribed in ink on the back, "President Andrew Johnson Inaugurated Apr. 15th 1865. Seventeenth President of the United States. Bought of Brady N.Y. June 5th 1865." **$125**

Presidents George Washington and Abraham Lincoln, engraving, fine condition. **$39**

Union, Other
"Hero of Gettysburg" John Burns

Beautiful signed cdv of the famous 70-year-old John Burns who grabbed his gun on July 1, 1863, to help the Union fight on the first day of Gettysburg. A couple very tiny tears in bottom of albumen, otherwise in very-fine condition and boldly signed. "Bogardus, New York" backmark. **$875**

This old War of 1812 veteran, who lived in Gettysburg, was furious about the Confederate invasion of Pennsylvania, so left his farm with musket in hand and fought valiantly with one of the Pennsylvania infantry regiments during the battle of Gettysburg. Photo is near full-length showing old John Burns standing with a bayoneted musket at his side. Brady/Anthony backmark, crisp clarity and contrast, bottom of carte lightly trimmed. Fine piece. **$275**

Captain Charles H. Morton, 58th Massachusetts Volunteer Infantry, wearing his nine-button frock coat with captain's shoulder straps. Morton was taken prisoner at Poplar Grove Church, Virginia, on September 30, 1864, and exchanged February 23, 1865. .... **$125**

Cavalry Private, Armed, full-standing pose with cavalry saber, sword belt, and a Model 1858 "Hardee" hat with a nice clear set of crossed sabers hatpin. The photo has an "Anthony Broadway, N.Y." backmark. **$85**

Chaplain John J. Hight, excellent ink-signed image taken in his Chaplain's uniform. Minor corner clips and slight trim to top of the image. **$195**

Chasseur, possibly a view of a "New England Guard" (has Boston photographer's backmark). View shows determined federal wearing classic chasseur jacket with Russian pattern shoulder knots, waist belt with two piece interlocking buckle, baggy trousers, gaiters, and sporting a light-color kepi w/dark band. Reverse note indicates soldier's name "Bradley Dean." ... **$125**

Chief Engineer, Union Naval officer with sword in complete uniform with hat. His rank is the pre-1862 Chief Engineer, card has been slightly trimmed, but doesn't affect the quality of the image at all. **$95**

First Lieutenant Sanford W. Newland, 34th Indiana Infantry, wearing his distinctive officer's Zouave uniform. He served from October 1861 until his death in May 1865, very-fine condition, image is signed in period ink and has a New Orlean's backmark. **$325**

Lieutenant, Unidentified, crisp, of a standing Union second lieutenant. He is wearing a nine-button officer's frock coat, and his shoulder straps are clearly visible, card is marked, "Gurney & Son N.Y." **$75**

Musician, soldier holding three-valve trumpet and wearing a musician's frock coat with fancy sleeve facings, hat has "LCB" on front, sits at his side. **$185**

Sergeant, 6th New Hampshire Volunteers, wears a frock coat, open to show his vest. His forage cap with "6 NHV" is on a pedestal at his side. His sergeant's chevrons are very clear. **$150**

Sergeant, wearing a frock coat with chevrons and holding his forage cap. Taken by D. Denison of Albany, New York. **$125**

Soldiers, combat-posed image of a bayonet about to plunge deeply into another soldier's chest. Both soldiers are fully equipped and appear to be taking themselves seriously. The image is from life and not a retouched or painting image. Appears to be a copy of a tintype, very-fine condition with excellent contrast and clarity, minor clipped corners. Dayton, Ohio backmark, with a two-cent orange tax stamp. **$550**

Spy Dick Turpin, superb image of one of the shady characters involved in espionage during the Civil War in the Tennessee area. Obviously famous enough to have his image taken and distributed at the time. Ink identified on the front as, "Dick Turpin (a union spy) Dept. of the Cumberland." No backmark. **$675**

Spy Pauline Cushman, excellent full-view with sword. Wonderful contrast and clarity to this image. Minor scratch in albumen near her head, no backmark.
.... **$395**

One of the Civil War's most famous females, excellent half-view of Cushman wearing a union major's uniform. This image is from life, minor corner wear, and usual foxing. Stamped backmark "G.W. Thorne Manufacturer of Photo. Albums & Photographs 60 Nassau St. N.Y." Imprinted on front bottom of carte, "Miss Maj. Pauline Cushman, The famous Union Scout and Spy of the U. S. secret service. Army of the Cumberland." **$350**

Surgeon Vanderkief, fantastic full-standing view showing the Army surgeon wearing his kepi with rain cover, commercial double-breasted blouse, and thigh-high boots. He also sports a long riding crop or Model 1860 staff officer's sword. Boldly autographed in ink on the bottom front, " Vanderkief Surgeon USA." Photo taken in Maryland. **$275**

Zouave, Unidentified, he wears the Zouave jacket with fancy braid trim with quarterfoils on the jacket front. A half-length photo. **$175**

Carte de visite, Governor Andrews of Massachusetts 1861, $50-$65.

PUBLISHED BY
E. ANTHONY,
501 *Broadway,*
NEW YORK.
FROM
PHOTOGRAPHIC
NEGATIVE,
FROM
BRADY'S NATIONAL
Portrait Gallery.

Carte de visite, Union navy lieutenant, $90-$95.

Carte de visite, unidentified Union infantry captain, $90-$105.

*Carte de visite, typical Union soldier, back marked Nashville, **$100-$125.***

Gallery of the Cumberland,
No. 25 Cedar St.,
Opposite the Commercial Hotel,
MORSE & PEASLEE,
Nashville.

*Fully cased, 1/9-plate
tintype, $265-$300.*

Tintypes

Tintypes were another version of the use of collodion. In this case, the medium was tin-dipped iron plates instead of glass as in the ambrotype. The advantage of tin was that it was not fragile, could be sent through the mail, and was easily carried. They were also relatively inexpensive, because multiple images could be made on a single plate and cut apart. This provided the sitter with duplicate images. The process came into popular use in the United States during 1856 and was still being used by some photographers as late as 1920.

Confederate

Tintype, 1/4 plate, Confederate Captain John S. Stansell, 52nd Tennessee Volunteer Infantry, 3/4-length seated pose of a very thin and gaunt looking rebel seated next to a studio table. He sports a classic Confederate gray six-button short jacket with three gold stripes on the collar (indicating a rank of captain), and a matching pair of gray trousers. The image is extremely clear and well contrasted and has some light surface "rubs" that only lightly affect the image. It is identified inside the back of the case in classic script, "Capt. John S. Stansell 52nd Regt. Tenn. Vol." This inscription is very nicely done. The regiment fought valiantly at such battles as Chickamauga, Atlanta, and with Hood at Franklin and Nashville. At Chickamauga the unit went into action with 270 men, and suffered a loss of 96 officers and men wounded or killed in the engagement. It surrendered to the Federals at Greensboro, North Carolina, in 1865. Housed in a ratty full leatherette case. **$1,175**

Tintype, 1/6 plate

Confederate Captain, handsome, 2/3-length seated pose. He is wearing a
Confederate officer's double-breasted gray frock coat with three rows of gold
braid on each side of the collar indicating the rank of captain. He also wears
a waist belt with two-piece interlocking tongue and wreath buckle, which is
probably a C.S. plate, but not visible due to light gilt-tinting on the buckle's
surface. The clarity, contrast, and condition are all excellent. The image is
nice and bright. The only defect is a slight bend running diagonally through
the center of the plate with a very slight abrasion in this area on the subject's
breast. Housed in a fine gilt mat, frame, and glass. **$1,075**

Confederate Prisoners of War, four Confederates posed at the P.O.W. Camp
Douglas near Chicago. Very clean image. At least three of the four appear
to be cavalrymen. Image is very clean, just a bit dark. Behind the image
is written, "Camp Douglas—Brandon 1863" in pencil Case is ornate
thermoplastic. **$760**

Confederate Private, clear, fully cased tintype of a Confederate private showing
his military vest and his gray frock coat. The neatest part of this photo is that
there is one large coat-size button visible, and it isn't gilted. The button is a
large-size, cast "I" Confederate button with the large letter "I" on the button
clearly visible. **$425**

Tintype, 1/8th plate

Confederate Private, Armed, housed in a nice, embossed, cream paper mat.
View shows knees-up standing, bearded, early war Rebel wearing tall top hat,
ten-button gray frock coat with fringed epaulets, waistbelt with roller buckle,
scabbard, square flat cap box, and the soldier is holding his Enfield musket
with bayonet, and has a Colt Root revolver clearly tucked into his belt. Image
has great clarity and contrast, with a couple minor bumps and blemishes
from not being under glass. Image is apparently a copy view of another tin or
ambrotype (subject is not reversed in image) but definitely war date. .. **$395**

Tintype, 1/9th plate

Confederate Soldier, young man in "battle shirt" tintype of young Confederate soldier, measures 2" x 2-1/2", condition is good. The image has excellent clarity and some light bubbling in upper right side. The case is crude, but in working order. **$350**

Confederate Private, crystal-clear fully cased, Confederate soldier wearing a butternut shell jacket open in the center. The buttons are gilted, but one is partially visible and appears to be a drooped wing eagle Confederate button. The photo is mounted in an excellent condition thermoplastic case marked, "Holmes, Booth, and Hayden." **$475**

Tintypes, Union

Tintype 1/4 plate

Soldiers, Armed, fine view showing four grizzly looking Yankees, two line officers, one sergeant, and an unknown rank. Three of these fellows are wearing M1858 U.S. Army Hardee hats, two with clearly visible infantry horns, company letters "H," and numerals "7" inside the horn. Interestingly these two also have the worsted wool hat cords that are almost never seen in photos, despite the fact that they are called for by regulations. One officer wears a classic round-top slouch hat with officer's embroidered bugle and "7" in the loop. The last fellow (line officer) has no insignia on his hat. Fine clarity and contrast. Good condition, but has two or three tiny chips and two or three minor bends in the tin. The backdrop is distinctive being an outdoor studio with white sheet background actual cut saplings or tree branches laid against the backdrop, housed in full case. **$495**

Musician, Armed, bugler with a Colt revolver in his belt, wearing a shell jacket with shoulder tabs (possibly a New York issue jacket), and an unusual hat. The bugle and Colt are very obvious. It is tinted and in a gilt frame. Unfortunately there is solarization, but the image itself is extremely sharp and clean. **$695**

NCOs, four soldiers (one seated three standing) posed in front of a fine camp-scene backdrop. Standing are well-worn, hardened Union soldiers including a corporal and sergeant. These fellows wear forage caps and frock coats, one wears a rectangular eagle buckle on the belt, and two are wearing boots. The seated fellow has no rank showing, and wears a kepi, un-piped infantry shell jacket, regulation trousers, and boots. Crisp clarity and contrast, one inconsequential slight bend, housed in full case. **$395**

Cavalry Soldiers, Outdoor, wonderful horizontal format outdoor view showing 14 war-ready cavalrymen posed in their camp in the woods in front of their Sibley tent, and having their national colors standing behind them. There are 13 enlisted troopers wearing shell jackets, bummer caps, sword belts, and holding their sabers— most have large full beards, a couple have high boots, and they are posed looking off to the left as though watching for some rebel cavalry to appear. At the left side of the view, is their company commander wearing his frock coat and holding his sword, also looking off into the distance. It is housed in a full leatherette case (spine split) with a beautiful, rich, green velvet cushion. **$3,500**

Officer, Armed, very crisp and close-up view showing a full-seated Union first lieutenant wearing a black slouch hat with clearly visible U.S. staff wreath insignia on the front, frock coat with clearly visible double border shoulder straps, regulation officer's sword belt with stitched designs, light-colored trousers, and gauntlets. He has his Model 1850-foot officer's sword propped upright next to him and proudly displays it to the camera. The image has excellent clarity, contrast, and condition, with a spot of staining on the right side of the image that does not affect the subject at all. This is housed in a full case with frame and glass. **$795**

Officers, Outdoor, really interesting outdoor image showing five officers and men, and one horse, posed outside a small log cabin. There is an officer and his wife near the doorway, a soldier holding his horse, and three other soldiers to the left of the cabin. Image is 100% solid and stable, but the lacquer coating on the plate has alligatored, leaving tiny lines and crackles in the surface of the lacquer coating. The image is not flaked or flaking in any form. Good contrast and a very appealing outdoor image, housed in mat, frame, and glass only. **$395**

Sergeant, Armed, pipe smoking union sergeant, contained in a full leather case. Weapon in hand, wearing all the proper accoutrements, this soldier is shown wearing his bedroll, haversack, and canteen. Great painted backdrop, this image has no flaws. **$1,450**

Sergeant, Cavalry, Armed, subject seated in front of a patriotic camp scene backdrop in his kepi with wreath insignia on the front, a commercially made shell jacket with narrow sergeant's chevrons on each sleeve, one button on the collar, and delicate-fine cuff piping. He wears an officer's sword belt and is cradling his cavalry saber in his lap. Excellent in all respects with some edge chips not visible under the mat, housed in a mediocre half case. **$425**

Soldier, Armed, full standing with patriotic camp scene backdrop. Shows soldier wearing regulation forage cap, nine- button frock, and holding a Model 1861 Springfield with bayonet in front of him. Very good in all respects, housed in mat, frame, and glass (no case). **$235**

Soldier

Full-standing, housed in full case, Yank wears forage cap, frock, trousers, and has rectangular eagle buckle and belt, very good with minor scuff to left of subject. **$125**

Really superb tintype photo shows a Yankee soldier the way he looked in camp posed in front of a great photographer's painted camp scene backdrop standing next to a studio chair wearing his issue trousers, a large cravat military vest open to expose his homespun shirt, and having a great pair of suspenders. In one hand he is holding a large wine bottle, and in the other he

Above: Fully cased, 1/6-plate tintype of Union infantry private (note pin in hand with photo), $375-$450.

Left: Half case, 1/4-plate tintype of standing Union cavalryman in shell jacket armed with saber, $550-$625.

Fully cased, 1/6-plate tintype of doubly armed Union infantryman with full belt rig, $450-$500.

is holding his worn out old black slouch hat. On the studio chair next to him he has laid his uniform blouse, which is draped over the back of the wooden chair. Excellent clarity, contrast, and condition with the edges of the tintype slightly trimmed to fit this in a photo album. No case. **$395**

Tintype, 1/6th plate

Private William F. Bowers, 21st Ohio Volunteer Infantry, fine, near-mint tintype in patriotic gutta- percha (thermoplastic) case (also perfect) showing William F. Bower, 21st Ohio, seated with musket and wearing belt with "OVM" buckle. Also comes with his eagle masthead discharge dated June 1865 (Bower served 3 years). Case has liberty cap and patriotic designs. **$650**

Sergeant Benjamin Thomas, New York Volunteers, seated pose shows a New York boy wearing light-color hat, N.Y. state jacket with huge homemade sergeant's chevrons, cross belt with circular eagle plate, waist belt with small-size oval buckle, and issue trousers. Image has dark tonal quality, but very viewable, and otherwise fine. A family note (recent) is on the back of the tin that reads, "Benjamin Thomas MD in civil war was prisoner in Andersonville. Father of Evan Thomas Fess grandmother of Dorothy Fess Herbert." Housed in a nice half case. **$185**

Cavalry Private, Double-Armed, fully cased tintype is clear, but just a little dark. The trooper is seated and wearing a cavalry shell jacket, a Hardee hat with a crossed saber hatpin, and a cavalry eagle sword belt rig. His cavalry saber is standing alongside of him, and a Remington Army Model revolver is tucked behind his belt. Although just a little dark, this is a nice photo with excellent content. **$395**

Drummer William H. Headly, 10th Vermont Volunteer Infantry, view shows William H. Headley of the 10th Vermont in a 2/3-length seated pose with his drum on a studio table next to him. Headley is posed wearing the elusive infantry musician's frock coat with "grid iron" piping on the breast. He also has his drum sling slung across his chest and a waist belt with eagle buckle

Fully octagonal, cased, 1/6-plate tintype Union private with Springfield musket, full belt rig, $350-$425.

clearly visible. The drum next to him is a full-size regimental rope-tension drum and it has the sticks stuck into the ropes for display. The clarity and condition are top-notch, and the contrast is very good with just a slight darkness on the coat and drum. This is not a dark image as his face, buckle, hands are all bright and clear. There is just a slight darkness to the coat and drum. Housed in a gilt mat only. **$1,275**

Tintype, 1/8th plate

Heavy Artilleryman, Armed, full standing soldier wearing black slouch hat with crossed cannon insignia, letter "M" and numeral "1," enlisted frock coat, U.S. belt with buckle and cap box, and having his cartridge box sling with plate visible across his chest. At his side is a Springfield musket with bayonet. The album that this came with contained all Ohio soldiers from northwest Ohio. Very appealing and artistically posed, but it becomes quite dark at the lower-right quadrant. It is housed in a fine mat, frame, and glass. **$145**

Private, Armed, standing Union soldier in full case. He is standing at attention with his musket at his side. He is wearing an enlisted man's nine-button frock coat with a U.S. belt plate and cartridge box sling plate visible. **$425**

Tintype, 1/9th plate

Private Thomas J. Naylor, 9th Indiana Volunteer Infantry, mint, crystal clear, shows Thomas J. Naylor, Company C, 9th Indiana from the waist up, in a very interesting pose. He is wearing a tall crown forage cap, state-issue shell jacket with shoulder tabs, and has his musket delicately displayed at his side with one hand grasping the fore stock and his other stretched across his body with hand caressing the lower stock. You can see the socket of his bayonet clearly below his belt. This is now housed in mat, frame, and glass, but was found inside the album. The album is beautifully inscribed in brown ink, "Thomas J Naylor Co "C" 9th Regt. Ind. Vet. Vols. Inft. 3rd Brig. 1st Div. 4th Army Corps June 2nd 1865." It is a fine gilt leather 1860s album in very nice condition
.... **$495**

Fully cased, 1/9-plate tintype,
$285-$315.

Cavalry Office, seated, almost full-length pose, he wears the frock coat and holds his slouch hat and a cavalry saber, housed in full leather case. .. **$165**

Tintype, 1/2 plate, Union 5th Ohio Volunteer Cavalry, rare outdoor image of the men of the 5th Ohio Volunteer Cavalry with their new 12 lb Mountain Howitzer. Image shows cavalrymen, their horses, outbuildings, and the Mountain Howitzer with caisson. This artillery piece was one of two purchased personally by Colonel Thomas Heath, naming one after his wife. **$3,000**

Tintype, Full Plate
Private, Armed, 6" x 7" image of uniformed and equipped Union infantryman holding a Short Enfield Rifle. Slight flaking to the emulsion at bottom left, otherwise perfectly clear. **$525**

Artillerymen, shows three soldiers in uniform, two seated, flanking one standing. They wear short jackets, vests, light trousers with stripes, and forage caps. Two hats are shown with crown insignia showing. This is a large, crossed cannon with "7" over top and "I" below. Standing fellow has instead, his 18th Corps badge showing. The photo was taken in studio setting simulating a garden bower. Two seated men rest against a decorative railing. Greens are arched over top. Good clarity for a full plate, which is rarely sharp. This is actually a photograph of a photograph. You can actually see the edges of the original tintype, and the tack heads holding it in place for this shot. **$475**

> "I could get my likeness taken by walking 5 miles in the mud twice and paying 6 dollars for a common case. I will have it taken the first opportunity that presents."
>
> —*Milo Grow*
> *51st Georgia Infantry*

Ruby ambrotype, 1/9-plate of Union corporal wearing slouch hat, $225-$250.

Fully cased, 1/6-plate tintype,
$425-$500.

Fully cased, 1/6-plate tintype,
$300-$350.

Double-cased, tintype of soldier and family,
$485-$515.

CHAPTER 11

SWORDS

During the Civil War, the sword served as both a weapon and a symbol of rank. Among the enlisted men, only cavalry troopers, some artillery soldiers, sergeants, and musicians carried swords or sabers. Officers, both combat and staff, carried swords, more as a privilege entitled by their rank than as a weapon of self-defense.

Though often used interchangeably, the terms "sword" and "saber" denote two very different forms of weapon. A sword is a long, straight-bladed weapon with the primary function to denote rank or status. A saber, on the other hand, is a weapon with a curved blade with the sole function being that of enabling the user to strike a blow. Sabers were most often carried by mounted troops during the Civil War.

Sword collecting offers many areas for the enthusiast. First, one can easily assemble a "type collection" of Civil War swords and sabers. This could include the Model 1850 staff and field sword, a Model 1860 staff sword, an 1860 Medical staff sword, a Model 1840 and Model 1860 saber, a Model 1840 NCO's sword, as well as a musician's sword, a foot artillery sword, a Model 1852 naval officer's sword, a Marine NCO sword, and a Model 1860 naval cutlass. From this point, a collector might focus on manufacturers or even inscribed presentation swords. The good news is that a lot of these swords have survived and are still available to a person just beginning a collection.

Confederate swords and sabers, however, will present some costly obstacles to collectors. Though many of the Confederacy's blades originated in U.S. arsenals, many were made after secession from the Union by southern manufacturers. These Confederate-produced blades are well beyond the means of an average or beginning collector.

Whatever approach one may decide for assembling a sword collection, one will benefit from years of research that is now available in any number of books on the topic. This is one area of Civil War collecting that is well documented, making it an ideal area for new collectors to safely enter the realm of Civil War relics.

Collecting Hints

Pros:
- Swords are impressive. More so than other relics, a sword will capture the attention of young, old, male, and female. There is a lot of "wow" factor for the dollar when you own and display a sword.

- Swords and sabers are relatively stable. As long as you don't handle the blades and you store the relics in a low humidity environment, deterioration will be minimal.

- Many swords and sabers have been handed down through the ages. There were a wide variety of makes and manufacturers during the war years, so there are plenty of choices for today's collector.

- Research has been intense in this area. Good references are available to assist a collector in determining origin, use, and scarcity.

Cons:
- Confederate swords and sabers sell for very large sums. The high values have lured some into creating swords by assembling pieces or by out-right manufacturing forgeries.

- The attractiveness of high-dollar prices has tempted many dealers to call anything "Confederate" that does not fit the immediate, accepted pattern of a regulation sword or saber.

- This is an area of the hobby where repairs and replacement of missing parts seems to be an accepted norm. It can be difficult to ascertain if the grip on a sword or all of the parts of it were always there, or if they had been expertly replaced in the last twenty years. This sort of alteration does not seem to be regarded as inappropriate within the hobby, so it is up to the collector (and not the dealer) to know exactly what they are examining.

Availability ★★★
Price ★★★
Reproduction Alert ★★

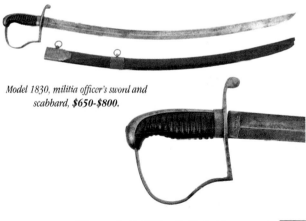

Model 1830, militia officer's sword and scabbard, $650-$800.

Confederate Cutlasses

Naval

Made by Thomas, Griswold & Company. The 21-1/4" blade is marked, "T.G.&Co./ N.O.," and has a dark-gray patina with scattered light pitting, markings are strong and blade is full. The brass hilt has an ocher patina. No scabbard, very-good-plus condition. **$2,400**

This Confederate copy of the U.S. Model 1841 Naval cutlass has a brass guard that is solid cast. A U.S. cutlass had three iron rivets that attach the blade to the guard. The blade is also smaller in width. The overall length is 26", the blade is 21", and the width at the hilt is 1-3/8". The patina is a soft gray and there is no pitting. **$3,500**

Confederate Sabers

Enlisted Man, Artillery

Single strand wire on grip, which is 95%+ intact. Unstopped fuller blade; crude lap-soldered scabbard with sand-cast brass mounts. Often called a "Dog River" and more recently, a "Boyle and Gamble, Richmond, Va.," pattern. Blade and scabbard most closely resemble the products of the Confederate States Armory at Kenansville, North Carolina, especially the pommel cap construction, fuller on blade, and scabbard construction details. It is documented that Kenansville produced artillery sabers, but nobody can specifically identify them at this point in time. **$9,500**

Model 1840 Light Artillery sword and scabbard, having the very rare early stamp, "Ames, Cabotville, 1845" Fantastic "WAT" script inspector mark in brass guard with full original grip leather and wire. Has initials "PAG" scratched in guard; family history attributes the sword to a relative with the last name of Gallagher, but only verbal provenance. Blade is brown and has light pitting overall; scabbard is correct type for the recessed guard model.

.... **$1,250**

Enlisted Man, Cavalry

Civil War cavalry saber manufactured for sale to the Confederate troops between
November 1861 and April 1865, in Columbus, Georgia. Haiman and Brother
was one of the largest Confederate manufacturers of swords during the
Civil War. This excellent example is based on the Model 1840 pattern. This
sword has a smooth, even, original patina. The guard is a reddish-umber
color showing typical high copper content. There is no pitting on the blade.
Casting flaws that are typical of Confederate manufacturers are present. This
is an attic example with original iron wire on the grip, and it also maintains
complete original oilcloth wrap. **$2,950**

"Dog River" style 34-3/4" blade with a wide unstopped fuller on each side of
the blade. Sand-cast brass three-branch guard and Phrygian helmet-shaped
pommel, very worn wood grip is missing all the leather and wire. Dark patina
on the blade with a few patches of corrosion, one branch of the guard is bent,
no scabbard. Good condition, likely Virginia made and came from that state
with the Reed and Watson Musket. **$350**

Cavalry saber made by B. Douglas & Co., Columbia, South Carolina. ... **$8,500**

Isaacs & Co. C.S. cavalry saber. **$4,400**

Haiman cavalry saber, 85% grip wrap complete, very-good condition. .. **$5,400**

Kraft, Goldsmidt & Kraft, Columbia, South Carolina, saber. **$8,800**

Mole cavalry saber with brass guard. **$2,750**

Overall very good with full oilcloth grip wrap (wire missing), full scabbard with
brass mounts (throat missing), and nice blade. This has traces of ancient
silver paint on areas of the scabbard. Classic, unmarked Haimann Georgia
saber. **$4,250**

Very fine example of an early Kenansville cavalry sword. The blade is excellent
and has no nicks or dings. The patina is a soft, uncleaned gray. It has the

original leather washer. The leather grip has single-strand iron wire. Brass guard has beautiful uncleaned dark brass patina. The sword is very tight with no wiggle in the guard. The scabbard has 60% original brown paint. Brass sword hangers have dark green patina. **$7,995**

This sword has a beautiful blade with a soft gray patina and a non-stopped fuller. No nicks or dings, with very smooth metal. It has the original leather washer. The brass guard has an aged-brass patina. The leather on the grip is very fine and is 98%. The twisted fine brass wire is complete and tight. The metal scabbard has a brass throat and brass hangers, the drag is iron. This sword has a lot of features of a Kenansville blade. **$5,400**

Model 1840 Cavalry saber and scabbard by William Glaze, Columbia, South Carolina, also known as the Palmetto Armory. Borderline fine blade with nice edge and just some scuffs from field use. Grip wire is 100%; grip leather has a few worn spots, but 75%+ intact. Original matching scabbard. **$3,750**

Officer, Cavalry

Kenansville cavalry officer's saber in mint condition. **$9,500**

Rare Thomas, Griswold & Co. Confederate cavalry officer's saber with "straight-line" stamp. There are fewer than ten examples known with the rare, straight-line Griswold mark. The blade has an attractive aged-gray/brown patina with a clear, "Thomas Griswold & Co. New Orleans," stamp. The guard is perfect with rich, dark, aged-bronze/brown patina. Grip professionally restored using original Civil War leather, looks absolutely original. **$8,500**

Extremely rare battlefield pick-up remains of a Nashville-produced College Hill Confederate cavalry officer's saber. This saber was picked up along the Confederate retreat route from Shiloh towards Corinth, Mississippi. The blade is broken 4" below the brass guard, and a portion of the guard is sheared off. Part of the, "C.S.A.," initials are intact, and remain clearly visible. This blade appears to have taken a severe impact. **$1,250**

Exceptionally attractive cavalry officer's saber was made by William J. McElroy of Macon, Georgia. William McElroy is well known for his deep, relief-etched infantry officer swords. This, his cavalry officer's pattern, is much rarer. Rarer still is the etched scabbard. Though it is now faint, the scabbard is etched with an old English script, "CS," crossed cannon, a battle flag and McElroy's vine pattern. The sword's complete and original grip is wrapped with oilcloth and single strand brass wire. The brass guard still retains traces of its original gilt. The sword knot is original to the sword. **$65,000**

Confederate Swords

Model 1832, Artillery
Artillery sword with tin-mounted, wooden scabbard. **$3,400**

C.S. copy of the 1832 short artillery sword with crude casting grip with eagle motif just like on the U.S. Model 1832. This one has no rivets and the tang end actually has a small cap on it. The space between the blade and the front of the grip has been filled in with lead to fill the void. The blade shows definite crudeness. There are stampings of "TP" and "127" on the grip. The blade has a dark patina present and some rust. **$995**

Officer, Artillery
Sword belonged to William Carnes, Captain of Carnes' Battery, C.S.A. Artillery. Captain Carnes commanded his battery at the battle of Perryville, October 8, 1862, where he was wounded in the foot, but remained with his command until after the battle. Though given a medical furlough, rumors of an impending battle sent the Captain back to the front where he effectively commanded his battery at the battle of Murfreesboro. At the battle of Chickamauga, Carnes' Battery lost 38 of 79 men taken into action Saturday afternoon, September 19th. He had 49 horses shot down and his battery captured when his infantry support gave way. When the Confederates counterattacked and retook the guns, Carnes' Battery was so badly cut up

it was removed from the field. After the battle, Captain Carnes was highly complimented by General Bragg for his work and given thirty days to recruit his command. As an additional compliment, the young Captain was given his choice of cannon from the battle captures and given command of a battalion of four batteries. He continued in this capacity until 1864, when he was reassigned to the Confederate Navy because of his pre-war naval experience. Carnes had been so effective as a battery commander, General Forrest specifically requested Carnes as the artillery officer he most desired for service with his command. The sword was purchased from the Carnes family and was later sold to well-known Confederate collector Kent Wall, who did all the subsequent historical research and documentation. The sword is completely original and unaltered. The leather grip wrap is flaking, but it retains all of its twisted-brass wire wrap. The blade and the original brass scabbard are excellent; the maker's name and full New Orleans address are exceptionally good. Captain Carnes' sword comes with full documentation and research done by Mr. Wall, as well as a first edition copy of *The Old Guard in Gray*.

.... **$13,800**

Foot Officer

Arsenal-produced Confederate foot officer's sword and scabbard that started out life as a standard three-branch Haiman-style cavalry saber. At the C.S. Arsenal, this sword was shortened to foot officer length, and the guard was refashioned to have two branches rather than three. The scabbard was appropriately fashioned to fit the sword. The blade is very nice with a gently aging gray-brown patina. The grip has long ago worn down to wood. The custom-fashioned brass guard has a rich uncleaned patina. The pommel cap has lots of small marks and dings from having been used to hammer something. The scabbard is classic Confederate lap seam, brass mount, and is in very nice condition. **$3,850**

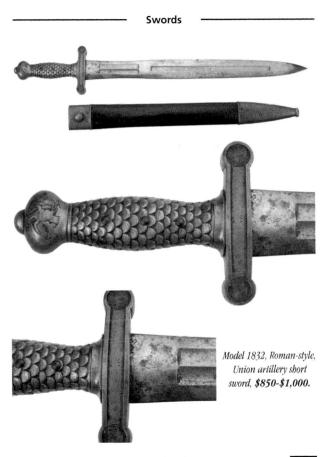

Model 1832, Roman-style, Union artillery short sword, $850-$1,000.

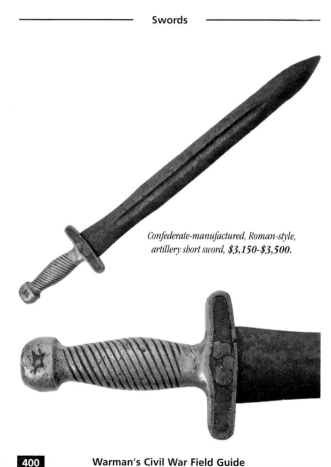

Confederate-manufactured, Roman-style, artillery short sword, $3,150-$3,500.

Boyle and Gamble Richmond, Virginia, field and staff officer's sword, $9,000-$10,000.

Though similar to a Federal Model 1850 foot sword, the handguard on a Boyle and Gamble sword is clearly Confederate.

Confederate Civil War McElroy infantry officer sword and scabbard, clearly marked, "W.J. McElroy Macon Geo.," on ricasso, 95% original tarred leather grip with full wire; scabbard is full length and unbroken (middle mount is unlike the other two, but original to the sword). Clear etching of tobacco vines and "CS" on blade. **$23,000**

Confederate Civil War officer's sword by Halfmann & Taylor, Montgomery, Alabama, and so etched on ricasso of blade. Noted importers of fine goods from buttons to swords, this firm imported this pattern of sword and etched the blades on site, clear, etched "CS." Guard is unusual, and may have been altered, 95% original ray-skin grip and full wire, fine scabbard. **$8,500**

Exceptionally rare Confederate foot officer sword and scabbard by McElroy, Macon, Georgia, and so marked on the ricasso. Extremely fine, deep etching on blade, "CS," scrolls, cotton plants, more! Beautiful hardwood maple grip never had leather; about 65% original wire remaining, original leather scabbard. **$12,500**

Officer, Field and Staff

Boyle and Gamble field and staff sword. **$16,500**

Extremely rare and beautiful C.S.A. "Kenansville" Field and Staff officer's sword with distinctive cast-brass guard made up of the letters, "C.S.A." The brass has a rich, dark uncleaned patina and has the Roman Numeral "XIX." It has the original blade that has been shortened a few inches. The blade also has a dark never-cleaned patina. The grip was, at some point prior to the 1930s, changed to a polished walnut. This is a beautiful "C.S.A." Kenansville in nice condition. **$4,950**

Pattern with the backwards "N" in Nashville and the flat-top scabbard with classic baby-size rings. There are only about ten known, complete examples of the short, straight Nashville Plow Works Field and Staff officer's sword. This example has a beautiful clean blade just beginning to gray with age.

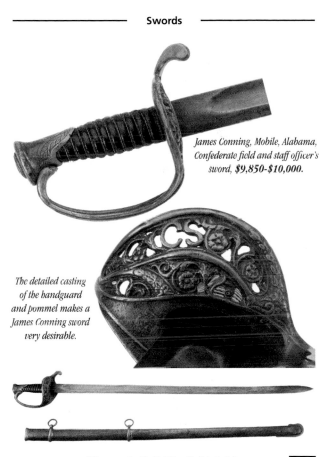

James Conning, Mobile, Alabama, Confederate field and staff officer's sword, $9,850-$10,000.

The detailed casting of the handguard and pommel makes a James Conning sword very desirable.

The brass guard is perfect with a rich, age patina, "C.S.A.," cast around the bottom and, "Nashville Plow Works," cast around the guard's top. The grip has original wrap and wire with approximately 70% of the original leather present and worn through to polished wood in the remaining areas. The grip has a couple normal small age cracks from the shrinkage of the wood with time. The scabbard is the early pattern with the flat brass top. The scabbard retains 80% of its original black enamel. **$22,500**

Staff officer's sword in original leather scabbard, once in the prestigious Norm Flayderman Confederate Sword Collection (still has the old tag from his collection hanging from the sword). The blade has a gently aging gray patina with original engraving visible in areas. The marking, "Made by Boyle & Gamble & Co. for Mitchell & Tyler Richmond, Va," can be seen faintly etched on the sword's ricasso. The grip is excellent with 100% original wrap and wire. The scabbard is complete and original, but does have some typical leather flaking, and the stitching is open in areas. **$15,500**

Officer

Identified Gettysburg Confederate sword that is likely the product of James Conning of Mobile, Alabama, or an unknown Louisiana maker. Full, original, brown leather- covered grip with original wire, top-brazed mounts on leather scabbard, and crudely cast pommel. Stopped fuller blade is plain and devoid of any decoration. Affixed to the scabbard is an old and faded paper tag, 100% genuine, that identifies the sword to a Union soldier in the 42nd New York Infantry. **$3,075**

Full, original, pigskin-leather grip and single-strand brass wire and fine original full-length leather scabbard with top brazed bandless suspension rings, typical of Southern construction. Totally plain blade and simple two-branch, single-knuckle bow guard with evidence of crude sand-casting. This item is totally unmarked, but virtually identical to several known marked, "Hyde and Goodrich, New Orleans, Louisiana," examples. **$2,500**

U.S. Cutlasses

Model 1860

The 26" blade is marked on the reverse ricasso, "Made by/AMES MFG Co./ CHICOPEE/MASS." The obverse ricasso is marked, "U.S.N./D.R./1862." The blade is clean with some age spots, a little fine pitting near the top. The Ames' markings are unusually well defined on this sword. The hilt shows small dents on the brass, the grip retains all the leather, but no wire (the wire was removed from many of these swords by the Navy). The guard is marked, "23M/783." No scabbard, very-good condition. **$675**

"Ames Mfg. Co.," 25-3/4" blade marked on the obverse ricasso with the naval anchor and date of 1862. The top front of the guard is rack numbered, "6M/125." The Ames markings are notoriously light on these swords, but are distinct on this one, except for a couple of letters. The grip is missing all the wire and has a 1/2" diameter hole in the leather. The brass cup guard shows small dents. The blade is gray with a little pinprick pitting near the tip. Very good with a reproduction brass-mounted, black-leather scabbard and frog. **$450**

Regulation enlisted cutlass by Ames, dated 1862, has the Ames firm marking on the ricasso. Blade is plain gray steel in nice shape and free from nicks. The brass basket guard is good with some honest dents and dings. The handle has most of the leather worn away, but still looks good, as the entire grip is a dark-black color. Complete with full and solid scabbard. Still with this is the original belt frog, which is worn and ratty, but still intact. **$745**

The 26" long blade is gray and has scattered light pitting, appears to have been plated at one time. The brass basket guard is in fine condition, with the lip of the guard marked, "16M/983." The grip is wrapped in black-enameled canvas (believed to be a Navy yard repair) with twisted wire binding. The black leather scabbard is the Navy yard-style with a row of copper rivets on the back. The leather shows some crazing and about 5% finish loss. **$800**

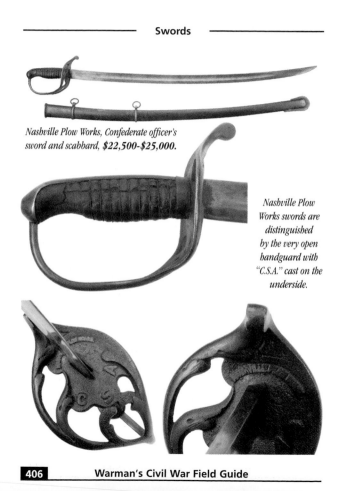

*Nashville Plow Works, Confederate officer's
sword and scabbard, **$22,500-$25,000**.*

*Nashville Plow
Works swords are
distinguished
by the very open
handguard with
"C.S.A." cast on the
underside.*

U.S. Sabers

Model 1833, Enlisted Man, Cavalry

Complete leather grip covering and the properly braided piano-style wire wrap. Most 1833 dragoons are found with this delicate piano-style wire broken or missing and current owners have replaced it with new twisted two-strand cavalry-style wire. The leather and wire on this one are perfect and original. The three-branch brass guard is free from bends or dents with, "ORD," and, "HKC," markings near the quillon. The blade is clean and shiny with full-engraved marking, "N.P Ames/Cutler/Springfield," and, "United States." The scabbard is free from dents and has the inspector's initials, "JM," on the drag. It is 50% covered with surface crud and crust. **$1,395**

Model 1840, Enlisted Man, Artillery

Overall 38" with bright, acutely curved 32" blade with a few tiny nicks, but is overall in fine condition. Crisp, "US/ADK/1863," markings on the right ricasso and, "Ames Mfg./Chicopee/Mass," in a panel on the left ricasso. Blade still retains the scabbard pad. Brass guard and pommel is a deep golden patina. Grips retain 90-98% dry original leather grip wrap and 100% double-twist brass wire wrap. Fine iron scabbard with an old original tin coating. Scabbard rack drag marked, "52". **$1,125**

Original metal scabbard, blade is clean and bright marked, "U.S. 1864 Ames." The grip and guard are original and in good shape, but do have remnants of old gold paint. The metal scabbard is in nice condition with dark, aged patina and no dents at all. Near the top of the scabbard are some old solder marks where a small plate was once affixed. **$795**

Model 1840, Enlisted Man, Cavalry

"C. Hammond"-type with clear stamping on ricasso. Full wire, but no grip leather remains, totally untouched. **$660**

Overall 42" with an iron gray 36" blade, unsharpened and in fine condition, would clean to brilliant. Right ricasso crisply marked, "US/ADK," left ricasso marked, "Ames Mfg. Co/Cabotville/1850." Deep mustard-colored patina on brass guard, pommel double inspected, "ADK," and, "JWK." Tine of knuckle bow has separated from the pommel, but could easily be pressed back in. Grips retain 100% original leather and double-twist wire wrap. Excellent heavy iron scabbard is a smooth almost blackish patina. **$1,450**

Complete Model 1840 "Old Wristbreaker" heavy cavalry saber. Blade is rusty, but very sound and complete. The brass guard is perfect with a brown-green patina. The wooden grip is decayed away, but remnants of the wire remain twisted around the tang. This is an early Shiloh find. **$325**

Exceptionally scarce 1859-dated M1860 Ames Light Cavalry sword and scabbard (most do not realize that the sword was actually in production prior to the model designation with examples known as early as 1858). This example is an honest, brown sword with clear maker and inspector markings. The grip is shrunk and has flaking to the leather, and the wire wrap is complete. On the reverse in old painted script is "Appomattox C.H. 1865." **$1,925**

The 32-1/2" long blade has a knight's head trademark on the obverse ricasso and is marked "Germany" on the reverse ricasso. The bright blade is in excellent condition, showing the original polishing marks. Grip retains all of the wire, but is missing about half of the leather, due to flaking. The steel scabbard has no dents and has quite a lot of spider webbing on the bright metal, overall condition is very good. **$225**

Model 1860, Enlisted Man, Cavalry
1861 Ames Manufacturing saber and scabbard, full original grip and wire wrap, and crisp and clear markings on ricasso. Scabbard lightly cleaned. Blade only average, but no big nicks or rust, hilt looks like it has been painted black.

.... **$600**

Made by Ames, 34-1/2" blade is marked on the obverse ricasso, "US/JH/1859," and has very good manufacturer's markings on the reverse ricasso. The blade is gray with several small nicks in the edge, which has been sharpened. The brass guard has the initials, "HC," scratched into the top and bottom and has a dark patina. The grip retains all the wire with three small areas of wear to the leather wrapping. The iron scabbard has two shallow dents and shows scuffing to an old covering of black paint. **$850**

Three-branch brass guard is dent free, and absolutely cruddy with patina, dirt, and grime encrusted over the brass. The leather grip covering is quite good. The wire is gone, the leather washer remains. Blade is outstanding with 80% mint factory luster. Blade is marked, "US JM 1864," and also, "Mansfield & Lamb Forestdale RI." The scabbard is dent free, though dirty, and appears to have a coat of hundred-year-old earth-tone paint under the dirt. **$595**

Blade nicely marked "US/CEW/1863." Also signed with full "Emerson & Silver Trenton N.J." maker's mark. Leather wrap is superb and the wire is still intact. Brass guard has a delicate patina and there is "JH" stamp on pommel and a tiny "167" rack marking. The blade is clean steel with one edge nick only, no leather washer present. The scabbard has a deep dark patina, no dents, one tiny push on the backside above the drag, and some pitting on the drag itself. A very appealing and solid specimen with really great leather grip. **$795**

The brass guard is excellent with moderate age patina and shows honest use. The leather grip covering is excellent with just a couple light scuffs. The twisted wire wrap is firmly in place. The blade is clean steel color and nicely marked at the ricasso, "US 1865 AGM," as well as with the Roby firm marking all clear and legible. The original leather washer is present at the hilt. The scabbard is very nice with a couple minor dents. It was painted black sometime in the distant past. **$625**

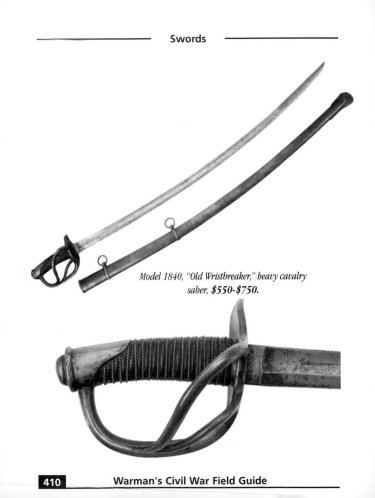

Model 1840, "Old Wristbreaker," heavy cavalry saber, $550-$750.

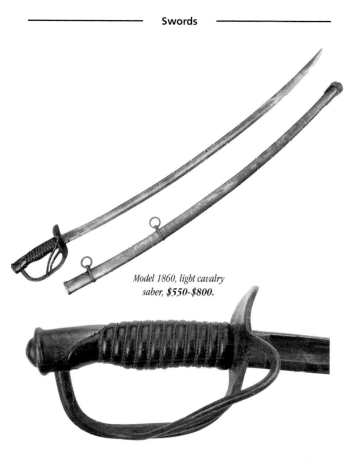

Model 1860, light cavalry saber, $550-$800.

The U.S. mark is clearly visible on the ricasso. The first part of the date, "18-," is visible as is a letter "J" for the inspector's mark. The maker mark on the reverse side is no longer visible, which could indicate that it is from Ames Manufacturing Company, Chicopee, Massachusetts. The blade remains unsharpened, has a few very minor nicks and remnants of silver paint. The leather-wrapped grip and wire are complete. The knuckle bow and pommel cap are both marked "44." Hilt and blade are firmly attached. The knuckle bow rattles a little. Blade is approximately 34-3/4" long. Overall length approximately 41", no scabbard. **$282**

Model 1860, Officer, Cavalry

38" overall with a curved 31-1/2" blade, black and steel patina with military etching on both sides of the flats. Right side features a spread-wing eagle surrounded by stands of arms. Left flat has a fine, "U.S.," encircled by an acanthus leaf decoration. German imported blade. Brass hilt has finely cast and chiseled acanthus leaf decorations on the guard, tines, and pommel. Grips retain 90-95% original rayskin wrap and 100% double-twist brass wire wrap. Smooth, plum iron scabbard with part of original sword sling, very-good condition. **$1,400**

It is a simple pattern, three-branch brass guard without casting or engraved decoration, rayskin grip covering with twisted-copper wire wrap (excellent with just light wear). The scabbard is very pretty with a plum-brown finish on the steel (no dents) and attractive brass throat, ring mounts, and drag. The drag looks like a standard drag as found on staff or foot swords. The blade is plain with an unmarked ricasso. Very nice with no rust or edge nicks, and also never having been etched, overall in excellent condition. **$975**

Shows honest wear and is very nice, full grip wrap and twisted wire. The brass guard has the Ames eagle incorporated (embossed) into the quillon area on the guard, which is a signature feature on this Ames pattern. Gray steel blade with full etching that is characteristically very faint. The brass mounted steel scabbard is very good with a few dents in the brass drag, missing the brass throat. **$1,695**

U.S. Swords
Militia, Officer

1840-1850 spread-wing eagle sword by Ames Manufacturing, Chicopee, Massachusetts, traces of heavy patina on all the gilt mounts. Nice, clear etching on blade with traces of original frosting as well—still has the original sword knot on it, as well as the chain guards. Family history states this item was carried by Assistant Surgeon F. A. McVeigh of the 46th Virginia Infantry who served from September of 1863 McVeigh was from Loudoun County, Virginia. The 46th saw action from Norfolk through Northern Virginia, North and South Carolina, Georgia and Florida. **$4,500**

Circa 1840-1865 Ames militia officer's sword, nice carved ivory/bone grip with repair to minor hairline crack. Brass hilt retains 60% of original gilt finish and has chain from knight's head pommel to quillon. Blade is in good condition with good etching of eagle, stand of arms, and floral design, marked, "AMES MFG CHICOPPEE MASS." There is some age staining on blade, no pitting or scabbard. **$535**

Model 1832, Enlisted Man, Artillery

Very nice Ames short with scabbard, part of the buff belt with frog and wreath, part of the two-piece belt buckle, 19" double-edged blade with three fullers in excellent shape and has great patina. The blade is marked with an eagle and, "Unite- Stat--, 1842, JCB inspector," as well as with traces of, "N.P. Ames Co. Springfield." Cast brass hilt in great shape with eagle on both sides of the pommel. Large "W.A.T." inspector's mark (Captain W.A. Thornton). The brass has beautiful patina. Excellent black leather scabbard with brass throat, drag, frog stud. The leather is in very nice shape and still supple. **$961**

Import, Model 1832, Artillery

French-made artillery short sword complete with the perfect condition, matching scabbard. Blade marked with Paris maker's cartouche, excellent condition. **$395**

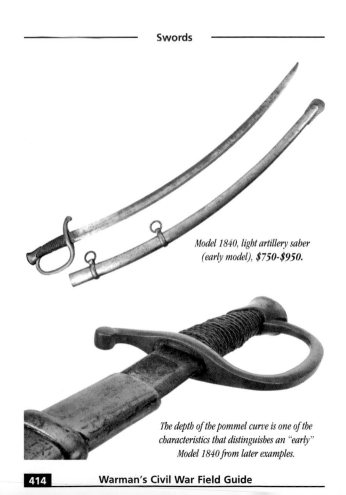

*Model 1840, light artillery saber
(early model), $750-$950.*

*The depth of the pommel curve is one of the
characteristics that distinguishes an "early"
Model 1840 from later examples.*

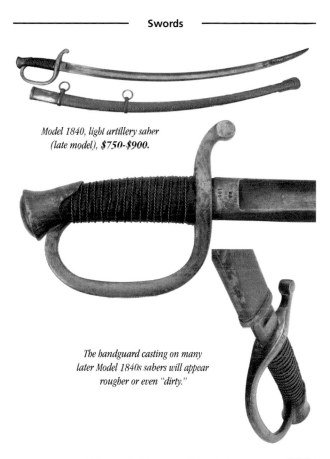

*Model 1840, light artillery saber
(late model), $750-$900.*

*The handguard casting on many
later Model 1840s sabers will appear
rougher or even "dirty."*

Very-fine condition, marked "329" on brass guard, blade is marked "1832" and "L" which is worn, but readable. **$350**

Model 1840, Musician

Blade is in very fine condition with no nicks or dings. The patina is gray to semi bright, with the usual age discoloring here and there, marked, "US/ AHC/1862," and the ricasso is marked with a very light stamping, "AMES MFG./CHICOPEE/MASS." The brass guard has a nice aged brass patina, no scabbard. **$295**

Sword without scabbard, brass is real nice as well as the Ames markings that include, "CABOTVILLE 1847," that makes this a Mexican War-dated piece. No scabbard is present and there is moderate pitting on the sword's tip. ... **$325**

Model 1840, NCO

The blade is sparkling bright, marked, "U.S. Ames 1864," cast brass guard is excellent with deep uncleaned patina. The leather scabbard is complete and in overall good sound condition. **$595**

Blade does not have a maker mark, but has a faint inspection mark and date, "US," and, "1863." The guard is inspection marked, "AHC," and there is the number seven on the pommel, guard, and grip. Nice patina on the guard, blade is bright with no pitting or rust, all the black paint is gone from the scabbard, missing screws. **$311**

Perfect leather scabbard, bright minty blade, boldly signed with full Ames firm marking, U.S. inspector's marks, and date of 1864. .... **$650**

The 31-3/4" straight blade is marked on the obverse ricasso, "U.S./DFM/1863," and the manufacturer's markings on the reverse ricasso are clearly stamped. The blade has a light-gray patina with some dried grease, should clean easily. The brass hilt is in fine shape with about 70% of the gilt remaining. The brass-mounted black leather scabbard is a reproduction in excellent condition. **$250**

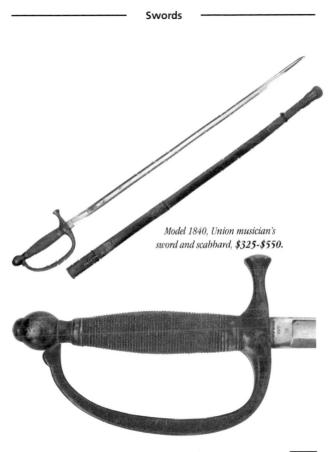

Model 1840, Union musician's sword and scabbard, $325-$550.

This sword has a mint blade with all the original factory luster, no nicks or dings, ricasso is marked, "U S/ G.W.C./1864," and the obverse is marked, "MADE BY/AMES MFG.CO./CHICOPEE / MASS." The brass guard has an uncleaned, soft brass patina, no scabbard. **$375**

Nice example of a pre-Civil War medical staff officer's sword. The flat, double-edged blade measures 28" long and 7/8" wide at the ricasso. It is profusely etched on the obverse side with floral designs, "U.S." and an eagle with outstretched wings and more floral designs. The etching runs for over half the blade length and shows much of its original luster and frosty contrast. Blade's reverse side is etched, "Medical. Staff," in a large panel. Above the panel is a nicely etched American flag with a liberty cap hanging from atop the flagpole. A couple of minor spots of dark staining. The heaviest staining is around the last "f" in the word "Staff." A couple very minor spots of pin-size pits between the etching's end and the blade tip. Unetched portion of blade shows 98% original full luster. No maker's marks on the blade. Nicely cast hilt retains about 80% of its original gold gilt. Applied silver "MS" on the front langet. At the top of the hilt, on both sides is a nicely cast eagle with outstretched wings. The dent-free, brass scabbard has a couple of minor scratches and pin-size nicks, mostly around the drag. Top mount lacks one ring mount. Brass scabbard shows the gilt only in protected areas, has a nice, soft patina. **$1,950**

Model 1850, Foot Officer

Manufactured by Horstmann & Sons. Blade is finely etched with standard U.S. motif with some salt and peppering, but no rust. Guard and pommel are heavily engraved with handle being German silver with triple-twisted wire wrap. Scabbard is iron with a dark-brown patina. A brass throat with heavily engraved brass hangers and drag. **$4,995**

Sword and scabbard by Horstmann, Philadelphia, circa 1862. Blade is about 90% mirror bright with crisp etching and frosting of U.S. military motifs.

Hilt retains 35% original gilt. Full sharkskin grip covering and wire wrap. Scabbard has minor flaking, but no cracks or breaks. **$1,350**

The blade is outstanding with 80% bright luster, superbly etched with military motifs, eagle, and "U.S." The guard has proper cast floral design with, "U.S.," incorporated into the casting. The scabbard is excellent. Steel finished with plum color, and adorned with attractive brass mounts. The brass has a delicate aged patina with great appeal. The pommel and guard are likewise absolutely beautiful with undisturbed aged patina. The rayskin grip covering is perfect and the triple wire wrap is intact with a small section repaired that is undetectable unless you look closely. The blade is signed on the ricasso, "PDL." **$1,950**

Superb color and patina, brass guard and scabbard mounts are truly beautiful, with a delicate undisturbed light age patina of uniform age and color. The leather grip coveting is near perfect with the fancy twisted wire wrap firmly in place. The wire is a double strand of twisted-brass wire flanked by single strands of brass wire. The blade is fine with bright steel color and etched with a widespread winged, federal eagle on one side and the letters, "U.S.," on the other. The spine is signed with a scarce Boston dealer's marking, "Palmers & Batchelders Boston." The leather scabbard is excellent with great life, strength, and finish. The finish is mostly smooth shiny leather, with just a few age crackles. The screw securing the drag is missing, and the previous owner put a spot of glue on it to hold the drag in place. **$1,295**

Presentation-grade infantry sword and scabbard, "Collins and Company, Hartford, Ct.," dated 1862. Etched blade includes a panel that reads, "Our Union Forever." Presentation plate on scabbard to, "Lt. W.H. Palmer from his Father, Feb. 1864." Palmer saw service in the 53rd Illinois Infantry at Corinth, Jackson, and Vicksburg. Also saw activity during the siege of Atlanta, Jonesboro, and the "March to the Sea." Above average blade, which shows honest light use and wear. **$5,000**

Model 1840, Union militia officer's sword,
$500-$700.

Presentation-grade sword and scabbard with exceptional gilt and overall condition with Tiffany-style statue hilt and perched golden American eagle on the pommel. Presented to, "Col. Jacob DeForest, 81st New York Infantry (Second Oswego Regiment; Mohawk Rangers)" in March of 1864. DeForest enlisted in August 1861 and was elected lieutenant colonel. He was promoted to colonel in July 1862, and served until he was dismissed for disability in September 1864. The 81st served in the Army of the Potomac, Department of North Carolina and Virginia, and Army of the James. **$20,000**

Model 1850, Officer, Field and Staff

Ames field and staff sword presented to, "Edmund Richard Pitman Shurly, Lt. Col March 1865 By his friends in England." Shurly enlisted May 4, 1861 with 26th New York Infantry and was severely wounded at Fredericksburg. Later, he served with the 8th Veteran Reserve Corp. Shurly was the last Commanding Officer at Camp Douglas, Ohio. He later went on to serve during the Indian Wars where he was again severely wounded at the Battle of Goose Creek, Wyoming. Shurly retired from active duty on December 2, 1868, due to wounds received in the line of duty, records included. **$10,000**

Presentation-grade field and staff sword presented to, "Lient. Col. Chas. H. Tay By the Enlisted Men of Co. E. 10th Reg. N.J.V. In the Field Maryland July 24, 1864." Records include copies of a letter from Tay's uncle asking for a, "Special Exchange of Prisoners," for his nephew with Confederate Col. George F. Maxwell and return letter to the uncle stating, "special exchanges are not approved except for such reasons of a public nature." **$11,500**

Excellent sword, crisp etching on blade and fine wide brass mounts on metal field scabbard. Original rayskin grip is easily 95% plus; full original wire. Company name stamped on guard, "J. Hoey, NYC." John Hoey supplied 1,800 cavalry sabers in 1861 under Federal contract and was known to sell many types of arms up through 1862 in New York City. Rare example in fine condition. **$2,500**

Civil War staff officer silver hilt sword. Exceptionally high, presentation-grade, silver-grip sword with eagle head quillon, "U.S.," in guard, German silver sheath with wide fancy brass mounts. Bright blade with crisp, "U.S.," and motifs. **$4,000**

Ames engraved sword presented to, "H. C. Keith 1, Lient. Co. B 121, N.Y.V. Aug. 1, 1862." Brass-mounted, blued metal, presentation-grade scabbard. Blade and etching are 95% with approx. 80% of gold gilt retained on hilt. **$6,500**

Presentation sword, blade by W. Clauberg with full etching of, "U.S.," eagles, and patriotic motifs. Silver hilt with original wire and a pommel cap inset with garnets and ruby in the filigree. The German silver scabbard has fancy high-relief cast mounts. **$5,000**

Fine sword and scabbard, presentation-grade, lots of hand engraving. Grip is 95% intact with minor wear in rayskin and a tiny portion missing on the top; wire is two strands of single and one of double twist, and 100%; blade is marked "Iron Proof" on the spine and etched with military motifs. Blade is gray-silver and uncleaned, showing use, but no nicks or pitting. Mounts are wide and scalloped, and deeply hand engraved. **$2,200**

Stunning presentation-grade inscribed sword made by Collins & Company, Hartford, Connecticut, and dated 1862 on the ricasso. Pressed leather scabbard is diamond shaped and a unique work of art, as are the gilt and strongly engraved patriotic mounts. Full original grip covering and wire, and superb inscription of "Presented to Capt. J.L. Yale by Co. K, 17th Vermont Volunteers, Sept. 23, 1864." Yale was originally mustered into the 13th Vermont in 1862, serving until 1863, then commissioned into the 17th Regiment seeing action at the Wilderness, Virginia, North Anna, Totopotomoy, Bethesda Church, Cold Harbor, Petersburg, Petersburg Mine, Weldon Railroad, Poplar Spring Church, and Hatchers Run. **$12,500**

Import, 37-1/2" overall with a nearly straight 33" blade. German blade handsomely etched with an eagle bearing an, "E Pluribus Unum," ribbon in panel on the right and broad, "U.S.," in panel on the left. Left ricasso stamped "Solingen," right ricasso has brass insert stamped, "proofed." Iron basket-style hilt with chiseled and engraved eagle, "U.S.," on guard. Iron pommel and back strap. Rayskin wrap nearly perfect and sword retains 100% of copper double-twisted wire. Excellent condition, bright iron scabbard. **$1,575**

Import, 37" overall with a slightly curved 31-1/2" brilliant blade. Blade heavily etched in a military motif 2/3rds of its length. On the right a stand of flags, surmounted by a stand of war trophies and a fine American eagle below beribboned, "E Pluribus Unum." Left side of the blade has, "PDL," within an oval maker's mark. Lunenschloss of Solingen at the ricasso. This is surmounted by a large American flag scrolled in acanthus leaves leading to an open panel with a large, block, "U.S." This is surmounted by a stand of arms and flags. Bright blade in excellent condition. Superb openwork brass guard with, "U.S.," set into the tines along with cast and chiseled floral and acanthus-leaf decoration. Grips retain 98-100% of the gray rayskin wrap and 80-90% of the gilt triple-twist wire wrap. Fine red-lacquered iron scabbard with gilt brass mounts at throat, drag, and rings. **$2,895**

Presentation-grade sword, French pattern, with exceptional brass scabbard with fine brass mounts; crisp and deep etching. Grip is rare white rayskin, 95% intact; full original wire as well. Hilt has fantastic eagle motif and form of an 18th Corps badge, exceptional example. **$4,500**

Model 1852, Officer, Naval

Produced by Horstmann & Sons with a Clauberg blade. Naval anchor and, "USN," etching on blade still sharp, but blade has some discoloration. Blade has no nicks or rust. Hilt has approximately 75% original gilt. Sharkskin grip has wear on back top toward pommel cap. Leather wire wrap is all there, but has some repair. Brass mounted leather scabbard is strong with some finish flaking on leather and a few minor dents on drag. **$1,895**

*Model 1850, Union, foot-officer's saber
with metal scabbard, $950-$1,800.*

Inscribed Civil War navy officer sword with generous original gilt and crisp blade etching, full original wire wrap, grip, and scabbard. Inscribed in guard, "Edgar K. Sellen." Sellen enlisted in September of 1864 from Hartford, Connecticut, as Acting Assistant Paymaster aboard the *bark Gemsbok* where he served until honorably discharged October 3, 1865. .... **$3,250**

Sword and scabbard clearly marked, "W.H. Horstmann," on ricasso. Fine scabbard with nice roped-brass mounts. Full original grip covering and wire wrap and beautiful etching. **$1,500**

Model 1860, Field and Staff

Straight blade staff sword carried by many officers and generals in the Civil War. Pattern stayed in use until the turn of the twentieth century. Sword has a very high-quality pommel, guard, and clamshell guard cast with great detail (eagle on pommel, leaves on "D" guard, eagle and flags on clam shell). The eagle and flags design on the clam-shell guard is highly detailed with a really crisp eagle's wings. The grip wrap is standard-style shagreen with double-twisted copper wire wrap. At the top and bottom of the grip are brass ferrules with intricate grooved designs. The blade has faint military etching and is signed, "W. Clauberg Solingen," with a standing knight motif marking associated with the 1860s and not the later period. The blade is quite wide with a subdued diamond cross section. The clamshell guard has one shell beautifully adorned with an eagle, and a smaller undecorated clamshell void of casting decorations. It is hinged identically to the 1840 foot officer's swords. The scabbard has high-quality, yet simple, ring mounts decorated with cast-raised floral designs, and the drag is totally symmetrical and is identical in design to those found on documented war-date inscribed specimens (the drag is made with open areas on the sides, so that there is a brass top and bottom which screws into the scabbard, but no brass on the side faces of the scabbard.) The scabbard is finished with a fine-smooth black paint that appears to be original to the date of manufacture. **$1,250**

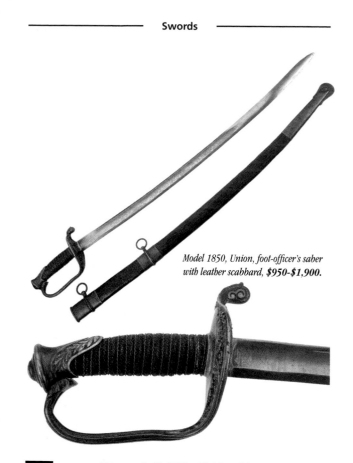

*Model 1850, Union, foot-officer's saber
with leather scabbard, $950-$1,900.*

Model 1850, non-regulation Union field and staff sword, $1,000-$1,250.

Though non-regulation, the cut-out federal eagle makes this sword a worthy addition to any Civil War collection.

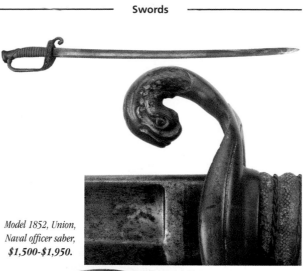

*Model 1852, Union,
Naval officer saber,
$1,500-$1,950.*

*The very delicate quillon
on the Model 1852 Naval
officer's sword testifies
to the quality of the
handguard's casting.*

CHAPTER 12

UNIFORMS

Little transmits the depth of personal association quite the way an original Union soldier's four-button blouse or a Confederate officer's kepi does. Highly sought after by collectors since the end of the Civil War, uniform groupings, jackets, coats, and headgear are both rare and expensive today.

Though it is oversimplifying to say that Union troops wore blue uniforms and Southern troops gray, it is not difficult to recognize that very few examples survived the war and the ensuing years. Collecting uniform pieces is an advanced form of the Civil War hobby, and it will become expensive in short order.

The upside of this, though, is that when pieces are found, they often have some sort of provenance. If you are looking for a representative piece such as a Union forage cap or a Confederate officer's frock coat, you will be able to find quality pieces available—provided you can afford the price tag!

Do exercise caution, though. As with any aspect of the hobby, fakes exist. Also, bear in mind that people have been reenacting the Civil War in an organized fashion for more than forty years. Some early reenacting clothing, if worn hard on the campaign and put away dirty, will begin to have some convincing looking patina. Learn to recognize appropriate period construction techniques, fabrics, and styles before making your first purchase. When one doesn't have the resources, either monetarily or physically, to collect Civil War uniforms, the next best thing is to collect insignia. Not

Confederate white drawers issued to Lieutenant Colonel Harrison C. Hobart, 21st Wisconsin Volunteer Infantry while he was a prisoner of war in Libby Prison, Richmond, VA. The cotton flannel drawers are hand sewn with black bone button closure. Such a utilitarian piece of clothing is rare. With strong provenance, such a garment would easily sell for $3,500-$4,500.

KP photo/Wisconsin Veterans Museum collection

taking up nearly the space or the capital that uniforms do, a person can spend a lifetime assembling a collection of shoulder boards, chevrons, corps badges, hatpins, or any number of other items intended to adorn a uniform.

One of the ironies of insignia collecting is that dug examples will often sell for more than non-dug examples. Take Union infantry hatpins, for example. A non-dug example from 1861-1865 with some patina is very hard to distinguish from a reproduction that spent ten years on a reenactor's cap. This is because the insignia on the reenactor's cap was struck from exactly the same dies as the original! Made from the same material, in the same design, only 150 years separates the original from the restrike. Now consider an excavated example of the same insignia. Resting underground for 150 years has some pretty noticeable effects on a brass hat pin that are awfully hard to replicate (apart from burying a reproduction for 150 years). Therefore, many collectors are willing to pay more for an item they know is original, rather than take a chance on a non-dug item.

Collecting Hints

Pros:
- Uniforms and uniform pieces are extremely personal and probably impact with some of the strongest emotional force of any Civil War artifacts.

- It is difficult, but not impossible or unlikely, to create fakes. A person familiar with nineteenth-century fashion and Civil War uniforms can usually spot questionable pieces.

- If you have the money, quality pieces are available.

Cons:

- Expensive! Uniforms, because of extreme delicate nature, have not survived in great numbers. When pieces become available, it is generally going to cost a lot to acquire them.

- Surviving examples of officer clothing far exceed the number of enlisted men's clothing. Therefore, it will be very difficult to assemble a representative Civil War soldier display complete with uniform.

- Uniforms are difficult to display. Special care has to be demonstrated in handling and storage. Proper storage materials can become costly.

Availability ★
Price ★★★★★
Reproduction Alert ★★★

Union issued thin brass insignia of the US Arms worn by infantry. The distance between the National Eagle wing tips is 2", $110.

KP photo/Wisconsin Veterans Museum collection

These stamped brass crossed cannons were worn on the headgear of artillery soldiers. Clean examples will sell for around $85-$150.

Headgear, Confederate

Chapeau de Bras, Officer, Infantry

Confederate "Chapeau de Bras" worn by Surgeon Henry DeSassussure Fraser. Les Jensen, Curator of the Museum of the Confederacy, calls this hat the, "rarest piece of Confederate headgear known to exist," as it was made early in the war conforming to South Carolina style and regulation. Hat is made of black beaver with a large black cockade sewn directly to the front. In addition, it is accompanied by its original box marked, "C.S. Army." An incredible rarity, this hat was worn by Surgeon Fraser, as a doctor in Anderson's Division, when he was captured on July 5th, 1863, during the Gettysburg campaign. (Les Jensen letter of authenticity). **$35,000**

Kepi

Enlisted Man, Artillery, Confederate Artillery Kepi worn by Private Robert Royall, Richmond Howitzers and signed by him inside the cap, "R RoyallRm'd Howitzers." He not only signed his name , but he also drew crossed cannons and, "Richmond Howitzers," inside the cap as well. A marvelous and historically important Confederate Artillery kepi gray wool cadet gray cap with a red band on top with confederate infantry "block" I pattern buttons both backmarked, "Extra Rich." Royall enlisted in the 1st Company of Richmond Howitzers in 1861 and served throughout the war. He fought briefly with the 23rd Virginia in 1864. He surrendered at Burkeville, Virginia, on April 24, 1865. Another identical kepi that belonged to Royall is now on display in the Museum of the Confederacy in Richmond. An extremely rare Confederate artillery man's cap made in Richmond, Capitol of the Confederacy, and worn by a member of one of the elite units of the Confederate Army of Northern Virginia. (Accompanied by Les Jensen letter of authenticity and research, with restoration by Jessica Hack.) **$35,000**

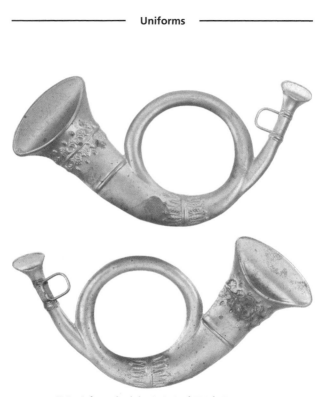

Union infantry, bugle hat insignia, $125-$150.

Enlisted Man, Infantry

Rare Confederate butternut kepi lined with red and white cotton checkered
print. This kepi is in remarkably good condition, and is a classic early war-
style Confederate headgear. Made with all Confederate materials, this kepi
with oilcloth chinstrap and intricate side buttons is a true rarity.
(Ex-Bill Turner Collection. Les Jensen letter of authenticity.) **$25,000**

Officer

Borderline pristine line officer kepi, early war pattern. Virtually no moth
damage, full silk lining, tarred linen sweatband, and incredible rows of
quatrefoil indicating the rank of major or lieutenant colonel. Buttons are
typical early pattern-lined shield eagle staffs. **$20,000**

Officer, Artillery

Confederate kepi worn by Captain Edward Owen of the famed Washington
Artillery of New Orleans. This attractive kepi has a red body with a blue
band around the base in accordance with Confederate uniform regulations.
Captain Owen was the brother of Colonel William Miller Owen who wrote
the acclaimed regimental history of the unit, *In Camp and Battle with the
Washington Artillery of New Orleans.* Exceedingly rare as an identified
Confederate artillery kepi worn by a member of the premier artillery regiment
in the Civil War; the Washington Artillery of New Orleans. (Les Jensen letter of
authenticity). **$30,000**

General Officer

Confederate general's kepi that is a beautiful dark blue wool with four rows
of gold braid signifying general's rank. The black leather visor is in good
condition and there is a red, black, and gray lining in the inside of the
crown, which could probably help identify the maker. (Les Jensen letter of
authenticity.) **$45,000**

Coats, Vests; Confederate

Frock, Officer, Georgia

Blue gray with red collar and cuffs and with Georgia State seal buttons, made in 1861 by Philadelphia tailor. **$15,000**

Frock, Officer, Infantry

Single star on each side of collar denoting rank of major, two rows of seven buttons and blue pointed cuffs. **$40,000**

Officer, Navy

Identified to a member of Whiteside's Naval Battalion of Columbus, Georgia, a period pencil note originally attached to the inside of the coat reads, "CONFEDERATE UNIFORM WORN BY LOUIS PHILLIPE HENOP." Research, all of which of course accompanies the coat, identifies Henop as an employee of the Columbus Naval Iron Works and as a member of this local naval militia battalion. The unit was activated and participated in the siege of Savannah. Subsequently, Henop was captured and paroled at Columbus, Georgia. The coat is of heavy cadet gray wool, double breasted with seven-button front. All buttons are Federal staff eagles with identical "Extra Quality" backmarks. All are original to the coat. Superb balloon sleeve cut. Body is lined with brown tabby-weave cotton, lightly padded in breast area. Tail pockets and breast pockets lined with unbleached osnaburg, as are the sleeves. Identical staff buttons used on the tails, though the coat never had cuff buttons. The coat's overall condition is truly remarkable, just some very minor nap mothing and a few very small seam openings. Shows no signs of ever having shoulder straps and doubtless saw very little use. The rolled collar coat was of course regulation for every Navy officer, but was also favored by many Army officers. Complete with the original belt and 1851 eagle belt plate with silver wreath, over the shoulder sling, but no provisions for sword hangers. Belt itself is unquestionably of C.S. manufacture. Coat is accompanied by a four-page letter from a leading authority on C.S. uniform/fabric/construction attesting to the authenticity of every detail of the coat. **$22,500**

Vest, Confederate, Officer

Single-breasted Confederate officer's vest is made of gray wool, lined with tan
cotton twill. It originally had nine buttons, but the top button is missing.
It has eight remaining Virginia state seal buttons including, "Mitchell &
Tyler/Richmond," "Scovill," "Extra Quality," and, "Horstmann," backmarks.
The reverse is made of black, glazed cotton twill. The pocket linings are
completely intact and are made of the same cotton twill as the vest's reverse,
half belt adjuster on the reverse is broken, tan cotton twill inner lining is in
excellent condition, with exception of collar and hem wear resulting from
much use. The style and cut is the standard three-pocket vest: an upper watch
pocket in the left breast and two at the waist. Waist pockets have scalloped
flaps with whipped interior eyelets, pocket buttons are missing, pocket linings
completely intact and made of same cotton twill as vest's reverse. **$9,900**

Headgear, Union

Cap

Enlisted Man, Model 1858, Artillery

Very solid example with fine silk lining and lots of padding, indicating high-
grade custom tailoring with original, full gilt eagle, "A" side buttons.
Exceptional gilt artillery officer false-embroidered insignia also on front of
cap. Cap has scattered moth or insect damage mainly on crown. **$2,850**

Enlisted Man, Model 1858, Sharpshooter

Excellent example of the Civil War Berdan-type forage cap as used by U.S.
Sharpshooters. Early war, double-seam construction with tarred inner
crown lining and original side buttons and chinstrap! Deep forest green,
now faded slightly. Upon close inspection in the protected seam areas, it is
green. Compared with another known and identified Berdan cap in a private
collection, crown construction and seam allowance are identical. **$7,500**

Enlisted Man, Model 1858

6.5" up the rear, 4.75" up the front, and 5.5" diameter crown. Generally
excellent, clean, and tight. Made from typical "shoddy" wool which shows
the under weave upon the least amount of wear to the nap. Hat body has two
holes in the right rear, one 3/4", one 1/2", with some fraying around the edge.
Crown has a couple worm holes (tracks) that go through the fabric. These
holes need to be backed, to match the rest of the undamaged hat. Visor is
flat, with edge binding, and dark green underside. Several wide heat cracks
in tar finish. Sweatband is thin leather, finished with a thick brown tar-like
substance. Interior lined with brown-black polished cotton, sweat stained, and
frayed along the lower edge on one side and a little on top of the other side.
Typical burlap stiffener inside the sweatband. **$2,250**

Dark blue wool with a bound leather visor, leather chinstrap with eagle side
buttons, and infantry horn insignia with "2" and "E"on the top. Has polished
brown cotton lining with drawstring top. Complete with leather sweatband,
few tiny nips. **$785**

Forage cap, a.k.a., a "Bummer's Cap." Overall excellent condition with full
lining, sweatband, and chinstrap. Excellent condition with just the smallest
amount of moth repair. **$2,950**

Standard-pattern blue wool "Bummer's" or "Forage" cap, having flat crown and
black polished cotton lining with original label reading, "G & S/No. 3/N.Y."
Leather sweatband and tarred leather brim intact. Leather chinstrap with
infantry buttons present. Crossed sabers cap device on crown. Condition is
very good. Shows a few scattered repairs and minor mothing. Lining shows
moderate wear with minor seam separations. Cap device is probably a later
addition. **$1,725**

KP photo/Wisconsin Veterans Museum collection

Model 1858 uniform hat ("Hardee hat") worn by Philander B. Wright, 1st Sgt., Co. C, 2nd Reg., Wis. Vol. Inf., Iron Brigade, at the Battle of Gettysburg. The hat is made of 1/16" thick black fur felt and has a blue infantry cord with tassels at base of crown. Beneath is a 1/4" black silk grosgrain ribbon. It has a 3" wide brim with a double row of stitching at 4-1/2 stitches per inch along the edge and 5-1/2" tall cylindrical crown. A brass number "2" on red wool disk is sewn in front with a brass letter "C" below. Two brass grommets have been inserted on the sides of the disk, and a third grommet in the center of the back, $25,000.

Kind of ratty, but still a great relic. Classic late-war forage cap, double-welted bands up rear seam, brown polished cotton side linings open to expose a tarred or oilcloth circular stiffener in crown. Wool faded blue, chinstrap with eagle side buttons present as is sweatband. Body has a few moderate moth holes. Crown has a couple large holes, visor has sewn, bound edge. **$795**

Officer, Model 1858

Cap has a great look being 5" from the top to the brim. The color is a rich blue with a few very small moth nip holes including one small moth hole on the seam in the rear of the cap. Retains its original chinstrap and bound brim. Label inside reads, "DICKSON/STATE-STREET/ ALBANY," and, "SEMPER FIDELIS." The silk lining is no longer present. **$2,600**

Officer, "Smoking"

Blue velvet with yellow rick-rack trim, an embroidered green, black, and yellow sideband, and a long yellow tassel. Worn in camp when officer was off duty. A nice example in excellent condition. **$125**

Hat

Officer

Simply superb Union officer's slouch hat with full, original trim. Magnificent officer-embroidered infantry insignia and "Hardee" cockade device. Fully embossed maker mark, "Tomes, Melvain & Company," noted high quality New York outfitters. Silk lining virtually flawless, only minor area of deterioration. Full, super tall sweatband has some loose stitching, but mainly in place. Original heavy bullion acorn hat cord! Oral provenance states hat was worn by Fred L. Atwood, 1st Lieutenant, Battery F, Pennsylvania Light Artillery, "Hamptons Battery." This battery was organized at Williamsport, Pennsylvania, December 7, 1861, to serve three years. Atwood was wounded at Chancellorsville and present at Gettysburg. Atwood died in 1871. .... **$15,000**

KP photo/Wisconsin Veterans Museum collection

Dark blue wool forage cap features an embroidered infantry bugle insignia with regiment number "2" in the center. The cap was worn by Col. Lucius Fairchild, 2nd Wisconsin Infantry during Gettysburg campaign. Because of the association with the famous Iron Brigade, this cap, which would normally sell for around $2,850 is valued at $18,000. This is a prime example of how provenance can affect the price of an item.

Officer, Cavalry

Black fur felt with 3-1/8" brim bound with silk braid, 4-1/2" crown dented front to rear, 3/8" silk hat band, 2-3/8" high black leather sweat band. The front of the crown has a gold bullion insignia on black velvet consisting of crossed cavalry sabers surmounted by a "1" in silver colored metal. The hat has three holes in the crown, the hatband is partially loose, but intact, the sweatband is partially loose with about 30% missing, the binding on the brim shows wear. Despite these shortcomings, a few minutes work with needle and thread will bind up the loose ends and give this hat a quite presentable appearance, would judge the overall condition as very good. **$1,200**

Enlisted Man, Model 1858, Cavalry

Standard pattern "Hardee" hat of black felt. On the inside there is a brown label reading, "U.S. Army/Extra/Manufacture/3." Hat has an enlisted man's yellow wool cord and cavalry device. Condition is very good, though it does show a few insignificant small splits in brim edge and minor repairs. Sweatband is intact with minor seam separations. Hat device may be a later addition.
....**$2,875**

Enlisted Man, Sailor

Extremely rare Civil War enlisted man's hat as seen in all the photos of the period. This all-wool example is in pristine condition with fantastic embroidered star design on the top. The lining is cloth with a black and gold pattern. It has the original bow attached and part of the silk ribbon around the outside. There is no label. Accompanying the hat is an old handwritten note stating that, "these effects belonged to my father who fought in the Civil War," dated 1926. ....**$4,995**

This all-wool example is in pristine condition with fantastic embroidered star design on the top. The lining is all cloth with a black and gold pattern. It has the original bow attached and part of the silk ribbon around the outside. There is no label. **$5,595**

KP photo/Wisconsin Veterans Museum collection

*This dark blue wool Model 1858 forage cap was Union army issued. The crescent-shaped visor is 2" wide and is made of heavy glazed leather, **$2,850.***

KP photo/Wisconsin Veterans Museum collection

This is a non-issue, private purchase hat worn by Maj. Frederick C. Winkler, 26th Wisconsin Volunteer Infantry. The hat was damaged in battle near Marietta, Georgia, June 23, 1864. In a letter home, Maj. Winkler wrote that a bullet "tore out a large piece of the brim and passed within half an inch of my head...Everybody looks at my hat, and dozens of men have stopped and looked and speculated upon the Major's close call. My nice hat, isn't it too bad?" **$9,500.**

Kepi
Chasseur

Identified Civil War officer Chasseur-pattern kepi very nice example with positive identification to Captain John Folcy, who served from 1861 until 1864, in the service of the United States. Cap is maker's marked as well, and missing the chinstrap. Comes in original box as found, with numerous calling cards of Captain Foley as a resident of New York. Research records included in portfolio format. **$4,500**

Absolutely wonderful war-dated officer's blue wool cap with quilted silk lining which bears the maker's mark, "James Y. Davis / 356 Penn. Ave. / Washington, D.C." The body of the cap is beautiful midnight blue wool in excellent condition with just a couple tiny moth nips. The lining is 95% intact. The sweatband is all there with one break in it. The visor is a little loose and could use a stitch or two to tighten it up, as is the case with part of the black piping. The chinstrap is missing, but the small kepi staff buttons are still present on the cap's sides. The cap is piped with narrow black quatrefoil piping on the top of the crown. It is circled with the same piping around the band of the cap, and up the sides of the capion. **$2,650**

New York, Zouave

Fine State of New York chasseur-style kepi, often associated with Zouave units or artillery officers. Beautiful deep blue wool body with scarlet trim, adorned with gilt New York state seal buttons. Lining is a bit tattered, but 95% intact. **$1,850**

Officer, Artillery

Blue wool with unbound leather visor, leather chinstrap and artillery officer's eagle, "A" buttons. Cardboard crown stiffener with black oilcloth covering, tan-polished lining, and deep leather sweatband. Has 1/4" hole in crown where insignia was attached. **$645**

Officer, Cavalry

Fine quality chasseur-pattern Cavalry Civil War officer's kepi with full chinstrap and virtually no moth or insect damage to the body. Sweatband intact, but many stitches are rotten and it is loose. Black silk quilted lining heavily padded, typical of a custom-tailored kepi, and is tattered and fragile. Illegible traces of gilt-embossed maker name remain. Cavalry "C" buttons in excellent form. Fine example, rich, deep blue broadcloth wool construction. .. **$2,450**

Officer, Engineer

Embroidered wreath and castle device affixed to the front. Chinstrap with buttons still present. **$5,500**

Officer, New York, Infantry

Civil War New York infantry M1859-pattern kepi with sky-blue trim, New York buttons, and rare New York front badge plate, all original and pre-1863, according to Les Jensen, former curator of the Museum of the Confederacy in Virginia. Sound overall, a few minor moth nips and some cracking to leather sweatband. Upper crown properly padded, lining fully intact. **$2,100**

Coats, Overcoats, Jackets, Trousers; Union

Coat, Frock
Enlisted Man

One of the rarest Civil War uniforms is the nine-button enlisted man's frock coat. This particular example is clearly maker and inspector marked in the sleeves, and there is an identification written in the left sleeve. Definitely issued and worn during the Civil War, not a surplus costume company coat. Overall condition excellent, only minor signs of wear in lining and a few tiny moth holes not detracting from condition. Buttons appear original and are Scovill marked; the light blue piping is all present and original. ... **$12,500**

Officer, Infantry

Uniform and effects of Captain VanDerzee, 44th and 25th New York Volunteers.
Outstanding set of material owned by one officer. This group includes his
regulation single-breasted line officer's frock coat with straps, two vests
(one blue wool army example and one summer weight linen example), a
fine 8" x10" oval albumen photo of him in uniform and armed, his bullion
embroidered officer's eagle side plate hat insignia, his GAR membership
medal, a loose portion of another medal, a wonderful 44th NYV GAR
miniature flag made up to look like a 5th Corps Headquarters flag, and a
Congressional record document. The coat is a regulation example in excellent
condition (some wear on the collar top), with eagle infantry officer's buttons
and double border bullion embroidered captain of infantry straps. The coat
has classic long skirts, ballooned sleeve elbows, functional cuff, and rich
quilted standard lining. It is as typical an example from the 1862-1863
period as can be found. The blue vest is outstanding, being the standard
army pattern with small NY state buttons on the front and brown polished
cotton back. The summer weight vest is a civilian example worn by him
during warm weather. The embroidered Hardee hat eagle side plate is an
outstanding example of the "tin back" variety covered with brown polished
cotton on the reverse. It retains both attaching loops as well as the brass
clips used to secure it to his hat. The albumen photo shows VanDerzee full
standing wearing this frock coat, and also sporting a regulation sash and foot
officer's sword. Excellent clarity, contrast, and condition housed in a period
oval walnut frame. This material was owned by Captain John VanDerzee of
the 25th New York, who served at the battles of Yorktown, Hanover Court
House, Mechanicsville, Gaines Mill, Malvern Hill, 2nd Bull Run, Seven Days
Battles, Antietam, Snickers Gap, Hartwood Church, Fredericksburg, Richards
Ford, and Chancellorsville! VanDerzee had previous service as a private in the
44th NY Volunteers during 1861 and early 1862. A superb and historic lot of
material. **$9,500**

Officer, Cavalry

Uniform and insignia of Captain Samuel N. Titus, 11th Pennsylvania Cavalry. The left sleeve bears a professionally printed (on cloth) label which reads, "T. McCormick / Merchant Tailor / Baltimore / 149 Baltimore Street." This label is inscribed in beautiful, ancient brown-ink script with the owner's name and location, "Lt. Titus / Portsmouth, Va." Included is the regulation Civil War line officer's frock coat of deep midnight blue wool in excellent condition, which has matching cavalry officer's eagle "C" buttons down the front (one missing), and small-size buttons on each cuff. It also has a pair of exquisite double-border, bullion-embroidered cavalry captain's shoulder straps on each shoulder with rich yellow velvet centers. The coat has a richly quilted and padded chest lining, wide elbows on each sleeve, and classic long skirts. In addition to the coat is included Titus' officer's embroidered crossed saber hat insignia on velvet in an oval with wire edge border and tin back covered with brown polished cotton, as well as his officer's eagle side plate (for the Hardee hat) also made of embroidered bullion on velvet with wire edge border and tin back covered with brown polished cotton. Includes a wealth of important historical and genealogical background which states that Titus enlisted as a private and rose through the ranks. He was wounded on October 7, 1864, in a fight on the Darbytown Road near Richmond by a gunshot wound through his right elbow, and he was taken prisoner at that time. He spent a short time in Libby Prison and then was exchanged. He nearly missed his appointment to major due to the fact that he had been wounded and captured, but his brigade commander saw to it that the promotion was indeed made. The regiment served in Virginia throughout the war, and one newspaper article states that Titus actually witnessed the battle between the Merrimac and Monitor. The 11th Cavalry was stationed at Portsmouth, Virginia, for much of 1862 and 1863 doing much raiding in southern Virginia and North Carolina, and fought at the Battles of Reams Station, Stony Creek, Petersburg, and others. **$15,500**

*These ornate buckskin trousers were worn by Lt. Charles King while serving with the 5th US Cavalry. The trousers, decorated with white, red, pink, blue and yellow glass beads, were given to King by "Buffalo Bill" Cody probably after the war, although there are documented instances of some officers wearing flamboyant trousers ranging from buckskin to leopard skin, **$18,000.***

KP photo/Wisconsin Veterans Museum collection

KP photo/Wisconsin Veterans Museum collection

Union army issued, regulation gray officer's uniform coat for militia.
The coat has captain's bars of black velvet sewn on each shoulder and
is lined with quilted brown polished cotton, ***$12,000.***

Officer, Infantry

Double-breasted lieutenant colonel's frock coat and shoulder straps in overall very good condition. Top of collar shows real wartime wear. Body is double-breasted with two rows of seven Union staff buttons down each side. Three staff buttons on each cuff and four staff buttons on tails. Shoulder straps very worn, single border lieutenant colonel examples with sky-blue centers. Coat has repaired tear on left shoulder (well-done) and scattered small moth holes and a couple larger holes, one on right cuff and one on the back. Lining is classic green quilted silk blend. **\$4,500**

Standard grade U.S. Civil War infantry frock coat, excellent original condition with minor mothing and a slight stain on upper left arm. Has wonderful gilt eagle "I" buttons of a line officer and fine double embroidered 2nd lieutenant of infantry straps. Lining is intact above average. **\$4,720**

Officer, Surgeon

Very high quality Civil War surgeon's frock coat belonging to Major Otis Humphrey, purchased originally from the family and passed through the collection of a well-known uniform collector. Comes with a letter from the seller and a letter from "The Horse Soldier of Gettysburg" and the original purchaser guaranteeing the authenticity and detailing the history of the coat. This is a dark-blue wool, double-breasted frock coat, unquestionably Civil War period. It has a plain dark green cotton lining, quilted breast area, plain white sleeve lining, and wide balloon sleeve, all the standard features of a Civil War frock. There is no moth damage and all the buttons are present, ("D. Evans" backmarks). The shoulder boards are for a major, and are not "MS" type. They have been added later. Dr. Humphrey enlisted at Lowell, Massachusetts and served as major with the 6th Massachusetts Infantry. He was surgeon in charge of the hospital at New Orleans, Louisiana and remained on duty until the end of the war. His records accompany the coat.
....**\$6,500**

Jacket, Enlisted Man
22nd New York Volunteer Infantry

Rare and custom-made enlisted man's jacket of the 22nd New York Infantry-
National Guard. It is single-breasted with New York state seal buttons made by
"Scovill Mf'g Co. Waterbury," with fancy blue trim, particularly on the jacket's
back, where it is very ornate. The collar has blue stripes, as well as similar
designs on each shoulder made to hold shoulder boards with a flat pocket
at right along with a custom made belt loop and polished green linen lining
inside. Organized at Troy, New York, the 22nd became part of the Army of
the Potomac and fought throughout Virginia against Lee's Army of Northern
Virginia, losing 102 men during the war. Their original uniforms were
strawberry-trimmed gray, which looked too much like Confederate artillery
uniforms. Therefore, they adopted this new style of uniform in the Chasseur
pattern. With their new style uniforms they were also issued two-band Enfield
rifles with saber bayonets, excellent condition. **$9,500**

Artillery

Civil War issue artillery shell jacket that is fully lined and bearing an inspector's
mark in the sleeve with size marking. All original red piping is present. All
buttons intact and appear with matching patina. No mothing nor stains.
Some wear to piping on rear of neck area likely from actual use.
....**$2,250**

Crisp and solid example of the regulation Union army artilleryman's coat
with 12-button front, red piped collar, cuffs, and edge. Full body lining
(slight fraying), full sleeve lining with inspector's stamp. 100% original and
complete. **$1,950**

Beautiful Civil War artillery shell jacket, vivid crimson piping and full lining.
Clear maker and inspector's marks in sleeve. **$2,650**

Cavalry

Mint example of the regulation cavalry troopers short jackets piped in yellow with 12 buttons down the front, two on each side of the collar, and two on each cuff. Bright midnight blue wool body is perfect with great color and no moth damage. This is complete with the full body lining, and the white muslin sleeve linings with clear-size number and inspector's mark. Absolutely top notch in all respects. **$2,950**

Regulation dark navy-blue wool coat body with dark yellow piping, 12 eagle buttons down front, two on each collar, and two at each cuff. Tall pillows are still in place on the rear. Light tan lining with some scattered thin spots intact. Marked in left shoulder lining with fairly legible ink stamp reading, "JOHN BOYLAN & CO./NEWARK, N.Y.," plus size mark "1." There is one 1/8" moth hole. **$3,495**

U.S. cavalry jacket in need of repair, 100% real jacket that has had some pieces removed. The jacket itself is in very good condition. The collar was cut down, the liner was removed, some of the burlap is still there. The buttons were removed and replaced with half round ones. There is only yellow tape on the right sleeve. **$323**

Enlisted Man, Zouave

Original Civil War Zouave jacket recently found in upstate New York. This pattern is standard issue to units such as the 5th New York, Duryea's Zouaves. Has inspector and quartermaster issue stamps in the sleeves! Unfortunately, the owner's name was removed from the inside by cutting out a section of fabric, scattered wear and insect damage. **$22,000**

Overcoat
Enlisted Man, Infantry

1851 pattern infantry overcoat manufactured by E. Tracy, Philadelphia, Pennsylvania. Coat is complete with outer cape and six original eagle cape buttons and five original eagle coat buttons; and two collar closing hooks. Kersey blue color has turned somewhat green, due to age, but original color can be seen in protected areas. Coat has some staining on front, which is slightly noticeable and a small hole in left front cape panel. Two small holes are on the back under the cape. Hem has some fraying with four tears approx. 2" long with old sewn field repairs. Lining is in excellent condition with good maker marks. Owner's name is lightly on the inside lining, and appears to be, "A Pelky." Sleeve markings inside are "E. Tracy Phila. Oct 21st, 64." This contract was for 100,000 infantry greatcoats. This coat is in good to very-good condition overall. **$6,595**

This fine enlisted man's infantry overcoat is identified to Private Franklin Denison of the 12th Vermont Infantry. It is made from satinette (the material used early in the war, only a few are known). The overall condition is excellent with a few minor moth holes, mostly under the cape and not visible. The coat has a red wool lining and is clearly marked with inspector's stamps and Denison's name on a sewn in label. Private Franklin Denison was born at Royalton, Vermont and enlisted at the age of 20 in Burlington on August 14, 1862. This regiment was present at the Battle of Gettysburg. Copies of the muster roll show his muster-out date of July 14, 1863. .... **$8,900**

Enlisted Man, Mounted

Fine original specimen once the property of the great military artist George Woodbridge who used it as the basis for his illustrations. It comes with a letter from Peter Hlinka attesting to this, dated in 1964, when he sold it to the collector who just recently released it from his collection. Heavy sky-blue Kersey wool, double breasted, with long cape. Six buttons are in a double row down the front and the cape has 12 buttons, 3-1/2" cuffs. Belt across the back, threaded through single wide belt loop. Upper body lined in a brown fabric abrasive to the touch. Off-white arm lining. "Size 3" stamp in right shoulder with a faded contractor stamp. Something on each shoulder is inked-out. Left shoulder has partial, illegible inspector's stamp. Condition is clean, excellent. One worn edge (bit on edge of cape) and 2" of seam needs to be resewn where the collar joins coat at edge. Couple of subtly faded spots, no mothing or frayed lining. **$8,450**

Regulation enlisted man's mounted sky-blue greatcoat with Connecticut identification. Fine condition with full lining, all the buttons, and only a couple minor moth nips. Nicely marked in the sleeves with maker-inspector. This was worn by a soldier in the 2nd Connecticut Light Artillery. **$6,850**

Very rare, standard-issue enlisted cavalry greatcoat, or overcoat. Unlike the infantry ones, this is a double-breasted garment. Standard eagle buttons and wonderful sky-blue wool body. Full lining has some field repairs as well as some light restoration, but overall extremely nice example of a very difficult item to find. Inspector marking in sleeves circa 1862. Full adjusting belt, outer cuffs, and cape. **$5,600**

Trousers

Enlisted Man, Zouave

Pants have "dished top" waistband and a slight reversed dish to the cuffs. Has a 1" woven gold bullion leg stripe. Red painted bone buttons (several of suspender buttons missing). A few scattered moth holes, but rates as excellent.
.... **$300**

Officer

Beautiful quality fabric, with extremely tight weave, thick, and with a rich, soft touch in one direction, and abrasive if rubbed the opposite way. Extraordinarily beautiful color between sky-blue and medium blue perhaps best called "Saxony Blue." Narrow waistband, bone suspender buttons inside, and tin-backed brass on the outside and down the fly. 1/8" golden cord welt down each outer seam. Side pockets along the side seam, and belt in back. Fully lined on top and at cuffs. Large size, clean, and in excellent condition showing light use. 1" tear at top of left pocket. **$1,950**

This 12-button front, blue wool uniform jacket with brown cotton lining features white cotton muslin sleeve lining and is trimmed with scarlet worsted wool twill lace, $2,450.

KP photo/Wisconsin Veterans Museum collection

One-piece Union Army issued cotton shirt worn by David Hotchkiss, Co. C, 13th Wisconsin Volunteer Infantry. Rectangular collar folded at top with single button and buttonhole, $3,500.

Drawers, Officer

Cotton, identified, and seldom encountered, pair of Civil War period drawers made of a cotton flannel and muslin combination, pieced together by both hand and machine. Front has a two-button closure and the back adjusts with a cotton tape tie. These drawers are very similar to the set pictured in *Echoes of Glory*. They were purchased in a lot of early clothing from upstate New York, and are inscribed in the waistband front "Col. W or N (?) C. Raulston (?) N.Y. Vol." Drawers in excellent condition, some minor yellowing and some minor stains but no tears or holes. Measures 37" from waist to cuff, waist measures about 30". **$405**

Uniform, Officer
Infantry

Exceptional, identified officer's frock coat and sky-blue pants. Coat is the standard nine-button with eagle "I" buttons, polished green lining and deep blue broadcloth construction. Captain of line (infantry) bars neatly sewn on, obviously a custom-tailored jacket—a lot of detailed and neat hand stitching throughout. Pants are typical, soft-brushed wool in sky-blue, with adjusting buckle on reverse with patent date of 1855. Button fly and slash front pockets. Bottom cuffs reinforced to reduce wear (worn with boots). Coat belonged to Captain Reynolds Laughlin, Company A, 103rd Pennsylvania Infantry. Laughlin mustered in service in September of 1861 and served until January of 1863. His unit saw action at Yorktown, Williamsburg, Fair Oaks, Seven Days Battles, Malvern Hill, Suffolk, and the 1862 Battle of Kinston, North Carolina, losing 53 officers and enlisted men killed in action during the term of service. Great condition overall, positive ID inked in upper sleeve area. **$7,500**

Quartermaster

Civil War Quartermaster uniform grouping belonging to a 164th Ohio Infantry officer. Exceptional grouping includes his beautiful frock coat with eagle "I" infantry buttons and super rare quartermaster bars; his vest; his trousers with blue officer welt down leg; his sword; his fine belt rig with eagle buckle (name inscribed on reverse), and officer's silk sash. Azariah C. Baker enlisted on May 02, 1864, as a Quartermaster. On May 11, 1864, he was commissioned into the Field & Staff of the 164th Ohio Infantry. He was mustered out on August 27, 1864, at Cleveland, Ohio. This regiment was organized at Camp Cleveland, May 11, 1864, to serve for 100 days. It was composed of the 49th Regiment, Ohio National Guard, from Seneca County and the 54th Battalion, from Summit County. On May 14, it left Cleveland and proceeded (via Dunkirk, Elmira, Harrisburg, and Baltimore) to Washington, D.C. on the 17th. It took position in the defenses on the south side of the Potomac and during its 100 days' service garrisoned Forts Smith, Strong, Bennett, Haggarty, and other forts. At the expiration of its term of enlistment, it returned to Cleveland and was mustered out on Aug. 27, 1864. His widow, Harriet K. Baker, applied for a pension on February 01, 1888, from the state of Ohio. **$22,000**

"**There was a man come by and told Chet that the secesh was coming...they come in sight and lo, they had the uniform of the U.S.A.—it was the Union soldiers.**"

—*Sirene Bunten*
French Creek, Virginia

Union Army officer's medium blue satinette trousers. The wool trousers have one flap pocket left and right with one watch pocket on right side. Trousers have 4" by 10" buckram reinforced lower legs and four button fly, black japanned buttons. There are also three wood-backed tin suspender buttons. The rear exterior features a waist adjuster buckle, *$1,950.*

KP photo/Wisconsin Veterans Museum collection

KP photo/Wisconsin Veterans Museum collection

Union Army sky blue wool vest with standing collar, three-slash pockets,
15 brass stud buttons and tan cotton back. The vest is typical of those
issued to enlisted Union soldiers, $1,100.

*Blue wool vest worn by Col. Lucius Fairchild, 2nd Wisconsin Infantry,
at the battle of Gettysburg. Col. Fairchild was wounded in battle. Note that the
left shoulder of the vest is cut. A surgeon needed to remove the vest prior
to amputating Fairchild's arm,* **$15,000.**

KP photo/Wisconsin Veterans Museum collection

Insignia

Corps Badges

U.S., 2nd

A red clover leaf (1st Division) with twisted gold wire borders and a blue wool backing. **$475**

Original 2nd Corps badge, all wool with just enough mothing to assure authenticity. Approximately 2" x 2". **$300**

U.S., 3rd

A silver-plated diamond, red enamel center, twisted wire border, pin backed, excellent condition. **$350**

Army of the Potomac silhouette corps badge, brass diamond with red wool center; tin-backed with a T-bar pin extending below the badge, excellent condition. **$425**

U.S., 4th

A Civil War 4th Corps, 3rd Division cloth corps badge still in its original paper packet from Horstmann's, 2-3/4" w, dark blue wool pyramid with internal stiffener, spun brass wire edging, brown fabric backing. Meant to be sewn to coat or hat, unused and good as new. Only the brass has toned a bit. Comes with 3" x 4" dark-tan paper envelope in which it was sold. Has ink-stamped, "HORSTMANN/PHILA" and black stamped corps badge design on one side. Shows some age stain only, first ever encountered. **$595**

U.S., 5th

A German silver bar with T-bar pin, engraved "52 Mass. Reg." from which hangs a Maltese Cross in a circle with a large "E" (Company E) in the center, 2-1/2" h. **$400**

KP photo/Wisconsin Veterans Museum collection

*This is a private purchase combination identification and corps badge belonging to William A. Craven, Co H, 8th Wisconsin Infantry Regiment. The top portion of the badge–the moon and star–is the only decorative element, **$2,200**.*

KP photo/Wisconsin Veterans Museum collection

Third Corps Union badge with gold wreath and green enamel leaves.
An eagle with spread wings is at the top of the badge and crossed swords
pointed down are at the bottom, $1,800.

U.S., 9th

Gilt brass, 1-1/2" h, die-struck crossed cannons and anchor with twisted rope, very sharp profile, T-bar pin. **$385**

Original wool and bullion 9th Corps badge, approximately 2"x 2", dark-red wool background with bullion crossed cannon and anchor with bullion border, minor moth damage, dark color to bullion with great aged patina. **$350**

U.S., 24th

24th Corps, 2nd Division badge, twisted wire border. **$595**

German silver heart with scalloped edges and white enamel center, T-bar pin extends below badge, usual age crackling to enamel, but otherwise excellent condition. **$450**

U.S., 25th

Brass silhouette-type badge with scalloped edges, red cloth center, T-bar pin extends below badge, some cloth wear, but in excellent condition. **$450**

Insignia of Rank

Chevrons, U.S.

Corporal

New condition, intended for an artilleryman, made of bright scarlet wool stripes sewn to dark navy-blue wool, thread is light, tan stripes are 11/16" w and 7" across the top. **$435**

Sergeant

Pair of infantry sergeant chevrons, three classic sky-blue worsted stripes sewn to the dark-blue woolen backing, excellent condition overall, shows just the right amount of age, with virtually no moth damage. **$650**

Epaulettes, U.S.
Enlisted Man

10th Volunteer Corps dress epaulettes, Civil War-era or earlier, gold bullion embroidery in excellent condition. **$425**

Officer

Dug in northern Mississippi, fine condition. **$85**

Comes with original tin box, embroidered cloth with gilded finish, buttons marked, "G and cie. Paris," by Schuyler, Hartley and Graham, cased in tin box with worn japanning, 6-1/4" x 7-1/2" x 9-1/4". **$165**

Civil War, field-grade officer's epaulettes made of gold bullion with gold-plated crescents and heavy gold bullion fringe (denoting colonel, lieutenant colonel, or major). Complete with hinged and padded mounting strap, super set in excellent condition. **$285**

Lieutenant

In original japanned tin case, silver bars of a 1st lieutenant, the insignia of the 5th Infantry Regiment, probably of Massachusetts, since that is where they were found. One of the buttons is a replacement naval button, fine condition. **$450**

Colonel

Mushroom-shaped brass gilt epaulettes with cloth of gold inside, topped with magnificent silver-embroidered eagle. Edges are bound with bright, gold-gilt binding, 3-1/2" brilliant gold bullion ringlets, red silk padding underneath. Red Moroccan leather under the connecting straps, left and right connecting straps are brilliant gilt, superb condition. **$1,100**

General

Japanned tin box with paper label that reads, "Horstmann Bros. Co./Fifty Cherry Sts./ PHILADELPHIA/MILITARY SOCIETY GOODS." The epaulettes are in fine condition with gold bullion fringe and a single silver bullion star. The tin case has remnants of a paper label inside, and has a large dent on the bottom front. **$425**

KP photo/Wisconsin Veterans Museum collection

*At top, Union issued pair of Brigadier General shoulder straps worn by Lucius Fairchild, **$1,900;** at bottom, Union issued set of 2nd Lieutenant of Infantry shoulder straps, **$400.** Both sets are 4-1/4" long by 1-3/4" wide.*

Sash, U.S.
Officer
Burgundy officer's sword belt sash, retains both knots and tassels, body remains, but is quite tattered and fragile. Reliable oral tradition identifies the officer who used this as Captain William Reuben Rowley who served as a 1st lieutenant in the 45th Illinois in 1861, a captain and aide-de-camp for General Grant in 1862, and as major when he served as Provost Marshal of the important Federal staging base at Cairo, Illinois beginning in November 1862; he resigned in 1864. .... **$225**

Infantry, burgundy officer's sword belt sash retains both knots and tassels, body remains, but is quite tattered and fragile. Reliable oral tradition identifies the officer who used this as Captain William Reuben Rowley, a 1st lieutenant in the 45th Illinois in 1861, a captain and aide-de-camp for General Grant in 1862. As major he served as Provost Marshal of the important Federal staging base at Cairo, Illinois, from November 1862 to 1864. .... **$225**

Shoulder Straps, U.S.
2nd Lieutenant, Artillery
Red cloth fields and heavy gold bullion borders, partial dark-blue wool undersides. Sewn together with crossed stitches, showing strap interiors, pair is in excellent condition. **$385**

Lieutenant, Cavalry
Smith's Patent strap with a bright-yellow wool field, gilt brass false embroidered borders, and silver oak leaves in false embroidery at either end. Blue wool underside, in excellent condition (a single). **$195**

Major, Cavalry
Single shoulder board insignia in excellent condition with mustard-color velvet backing, and oak leaves in fine gold bullion. **$245**

2nd Lieutenant, Infantry

Dark-blue wool fields with heavy gold-bullion borders, blue undersides go only partly across the back, dome gold bullion missing, but still a great set of straps. **$225**

Lieutenant, Infantry

Unique and important example in marvelous condition. Designed to reduce the high casualty rate among frontline combat officers, rank insignia was made smaller without bullion, and often worn less conspicuously. Borders are contoured navy-blue felt, tightly edged by spun-brass wire, that also outlines the lieutenant's bars against the black velvet facings. Navy-blue fabric backsides are folded over and hand sewn, some stiffener at center, one has a few moth holes, clean and excellent condition. 1-1/2" x 3-11/16". **$875**

Gilt ribbed frame (false embroidered), medium-blue wool field and dark-blue wool backing. Marked, "Jas. Smith Pat. June 16 1861 16 Dutch St. N.Y.," a single. **$115**

Captain, Infantry

Single, dark-blue velvet with heavy gold-bullion border and gold-bullion captain's bars, shows use. **$135**

2nd Lieutenant

Possibly used by a Zouave unit, this pair of straps has red cloth undersides (open in the center) intended for use on a red uniform. Centers are black velvet with fancy gold bullion borders, size 1-3/8" x 3-1/2", shows wear and age. ... **$475**

Captain, Assistant Surgeon

Ribbed brass (false embroidered) borders and captain's bars on blue velvet field (assistant surgeons were captains of staff), tin backed (a single). **$145**

2nd Lieutenant, Rifleman

Smith patent with ribbed metal frames (imitation gold embroidery), rifleman green field, pair marked, "Jas. Smith Pat. June 18, 1861 15 Dutch Sts. N.Y.," on the blue backing, excellent condition. **$425**

Hat/Cap Insignia

Hat Cord, U.S.
Enlisted Man, Artillery
Bright red hat cord, great condition, no moth damage. **$60**

Perfect surplus example of red, worsted-wool artillery hat cord for use on the
  Hardee hat. **$45**

Enlisted Man, Cavalry
Mint condition, yellow cavalry hat cord. **$185**

Yellow, worsted-wool cord with tassels and adjustment slide, original unissued
  Civil War cord with storage wear only. **$80**

Enlisted Man, Infantry
Medium-blue worsted wool hat cord for the Model 1858 Hardee hat, tassels
  retain original cord ties, unissued example from old Bannerman's Island
  stock. **$45**

Officer
Original hat cord, single strand that goes around the hat in black and gold and
  has a black and gold slide, acorns are also gold with black webbing.
  .... **$125**

Hat Insignia
Confederate
Rare 3rd Dragoon hat pin, dug in a camp of C.S. General Tom Green's Texas
  Cavalry from the Red River Campaign in western Louisiana, made of heavy
  cast brass, not the thin stamped variety, and is fashioned to look like a
  rectangular belt plate such as the 1851 sword belt plate. All four hooks are
  on the reverse, very-fine brown patina with green bits of patina on the edge.
  Measures 1-1/4" l x 7/8" h x 1/8" w. **$600**

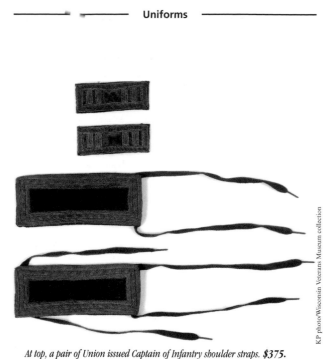

At top, a pair of Union issued Captain of Infantry shoulder straps. $375.
At bottom, a pair of Union issued 2nd Lieutenant shoulder straps
("extra rich" type), $400.

KP photo/Wisconsin Veterans Museum collection

Confederate, Enlisted Man

Louisiana, very rare hatpin dug in Louisiana camp in middle Louisiana during the early 1980s, very good condition, pin retains about 40% of the gold gilt. Loop attached to the back is still present. Pin is 5/8" w x 3/4" h. **$1,600**

Letter "S"

Large-size, cast letter "S," dug from a Confederate Army of Tennessee winter camp. **$65**

Letter "T"

Excellent condition, non-dug, lead-filled, stamped brass letter "T." **$65**

Number "1"

Nice condition, dug, large-size, stamped brass Union cap, smooth brown patina. **$38**

U.S., Enlisted Man, Artillery

Bannerman's surplus Civil War headgear insignia, never had the attaching wires attached to the back, but were added later by the Francis Bannerman Military Surplus company. **$85**

Large crossed cannons in brass, 3-1/2" across, heavy trunions, and smaller horizontal intersection angles than the more common specimens. Complete with four flat, original wires attached to the back. **$250**

Stamped, sheet brass, crossed cannons, excellent condition with most of the original shellac and all four soldered attaching loops. **$185**

U.S., Officer, Artillery

2-1/2" w, stamped brass, crossed cannons with embossed surface simulating bullion embroidery. Wide, wire pin-back fastener, number "8" soldered to a horizontal bar above center, for 8th Artillery, dark, even coppery patina, very-fine condition. **$295**

Brilliant gilt artillery insignia that retains all four brass mounting wires on the back, near perfect condition. **$360**

False embroidered, stamped brass "crossed cannons" with 90-99% bright original heavy gilt finish, retains all four mounting pins on the back, super condition. **$360**

Original Civil War period artillery officer's false-embroidered, crossed-cannon headgear insignia. Retains its original gilt, except raised edges. All four original attachment wires present with old light gray solder, cannon barrels measure about 2-1/2" across at the muzzles. **$150**

U.S., Enlisted Man, Cavalry

Original and mint example of the Civil War cavalry hat badge with the stand up attachment loops on the back. **$275**

Bannerman's surplus Civil War headgear insignia, never had the attaching wires attached to the back, but they were added later by the Francis Bannerman Military Surplus company. **$150**

Stamped-brass crossed sabers, fine umber patina, retains one iron mounting pin on back, in Riker display case. **$260**

Stamped-brass, crossed sabers, 3-3/8" w, four thin-brass wire loops soldered on back, light patina, fine example. **$325**

U.S., Enlisted Man, Infantry

Excellent condition, non-dug, stamped-brass bugle infantry hat insignia, both loops intact. **$95**

Dug, large-size Union infantry bugle hatpin with brown-green patina, very solid, but does appear to have an old repair to the mouthpiece tip. **$125**

Bannerman's surplus Civil War headgear insignia, never had the attaching wires attached to the back, but were added later by the Francis Bannerman Military Surplus company. **$45**

Gilt, sheet-brass stamped in the false embroidered pattern. Very fine strike with beautiful detail, bugle retains almost all its original gilt, which is slightly tarnished to a gold patina. Perfect attaching wires on the back, excellent condition. **$285**

Mint, unissued stamped brass infantry bugle insignia from the Wm. H. Horstmann stock, excellent condition just lacking one attaching loop. ... **$49**

U.S., Officer, Infantry

Mint and unused, this embroidered bugle is in the exact state it was sold to an officer, still untrimmed for sewing to a hat. Large and impressive, the bugle is on a 3-1/8" x 4-1/4" rectangle of prime-quality black wool with stiffener layer behind. The gold bullion infantry horn is embroidered in unbelievable three-dimensional, high relief. It is almost as if the horn were laid on the backing. Gorgeous condition with the slightest, even muting. **$495**

Rounded oval 2-5/8" w, black velvet facing over internal stiffener, affixed to the face is a stamped sheet-brass infantry horn, with embossed surface raised to simulate bullion embroidery. Nice toned patina, fastening wires bent over on back. Within the horn's loop is a false embroidered, silver number "5." The entire thing is bordered by a line of thin spun brass wire...this now aged to a coppery tone. Reverse faced with thin black wool, excellent overall. **$545**

U.S., Officer, Engineers

A silver anchor with a ribbon running from fluke to fluke and with crossed oars overlay, T-bar pin on back, very scarce badge, excellent condition. **$350**

Appears to be silver, or more likely, silver-plated sheet brass, has dark silvery-gray tarnish distinctive of silver or silver plate. A most handsome insignia worn by a very small, select group of army engineer officers before and during the Civil War period. Also by officers at West Point since 1842, 3-1/4" w, 2-1/4" h. Classic engineer's castle bent a bit to take the hat's contour, two original wire fasteners soldered on back. Fine overall, and very rare. ... **$645**

U.S., Officer, Rifleman
Consists of a bugle standing vertical with the cords forming the letter "R," all embroidered in gold bullion on a rectangle of black wool, very-fine condition, minor tarnish, fabric stiffener on back and a bit of adhesive residue from album display. **$535**

U.S., Enlisted Man
Eagle hat plate for the Model 1858 "Hardee" hat, classic stamped-brass eagle with loop and "fish hook" loop on the reverse, non-dug, beautiful.
.... **$295**

Shako Plate
U.S., Model 1851, New York, brass shield almost 4" h, eagle on a demiglobe above and "Excelsior" on a ribbon below. Worn on the shako into the Civil War and pictured in *General Regulations for the Military Forces of the State of New York,* excellent condition. **$385**

Personal Identification

Identification Disc
Enlisted Man
Ohio. Pewter dog tag embossed edge, "War of 1861." Wreath is marked, "Engaged in the above Battles." Filled in here with, "Enlisted Jan 26th 1865 under Capt Green at Fremont, Ohio." Reverse marked, "Henry Spade Co "E" 186th O.V.I. Fremont Ohio." Tag is cast with a small nib (drilled with hole) protruding above the disc's edge (designed to pass a neck cord through). Attached to this nib is a small link of chain attached to a stamped German silver shield (pin back) with Grant bust and words "Lt. Gen. Grant." ... **$475**

Vermont, War of 1861-style, made of brass, 28 mm diameter, non-excavated specimen, mellow patina, disc marked, "G.C. Richardson Co. H. 6th Reg

Roxbury, VT. Vol." George C. Richardson, was a private in the 6th Vermont Infantry. He enlisted August 8, 1861, into Company H and was discharged December 6, 1862. He died three days later on December 9, 1862. The 6th Vermont had been engaged in battle at Williamsburg, Malvern Hill, Alexandria, and Antietam just prior to Richardson's death. **$855**

Maine, 1-5/8" diameter, cast, lead alloy, face has side-view bust of General Grant surrounded by three narrow rings, the inner reads, "LIEU. GEN. U.S. GRANT," within gnarled-edge wreath. Other side has complex design of shield at center, flanked by a panoply of U.S. flags on staffs, under a spread eagle. Stamped in tiny letters is, "F. H. OLIVER/UNATTACHED/MAINE/VOLS/19/ARMY CORPS." Fine detail, tarnished to dark gray, minor wear. **$675**

Identification Tag
U.S., Enlisted Man

Pennsylvania, "J. Standring" is engraved on the badge's top. Standring was a member of the 124th Pennsylvania Volunteer Infantry, measures 2" x 1-1/4" and appears to be silver, but is unmarked. **$464**

Connecticut, identification tag made of reinforced paper, handed out to soldiers by the Christian Commission to wear in case they were killed or wounded. Many soldiers simply wrote a note and kept it on their person in case of injury or death. This one has been filled out by a private in Company K, 18th Connecticut Volunteers. They saw extensive service in the Shenandoah Valley against Jackson. Extremely rare as this is paper and few survived. Complete with its original carrying envelope. **$1,300**

"By order of General Bernie, we have permission to wear a red patch on our caps as a badge of honor."

—*J.S. Hobbs*
17th Maine Volunteer Infantry

Shoulder Scales

Though not exactly a badge of insignia, shoulder scales were worn only by soldiers who ranked as non-commissioned officers or lower. Therefore, just by glancing at a soldier who had on a pair of scales, one would immediately be able to determine that the soldier was not of a "gentleman's rank."

U.S., Enlisted Man

Exact style worn by the U.S. Marines, but these are nickel plated, which suggests wear by a fancy militia unit. Excellent, complete, and untouched, with haze of storage grime and patina. **$275**

Excavated, pieces separated, fit nicely together, in Riker mount. **$48**

Nice and near-mint matched pair of brass shoulder scales, seen being worn in early war photos. **$350**

This model was used by enlisted men of the U.S. Marine Corps, and some militia units also adopted them. They are distinctly different from U.S. Army models in that they are a bit larger, and the undersides of the crescents are open allowing a removable second plate that carries a corded fringe to slip into place. Thus, the epaulettes can be worn with fringe, or without. A very excellent, complete set, no dents on crescents. Medium brass patina that can be polished good as new, fringe is yellow (cavalry), excellent, lightly faded. Retains springs on back, marked, "HORSTMANN/PHILA." **$370**

> "This was General Inspection Muster day. We all had to don the regalia such as shoulder straps, badge and sword!"
>
> —*Dr. David Warman*
> *Contract Surgeon, U.S. Army*

Set of Union brass shoulder scales, $275-$350.

GLOSSARY OF TERMS

ADS: "Autograph Document Signed."

ALS: "Autographed Letter Signed."

Ambrotype: A positive image achieved on glass coated with light-sensitive collodion, backed with black paint, fabric, or paper. Patented by James Ambrose Cutting of Boston, 1854. Encased in the then widely available daguerreotype cases, they are often confused with the early daguerreian photographs.

Armory brown: A term used today to describe a soft, even discoloring of a weapon's metal. Originally, bright metal was treated at the arsenals with a protective coating of brown lacquer.

Armory: The place where firearms are built.

Arsenal: A government location where weapons are stored. May also contain an armory where weapons are built.

Attributed: This term is used to associate an item to a particular soldier even though it is not marked as having belonged to him.

Backmark: Wet plate photographers often imprinted their name and address on the cards on which they mounted their photographs. These imprints served as an advertisement and today, can help identify the origin of a particular image. Abbreviated, "B/m."

Backstrap: (1) A metal strap running down the back of the handle resting in the palm of the hand. (2) That part of the revolver or pistol frame that is exposed at the rear of the grip.

Bannerman's: Francis Bannerman was an early surplus dealer, beginning his business in the late nineteenth century. He bought vast supplies of Civil War goods direct from the government and manufacturers for resale to early Civil War buffs. Bannerman was also the first individual to reproduce Civil War items on a large scale.

Barrel band: A metal band, either fixed or adjustable, around the forend of a gun that holds the barrel to the stock.

Battle honors: The names of battles or engagements in which the unit fought; honors are sewn or painted onto the flag or attached by streamers.

Belt plate: A belt plate is intended for wear on a leather belt, and generally has a decorative face.

Blank cartridge: A cartridge filled with powder, but having no projectile.

Blind shell: A projectile with a hollow cavity that was plugged and not intended for fitting with a fuse. This projectile weighed less than a solid shot of the same caliber, thereby increasing its velocity when it was fired.

Blouse: Period term used to describe a waist-length outer garment. Blouses are not fitted at the waist.

Bluing: The blue or black finish of the metal parts of a gun. Bluing minimizes light reflection, gives a "finish" to the bare metal, and protects somewhat against rust.

Bolt: An elongated, solid, rifled projectile that contains no explosive material that would fragment it. They were best used in counter-battery fire and against fortified positions. Because there are no explosives involved, they are also the safest artillery rounds to dig and collect.

Bormann fuse: This fuse is the invention of an officer of the Belgian service. The case is made of an alloy of tin and lead, cast in iron molds. Its shape is that of a thick circular disk. A screw thread is cut upon the edge, allowing it to be fastened into the fuse-hole of a projectile.

Breechloader: A long arm that is loaded from the area nearest the ignition system, rather than down the muzzle of the weapon. Most often involves a pre-made cartridge.

Broadside: Single-sheet notices or announcements printed on one or both sides, intended to be read unfolded.

Brogan: An early nineteenth century term meaning shoe. Somewhat erroneously, collectors and reenactors often refer to federally-issued Jefferson Pattern shoes as "brogans." The error, though, is very slight as many soldiers also referred to their government-issued footwear as brogans.

Bundle: Period term to describe a sealed package of cartridges.

Bunting: The woolen fabric from which flags were traditionally made.

Caisson: A two-wheeled vehicle designed to carry artillery ammunition. It was pulled by a limber and team.

Canister: A metal cylinder made of tin, iron, or lead, with a removable thin iron top. A heavy iron plate is usually located between the canister balls and the wooden sabot at the bottom. The cylinder contains iron or lead balls that are arranged in rows with sawdust packed between them. The top edge of the vertical cylinder wall is bent over the iron top plate to help keep the canister contents in place and the bottom edge is nailed to the wooden sabot. Canister was designed to be used against infantry at close range.

Canton: Any quarter of the flag, but commonly refers to the upper-left corner. On the U.S. flag, it is the blue section.

Cap pouch: Small leather box carried on the waist belt for the storage and easy retrieval of percussion caps.

Cap: Short for percussion cap, the primer that when placed on the nipple and struck with the hammer, provides the fire to ignite the gunpowder charge.

Carbine: A breech or muzzle-loading shoulder arm having a smooth or rifled bore, using externally primed ammunition. Originally designed for horse-mounted troops.

Carte de visite: Also known as "cdv." A 2-1/2" x 4-1/2" photographic calling card, usually created as one of a number of images on a single photographic plate. Their introduction dates to 1854 by French photographer, Adolphe-Eugene Disderi, though their popularity in America started in 1860. Their major competition was the lower-cost tintype.

Cartouche: A marking impressed on a firearm, usually denoting an inspector's initials.

Cartridge box plate: Similar to belt plates, cartridge box plates are decorative and generally have loops for fastening to a cartridge box flap. Though decorative, a cartridge box plate provided weight that kept the box flap closed.

Cartridge box sling plate: These are intended to be worn on the shoulder sling of the cartridge box strap. Its function was strictly decorative.

Cartridge box: Leather box carried on the waist belt or suspended from a shoulder strap for the storage and easy retrieval of cartridges.

Cartridge: A case usually made of paper for muzzleloaders and of copper, brass, or combustible paper for breech-loaders that contains the powder charge, bullet, and sometimes, the primer.

Case shot: Also known as spherical case shot. Similar to the common shell except that the walls of the projectile were thinner. In both spherical and rifled projectiles, the bursting charge was usually located in a thin tin or iron container and placed in the center of the internal cavity. The case shot was placed around this container. The Confederates usually drilled into the case shot to form the bursting charge cavity. Due to the shortage of lead needed by the Confederates for small arms ammunition, iron case-shot balls were often substituted for lead.

Case: Due to the fragile nature of the photograph, and the familiar practice of housing a painted miniature in a jewel-like case, early photographers packaged daguerreotypes, ambrotypes, and many tintypes in a protective case. First, a thin brass mat was placed over the image, followed by a protective cover glass. After 1849, this sandwich was held together by a thin brass rim known as a preserver. A miniature case was then selected to house this package. The image was slipped into the right half opposite a pad, usually of velvet, on the left. (Some, however, were made to hold photographs on both sides.) The cheapest examples were made of embossed paper applied over a wooden shell. Leather was used as a covering as well. A molded thermoplastic (sometimes called "gutta-percha") "Union" case was the most expensive choice.

Centerfire: A design of ammunition in which the primer is centrally located in the base of the cartridge case.

Charge: An emblem or design added to the basic flag.

Chipped: Used to describe where small pieces are missing or where fraying has occurred on a dust jacket or the edge of a paperback.

Color: During the Civil War, this was the national, state, or regimental flag carried by dismounted units.

Combination fuse: Combination of the time fuse and percussion fuse system. The inertia of firing caused the plunger in the fuse to strike a chemical composition, thereby igniting the powder train. The fuse was designed to act as a percussion fuse if it struck an object before the preset time.

Concussion fuse: A chemical fuse designed to activate from the shock of striking an object. The chemicals were kept separate until impact when the action of the chemicals upon each other caused a flame.

Conversion: In terms of Civil War firearms, a conversion is where the ignition system of a weapon (usually a flintlock), is modified into a more modern system (usually percussion).

Corps badge: In 1863, the Union Army instituted a system of denoting corps affiliation by displaying specific symbols. These symbols, cut of wool felt, were initially issued to soldiers. Enthusiasm caught on for the idea and soldiers soon began buying commercial corps badges to decorate their hats, caps, coats, and jackets.

Cut-down: A collector term to describe a long arm that has had its original barrel length modified. In almost every case, a cut-down will not be worth as much as an original full-length weapon.

Cylinder scene: Many revolvers of the Civil War era had various pictures, or scenes engraved on the cylinders.

Daguerreotype: The first practical system of photography with a positive image produced on copper clad with a layer of burnished (mirror-like) silver, treated in the manner developed in France following successful efforts by Nicephore Niepce and J.L.M. Daguerre, announced to the world in 1839. Without a negative, the superior wet-plate system introduced about ten years later soon brought daguerrean era to an end.

D-Guard: This is the term applied to the over-the fist guard on some Bowie knives. Most often associated with Confederate knives, there are many photographs of Union soldiers posing with D-Guard knives as well.

Double action: A revolver that may be fired by just pulling the trigger to cock the hammer and rotate the cylinder to the next chamber.

Drop: This is a collector term to describe a bullet that was dug and found to be in unfired condition. The idea is that the soldier who originally handled the round somehow dropped it and never recovered it.

DS: "Document Signed."

Dug: Any item that has been excavated, usually using a metal detector. Many collectors prefer dug items, because such pieces are more difficult to fake.

DuoDecimo: A book or document approximately 7" to 8" tall.

Edges: The outer surfaces of the leaves of a book.

Ensign: A flag flown on ships or boats.

Epaulette: Worn on the shoulder and fringed, epaulettes are part of a dress uniform. Rarely would they ever be worn in a combat situation.

Ephemera: Items that were intended to be used for a short period of time, then disposed.

Face: The front of a button on which the design is stamped or cast.

Ferrule: (1) A metal tip at the bottom of a staff used to plant the flag in the ground or rest the flag in a sling around the neck. (2) A metal washer between the guard and handle. It is there to make sure the handle doesn't move.

Field: The background color on a flag.

Finial: An ornamental device attached to the head of a flagstaff.

Fixed ammunition: A pre-assembled (or fixed) combination of a smoothbore projectile, sabot, and powder bag. This assembly allowed an increase in the rate of fire of the artillery crew by eliminating two steps in the process of loading and firing.

Flank markers: Small flags carried at each end of an infantry regiment's line of battle to mark the flanks

Flintlock: A firing mechanism used primarily on martial firearms prior about 1848. It uses a shower of sparks created when a piece of flint strikes a steel frizzen to ignite a priming charge, which in turn, ignites the main powder charge.

Flyleaf: A blank leaf, sometimes more than one, following the front free endpaper, or at the end of a book where there is not sufficient text to fill out the last few pages.

Fly: The part of the flag furthest from the staff.

Folio: Has several meanings: (1) a leaf numbered on the front; (2) the numeral itself; and (3) a folio-sized publication. When used as this third definition, it refers to the largest size of printed material. By the mid-1800s the normal folio size had increased to about 17" x 21", the size that is still standard to this day.

Foxing: Brown spotting of the paper caused by a chemical reaction, generally found in 19th century books, particularly in steel engravings of the period.

Frame buckle: This is simply a utilitarian buckle that was not intended to have any decorative value. Often associated with Confederate accoutrements, there are a wide variety of frame buckles.

Friction primer: A small brass or quill tube, known as the priming tube, filled with gunpowder and used to send a flame to the powder charge inside the bore. An artilleryman used a lanyard to pull the wire, thereby, igniting the fuse.

Frock coat: A thigh-length outer garment fitted at the waist. Military examples will usually have a standing collar.

Frog: Generally, a frog is a leather item that slips onto a belt and provides a means for carrying a bayonet scabbard or straight sword scabbard on the belt.

Fuller: A groove down the center of a blade, for strength and lightness. Usually misnamed the "blood groove."

Fuse: Device used to detonate a shell or case shot. Fuses for projectiles are classified as time fuses, percussion fuses, and combination fuses. The time fuse serves to explode a projectile during flight, or at the end of a given period of time after its discharge from the gun. The percussion fuse, rifled guns serve to explode a projectile either during flight or on impact. The combination fuse involves both of these elements.

Gemrig bone surgery set: A specialized surgical set issued to military surgeons for bone resection or removal. J. H. Gemrig was a supplier of military and civilian surgical sets before and during the war.

Gilt: The gold wash applied to the face of a button.

Grapeshot: Iron balls that, when bound together, formed a stand of grapeshot.

Grouping: The term used by collectors to identify items that are historically associated.

Guidon: A small flag or banner carried by military units to identify their origin or affiliation.

Hammer: The part of a gun's mechanism that, after being cocked, flies (usually) forward to strike the percussion cap or primer, thus firing the gun.

Haversack: A bag used primarily for an individual's eating tools and foodstuffs. Generally carried by means of a shoulder sling.

Hernstein military amputation set: Strictly for field amputation, marked instruments for U.S. Army Hospital Department. H. Hernstein was a supplier of military and civilian surgical sets before and during the War.

Hoist: The part of the flag nearest to the staff or flagpole.

Housewife: A small, usually rolled-up, portfolio for storing sewing supplies.

Identification disc: These are the precursors to the issued "dog tags." These items were not issued during the Civil War. Rather, soldiers purchased and made a variety of identification tags to wear while in service.

Identified: When a collector or dealer refers to an "identified" item, that means that the name of the soldier associated with the item is known.

Import: In Civil War terms, any weapon not produced in a Northern or Southern armory.

Imprint: A term that can refer either to the place of publication or to the publisher.

Jacket: A fitted, waist-length outer garment.

Keeper: Some belts were issued with a brass fitting that accepted the hook of the belt plate. This fitting was called the keeper.

Kepi: Drawn from the style of the French military, a low cap. Shaped with reed or wire to have a sharp rise on the rear, a standing front and a round crown.

Kern trepanning set: Civilian set for surgery of the skull. H. Kern was a supplier of military and civilian surgical sets before and during the War.

Kit: Term used to describe the entire trappings of accoutrements assigned to one soldier.

Knuckle bow: Single strap running from the quillon to the pommel. It guards the front of the hand.

Kolbe military set: Intended for major bone surgery, trepanning, amputation, a specialized set for bone resection or removal. Marked for U.S. Army Medical Department. Date of manufacture determined by label address of maker. D. Kolbe was a supplier of military and civilian surgical sets before and during the War.

Limber: A two-wheeled vehicle to which a gun or caisson is attached.

Lock: The firing mechanism of a muzzle loading firearm.

LS: "Letter Signed."

Married: Items that were not historically together, but rather, put together some time after the Civil War.

Minié bullet: Perfected by Captain Claude Etienne Minié of the French Army in 1848. The U.S. Army adopted the design in 1855. The bullet was elongated, but was hollow at the base for about one-third of the length. When fired, gasses forced the lead into the rifling grooves in the barrel.

Musket: A muzzle-loading, smoothbore long arm that is equipped to support a bayonet.

Musketoon: A muzzle-loading shoulder arm having a smooth or rifled bore and a maximum barrel length of 26.5 inches.

Nipple: A small metal tube extending through the breech of a percussion firearm also called the cone.

Obverse: The right-hand page of a book, more commonly called the recto.

Octavo (8vo): A book or document of about 5" x 8" to about 6" x 9". Octavo is the most common size for current hardcover books. To make octavo books, each sheet of paper is folded to make eight leaves (sixteen pages).

Pamphlet: Published, non-serial volumes with no cover or with a paper cover, usually five or more pages and fewer than 49.

Paper boards: Stiff cardboard covered in paper.

Pennant: A flag made in the shape of an isosceles triangle, which has two equal sides.

Percussion cap: A slightly conical copper cap, shaped like a top hat, that contained fulminate of mercury. The cap was placed on the nipple of the fuse slider in the percussion fuse or simply the nipple of a musket. When struck, it sent a spark to the charge.

Pinfire: The pinfire system is one in which the firing pin is actually a part of the cartridge.

Plate sizes: Full (whole) plate 6-1/2" x 8-1/2"; half plate 4-1/4" x 6-1/2"; quarter plate 3-1/4" x 4-1/4"; one-sixth plate 2-3/4" x 3-1/4"; one-eighth plate 2-1/8" by 3-1/4"; one-ninth plate 1-1/2" x 1-3/4"; and one-sixteenth plate 1-5/8" by 2-1/8".

Pommel: The part of the handle that keeps your pinky from sliding off. Also holds the whole sword together.

Primer: Device that when placed in the vent hole of a field piece and attached to a lanyard, is used to fire the gun. It replaced the process of priming the vent hole with fuse and powder and igniting with a slow match.

Provenance: The history of an item. Usually, provenance will identify the original owner and in some cases, subsequent owners of an item.

Puppy paw: Consisting of two studs, this is a style of attachment found on some U.S. belt plates.

Push: Slight dent, usually used to describe damage to a dug button.

Quarto (4to): A book or document between octavo and folio in size; approximately 11" to 13" tall. To make a quarto, a sheet of paper is folded twice, forming four leaves (eight pages).

Quillon: The cross piece on a sword, also thought of as a guard.

Ramrod: A wood or metal rod used to force a bullet down the barrel of a muzzle-loading firearm.

Receiver: The housing for a firearm's breech (portion of the barrel with chamber into which a cartridge or projectile is loaded) and firing mechanism.

Recto: The front side of a printed sheet or the front side of a leaf in a bound book; in other words, the right-hand page of an opened book. Also called the obverse.

Repeating firearm: A firearm that may be discharged repeatedly by recharging through means of deliberate, successive, mechanical actions of the user.

Ricasso: The flattened portion of the blade that assists in the manipulation of the weapon. Often, one will find the maker's mark stamped here.

Rifled musket: A muzzle-loading, rifled long arm that is equipped to support an angular bayonet.

Rifle: In terms of Civil War weaponry, a two-banded weapon (or of similar length to a two banded weapon) equipped to support a saber bayonet.

Rimfire: A rimmed or flanged cartridge with the priming mixture located inside the rim of the case.

Ring: On the base of a conical bullet, rings will often be found. The idea is that, when fired, these rings expand and engage the rifling grooves in the barrel.

Rmdc: Used to describe hallmarks, usually on buttons. It means, "Raised mark depressed channel."

rm: Used to refer to hallmarks, usually on buttons. This refers to a "raised mark" maker's mark.

Saber bayonet: This is a wide-bladed (most often with a fuller) bayonet that has a handle that attaches to a lug on the side of a rifle barrel.

Saber belt: An enlisted man's grade leather belt fitted with straps for attaching a saber and often, also fitted with a shoulder strap.

Saber: A cavalry sword with a curved blade.

Sabot: The sabot served as the driving band for an artillery projectile. Generally, a sabot was made of wood, brass, copper, lead, or wrought iron. The sabot for a rifled projectile was attached directly onto the projectile. When the weapon was fired, the gases from the explosion caused the sabot to expand into the rifling grooves of the barrel.

Sack coat: Period term for a "blouse." Federally-issued, Union sack coats had four-button fronts. Most, but not all, were lined.

Sash: A sash was worn by officers and NCOs wrapped around their waist and under the sword belt.

Scabbard drag: Tip of the scabbard that is reinforced. It is the part that literally drags on the ground.

Sextodecimo (16mo): A small book or document, approximately 4" x 6". To make it, each sheet of paper is folded four times, forming sixteen leaves (32 pages).

Shako: Similar to a kepi, but generally taller, often standing 6" from visor to crown.

Shank: The loop on the back of a button for attaching to material.

Shell: A hollow projectile cast iron containing a bursting charge that was ignited by means of a fuse.

Shoulder scale: Not actually an insignia (though they were worn only by NCOs and lower ranks), shoulder scales were more of a form of body armor. The idea was that if a soldier wearing these was struck down by a swordsman, the blow would be diminished by the protecting scales.

Single action: The hammer has to be cocked manually on a single action revolver. Depressing the trigger will only fire a fully cocked revolver.

Solid shot: A solid projectile cast without a powder chamber or fuse hole. Also known as a "shot" or "cannonball."

Standard: This was the national, state, or regimental flag carried by mounted units.

Sword belt: An officer's grade belt fitted with straps for carrying a sword. Often, there will be provisions for a shoulder strap.

Tang: A metal strip extending rearward from the breech plug that attaches to the stock of the weapon.

Tarred: Nineteenth century term used to refer to painted cloth.

Tax stamp: Images bearing a U.S. postage stamp on the back can be dated as having been produced before or during the period September 1, 1864, to August 1, 1866, when all such photographs transported in the U.S. mail were subject to this form of government tax in order to raise additional wartime revenue. Mainly found on cartes de visite, but also on some tintypes and ambrotypes as well.

Tintype: Also known as "Ferreotype" and "Melainotype" it is a direct-positive (that is, without a negative) photograph on a thin, tin-dipped iron sheet developed by a French process of 1853. Introduced to America beginning in 1856, its tonal range, durability, and low cost made it a popular process that continued in many places well into the early twentieth century.

Tongue: On a two-piece buckle, the "tongue" is the male half.

Trappings: Nineteenth century term used to described the sum of belt, cartridge box, cap pouch, bayonet scabbard, canteen, and haversack.

Trigger guard: A metal loop around the trigger designed to protect it.

Tube: Refers to the barrel of a gun, generally of bronze or cast iron.

Verso: The back of a printed sheet or the rear side of a leaf in a bound book; in other words, the left-hand page of an opened book.

War log: The term was first used in the early days of the Grand Army of the Republic and United Confederate Veterans to describe souvenir pieces of wood recovered from battlefields that showed the impact of bullets or artillery pieces. These early specimens served as reminders of the perils the veterans had faced. Today, war logs are reemerging on the market. No longer the branches or stumps stripped of bark, these are battlefield recovered specimens where the tree had actually "healed" around the projectile. Split open, these branches reveal the bullet, and often, the path it took to enter the wood. Definitely possessing a different feel than the earlier veteran-acquired specimens, they are, nonetheless, a true testament of the deadliness the soldiers had faced.

Water stained: Discoloration and perhaps actual shrinking. A greater degree of damp stained.

Wraps (a.k.a. Wrappers): The outer covers of a paperbound book or pamphlet. Not to be confused with the dust wrapper, which protects a hardcover book.

Zouave: A French soldier who wore a rather outstanding uniform consisting of short jackets, baggy pantaloons and a fez and/or turban. Both Union and Confederate regiments were raised, uniformed and drilled in the manner of the Zouave.

CIVIL WAR MEMORABILIA RESOURCES

Advance Guard Militaria
270 State Hwy. HH
Burfordville, MO 63739
Phone: 573-243-1833
E-mail: orders@advanceguardmilitaria.com
Web site: www.advanceguardmilitaria.com

**Dale C. Anderson Co.
Militaria and Americana**
P.O. Box 3516
Gettysburg, PA 17325
Web site: www.andersonmilitaria.com

Antebellum Covers
Box 3494
Gaithersburg, MD 20885
Phone: 1-888-268-3235
E-mail: antebell@antebellumcovers.com
Web site: www.antebellumcovers.com

Barry'd Treasure—Civil War Relics
Barry L. Anderson
P.O. Box 16569
Louisville, KY 40256
Phone: 502-448-8772
E-mail: btreasure@iglou.com
Web site: www.iglou.com/btreasure

Battleground Antiques, Inc.
Will Gorges, Scott Ford
3910 US Hwy 70 East
New Bern, NC 28560
Phone: 252-636-3039
E-mail: rebel@civlwarantiques.com
Web site: www.civilwarshop.com

Blue Gray Relics
Mark Shuttleworth & Jocelyn Shuttleworth
3321 N. Reynolds
Mesa, AZ 85215
Phone: 480-641-8752
E-mail: mshutt3@aol.com
Web site: www.bluegrayrelics.com

**Mike Brackin
Civil War Americana**
Mike Brackin
P.O. Box 23
Manchester, CT 06045
Phone: 860-647-8620
E-mail: info@mikebrackin.com
Web site: www.mikebrackin.com

Brian & Maria Green, Inc.
P.O. Box 1816
Kernersville, NC 27285-1816
Phone: 336-993 5100
E-mail: bmgcivilwar@triad.rr.com
Web site: wwwbmgcivilwar.com

Caldwell and Company Civil War Antiques

816 Pleasant St.
Lebanon, IN 46052
Phone: 765-482-0292
E-mail: civilwr@in-motion.net
Web site: www.caldwellandcompany.net

Carolina Collectors

Rick Burton & Warren Vestal
P.O. Box 21864
Greensboro, NC 27420
Phone: 336-996-0787
E-mail: ccrelics@collectorsnet.com
Web site: www.ccrelics.com

The Carolina Rebel

Joe Haile
5426 Main Street
P.O. Box 1659
Spring Hill, TN 37174
Phone: 931-486-1561
E-mail: caroreb@aol.com
Web site: www.civilwarrelics.com

Civil War Artillery Man

Shane Cooper Neitzey
7595 Centreville Rd.
Manassas, VA 20111
Phone: 703-335-8185
E-mail: shanessigns@mindspring.com
Web site: www.cwartilleryman.com

The Civil War Connection

Dan and Teresa Patterson
128 Meadowdale Dr.
P.O. Box 2468
Madison, MS 39110
Phone: 601-856-0094
E-mail: cwtrader1863@E-mail.com
Web site: www.civilwarconnection.tripod.com

The Civil War Relicman

Harry Ridgeway
124 Selma Drive
Winchester, VA 22601
Phone: 540-662-6786
E-mail: relicman@shentel.net
Web site: www.relicman.com

CivilWarTokens.com

Steve Hayden
P.O. Box 571
Mauldin, SC 29662
Phone: 864-288-4375
E-mail: steve@civilwartokens.com
Web site: www.civilwartokens.com

CSA Military Collectables, Inc.

Robert S. Dodson, S. K. Dodson
P. O. Box 1111
Acworth, Georgia 30101
Phone: 678-354-2959
E-mail: info@csamilitary.com
Web site: www.csamilitary.com

Damon Mills
Fine Antique Arms
Damon Mills, Antique Arms Dealer
Montgomery, AL
Phone: 334-281-0804
E-mail: damonmillsantiques@home.com
Web site: www.damonmills.com

Dave Taylor's
Civil War Antiques
P.O. Box 87
Sylvania, OH 43560
Phone: 419-878-8355
E-mail: davetaylor.civilwar@Sylvania.sev.org
Web site: www.civilwarantique.com

Deep South Artifacts, Inc.
Keith B. Kenerly
11612 New Bond St.
Fredricksburg, VA 22408
Phone: 540-710-7841
E-mail: kbkdsa@aol.com
Web site: www.DeepSouthArtifacts.com

Drumbeat
Civil War Memorabilia
Eric P. Kane
P.O. Box 119
Bayport, NY 11705
Phone: 631-472-3087
E-mail: info@DrumBeatMilitaria.com
Web site: www.erickaneantiques.com

N. Flayderman & Co., Inc.
P.O. Box 2446
Fort Lauderdale, FL 33303
Phone: 954-761-8855
E-mail: flayderman@aol.com
Web site: www.flayderman.com

Frohne's Historic Military
1963 Amy Jo Drive
Oshkosh, WI 54904
Phone: 920-232-9839
E-mail: modoc1873@charter.net
Web site: www.modoc1873.com

Greybird's Relics
P.O. Box 126
Acworth, GA 30101
E-mail: greybirdrelics@mindspring.com
Web site: www.greybirdrelics.com

Gutterman
Historical Weapons, Inc.
Neil & Julia Gutterman
P.O. Box 1022
Pearl River, NY 10965
Phone: 845-735-5174
E-mail: host@19thcenturyweapons.com
Web site: www.19thcenturyweapons.com

Heller's Antiques
Steve E. Heller
231 Juniata Park Way East
Newport, PA 17074-8725
Phone: 717-567-6805
E-mail: seheller@tricountyi.net
Web site: www.civilwarantiqueshop.com

Hendershott
Museum Consultants

2200 N. Rodney Parham Rd., Suite 209
P.O. Box 22520
Little Rock, AR 72212
Phone: 501-224-7555
E-mail: hmc2000@swbell.net
Web site: www.garyhendershott.com

The Horse Soldier

Chet, Pat, Sam & Wes Small
777 Baltimore Street
Gettysburg, PA 17325
Mailing address:
P.O. Box 184
Cashtown, PA, 17310
Phone: 717-334-0347
E-mail: info@horsesoldier.com
Web site: www.horsesoldier.com

Steven L. Hoskin

P.O. Box 2148
Venice, FL 34284
Phone: 941-496-8427
E-mail: slhdoc@home.com
Web site: www.civilwarautographs.com

Jacques Noel Jacobsen, Jr.

Collector's Antiquities, Inc.
60 Manor Road
Staten Island, NY 10310
Phone: 718-981-0973
E-mail: Jjacobsen@SI.RR.com
Web site: www.home.fiam.net

J.C. Devine Inc.

P.O. Box 413, 20 South St.
Milford, NH 03055
Phone: 603-673-4967
E-mail: jcdevine@empire.net
Web site: www.jcdevine.com

JS Mosby's
Antiques & Artifacts

Stephen W. Sylvia
125 East Main St.
Orange, VA 22960
Phone: 540-672-9944
E-mail: info@jsmosby.com
Web site: www.jsmosby.com

J & W Relics

Jack Masters
1049 Robertson Road
Gallatin, TN 37066
Phone: 615-748-3532
E-mail: jack@jackmasters.net
Web site: www.jackmasters.net

Keemakoo's Civil War Antiques
James Dews

459 West Commodore Blvd.
Jackson, NJ 08527
Phone: 732-928-8973
E-mail: keemakoo@aol.com
Web site: www.hometown/aol.com/
keemakoo/page3.html

Phillip B. Lamb, Ltd./
Col. Lamb's Antiques

P.O. Box 206
Montreat, NC 28757
Phone: 504-236-6014
E-mail: lambcsa@aol.com
Web site: www.plamb.com

Lawrence Of Dalton

Lawrence Christopher
4773 Tammy Dr. N.E.
Dalton, GA 30721
Phone: 706-226-8894
E-mail: cw1861@vol.com
Web site: www.cw1861.com

McGowan Book Company

R. Douglas Sanders
P.O. Box 4226
Chapel Hill, NC 27515
Phone: 1-800-449-8406
E-mail: mcgowanbooks@mindspring.com
Web site: www.mcgowanbooks.com

Middle Tennessee Relics

Larry & Debbie Hicklen
3511 Old Nashville Hwy.
Murfreesboro, TN 37129
Phone: 615-893-3470
E-mail: DebHicklen@comcast.net
Web site: www.midtenrelics.com

Military Antiques & Museum

300 Petaluma Blvd North
Petaluma, CA 94952
Phone: 540-740-8065 (EST)
E-mail: WarGuys@sonic.net
Web site: www.militaryantiquesmuseum.com

Old South Books, Inc.

Larry and Vivian Wandling
Address: P.O. Box 757
Shalimar, FL 32579
Phone: 850-651-0709
E-mail: wandlinv@cybertron.com
Web site: http://home.cybertron.com/
~wandlinv

Old South Military Antiques

Shannon and Lesia Pritchard
P.O. Box 175
Studley, VA 23126
Phone: 804-779-3076
E-mail: oldsouthantique@mindspring.com
Web site:www.oldsouthantiques.com

Barbara Pengelly, Autographs

13917 NO. Meadow Rd.
Hagerstown, MD 21742
Phone: 301-733-9070
E-mail: barbpengly@aol.com
Web site: www.autographdomain.com

The Powder Horn Gunshop, Inc.
Bob Daly, Owner
Cliff Sophia, Manager
Box 1001, 200 W. Washington St.
Middleburg, VA 20118
Phone: 540-687-6628
E-mail: info@phgsinc.com
Web site: www.phgsinc.com

Reb Acres
Sue Coleman
P.O. Box 215
Raphine, VA 24472
Phone: 540-377-2057
E-mail: scoleman@rebacres.com
Web site: www.rebacres.com

RelicAuction.com
Carson Jenkins & Steve Sylvia
Springfield, VA 22152
E-mail: auctioneer@relicauction.com
Web site: www.relicauction.com

Sharpsburg Arsenal
101 W. Main St. P.O. Box 568
Sharpsburg, MD 21782
Phone: 301-432-7700
E-mail: sarsenal@mip.net
Web site: www.sharpsberg-arsenal.com

Shiloh's Civil War Relics
Rafael & Lori Eledge
4730 Highway 22
Shiloh, TN 38376
Phone: 731-689-4114
E-mail: relics@shilohrelics.com
Web site: www.shilohrelics.com

Shotwell's Antiques & Civil War Memorabilia
Olin Shotwell
2935 Sycamore Lane
Bloomsburg, PA 17815
Phone: 570-387-1112
E-mail: OSCIVWAR@aol.com
Web site: www.shotwellsantiques.com

Jim Stanley & Associates
Jim Stanley
7613 Ensign Court
Fort Wayne, IN 46816
Phone: 219-447-7202
E-mail: cwartifax@home.com
Web site: www.cwartifax.com

Stone Mountain Relics, Inc.
John Sexton, Charles & Nan Nash, Lori Nash Cosgrove
968 Main Street
Stone Mountain, GA 30083
Phone: 770-469-1425
E-mail: SMRelics@aol.com
Web site: www.stonemountainrelics.com

Stones River Trading Company

Tom Hays
3500 Shacklett Rd.
Murfreesboro, TN. 37129
Phone: 615-895-7134
E-Mail: Whays@aol.com
Web site: www.stonesrivertrading.com

Sumter Military Antiques

Ray Davenport & Jay Teague
45 John Street
Charleston, SC 29403
Phone: 843-577-7766
E-mail: cwantiq@bellsouth.net
Web site: www.sumtermilitary.com

Sword and Saber

John Pannick, Betty Pannick
2159 Baltimore Pike
Gettysburg, PA 17325
Phone: 717-334-0205
E-mail: swordandsaber@blazenet.net
Web site: www.swordandsaber.com

Trader Ben's Civil War Relics

B. Thomas Martin
P.O. Box 7593
Garden City, GA 31418
Phone: 912-961-9868
E-mail: traderben@yahoo.com
Web site: www.trade4relics.com

Uniformbuttons.com

Ronald P. Pojunas
1605 Edwin Ct.
Bel Air, MD 21015
Phone: 410-893-0923
E-mail: pojunas@uniformbuttons.com
Web site: www.uniformbuttons.com

www.civilwarbuttons.com

William Leigh
P.O. Box 145
Hamilton VA 20159
Phone: 540-338-7367
E-mail: wleigh@mindspring.com

Index

A

Accoutrements, 15-76
Ambrotype, 1/9 plate, 387
Amputation
    catlin, 334
    knife, 334
    set, 340, 343-344
Artillery, 195, 204, 394, 397, 400, 433, 435, 437, 445, 452
Autographs, 222-224

B

Banner, regimental, 318
Bayonet, 76-92
    .54 rifle, Model 1841, 81
    .58 rifle, 80-81, 85
    .58 rifle, Model 1855, 85
    .58 rifle, Model 1863 Remington, 85
    .58 rifle, P.S. Justice, 85
    .69 musket, Model 1795, 85
    .69 musket, Model 1816, 86
    .69 musket, Model 1835, 86
    Austrian, 89, 92
    Brunswick, 91
    Enfield, 91
    French import, 91
    Model 1816, 87
    Model 1835/42, 88
    Model 1842, 88
    Model 1853 Enfield, 89
    Model 1855, 88
    Model 1858 Enfield, 91
    Model 1861, 88
    Model 1863, 88
    Plymouth/Whitney, 89
    Springfield, 90

Belt
    buff leather, 21
    harness leather, 21
Belt plate, 100-135
    Alabama, 118
    Georgia, and belt, 118
    Louisiana, and belt, 119
    Mississippi, 119
    Model 1851, 131
    New York, and sword belt, 132
    North Carolina, 119
    Ohio, 134
    oval, 105-107, 109-110, 123, 125-126, 135
    Pattern of 1839, 121-122
    Pattern of 1839, and belt, 121
    Pattern of 1841, 122, 124
    Pattern of 1841, and belt, 122, 124
    Pattern of 1851, 129, 132, 134
    Pattern of 1851, and sword belt, 127, 129, 132, 134
    Rectangular, 102, 111-115, 130
    Rectangular, and belt, 112
    Sword, 117, 133
    two piece, 112, 116
    Virginia, 119-120
Belt rig, 69
Blade director, 334
Bone file, trepanning, 336
Bone hammer, 334
Bottle, medicine, 341
Bow saw, Gemrig, 335
Bowie, 93-95, 97, 99
    D-Guard, 93-94
    Sheffield, 93
Box, pill, 341

Breastplate, 128
Brush, 20
Buckle, 20, 68, 70, 100-101,
    103-105, 108, 121
  belt, fork-tongue frame, 105
  belt, frame, 101, 103-104, 108
  belt, M1855 rifleman, 121
Bugle, 315, 321-322
  cavalry, 315, 322
Bullet, 136, 137, 162-167
  .36 caliber, 137, 163, 165
  .36 caliber, Confederate, 163
  .36 caliber, Hayes, 163
  .36 caliber, Manhattan, 165
  .36 caliber, Remington, 163
  .36 teardrop revolver, 162
  .44 caliber, Starr, 165
  .44 caliber Model 1860, 147
  .44 Deane, 162
  .45 Whitworth, 162
  .50 caliber, Maynard, 163
  .50 caliber, Smith, 166
  .52 caliber, Spencer
    154
  .52 Sharps, 162
  .54 Burnside   162
  .54 caliber, Merril, 162, 164
  .54 caliber, Sharps, 166
  .54 caliber, Starr, 164
  .55 caliber, Suhl, 164
  .56 caliber, Colt, 165
  .577 rifle, 162, 167
  .58 caliber, 137, 140
  .69 Gardner, 167
  .69, 162
  Burnside, 147
  Shotgun, 167
  extractor, 17

Minié, 151
  mold, 139, 167
Button, 190-210
  CSA, 202
  dragoon, 205
  eagle, 210
  general service, 195, 204
  pattern, 201
Button, branch of service
  artillery, 195, 204
  cavalry, 195, 197, 204
  engineer, 195, 205
  infantry, 196-197, 205, 207,
    210
  national guard, 205
  rifleman, 196, 205
Button, state seal
  Alabama, 200
  California, 206
  Connecticut, 206
  Georgia, 200
  Kentucky, 200
  Louisiana, 200
  Maine, 206
  Maryland, 200
  Massachusetts, 206, 208
  Michigan, 208
  Mississippi, 203
  Navy, 191, 196, 198, 205
  New Hampshire, 208
  New York, 208
  North Carolina, 203
  Pennsylvania, 209
  Rhode Island, 209
  South Carolina, 203
  Vermont, 209
  Wisconsin, 209
Button, staff, 194, 198-199, 202,
    205-206

C

Cannonball, 179
Canteen, 17, 46-50, 52-54, 56-59, 341
  M1858, 56
  bull's-eye, 52, 56-58
  drum-style, 17
  Medical, 341
  Model 1858, 47, 53, 56, 59
  tin drum, 46-47, 50-51, 56
  wood drum, 47-49, 54
Cap
  enlisted man, Model 1858, 437-438, 440
  forage, 441, 443
  Officer, "Smoking", 440
  Officer, Model 1858, 440
Cap box, 22-23, 25, 29
Cap pouch, 24, 26-28
Caps, Percussion, 168
  Lawrence Pellet Primers, 168
  Maynard Priming, 168
  Revolver, 168
Carbine
  Austrian, Froewurth, 244
  Ballard, 231
  British, Greene, 245
  British, Model 1856 Enfield, 245
  Burnside, 2nd Model, 231
  Burnside, 3rd Model, 232
  Burnside, 5th Model, 232-233
  Gallagher, 233
  Gwyn and Campbell, Type I, 233-234
  Hall, Model 1840, Type II, 234
  Hall, Model 1843, 234-235
  Jenks, Navy, 235

  Joslyn, Model 1862, 236
  Joslyn, Model 1864, 236
  Keen, Walker and Co., 229
  Maynard, 2nd Model, 237
  Merrill, 1st Type, 237
  Morse, 229
  Morse, Type III, 229
  Musketoon, 229
  Palmer, bolt action, 237-238
  Sharps, Model 1853, Slanting Breech, 239
  Sharps, New Model 1859, 239-240
  Sharps, New Model 1863, 240
  Sharps, Richmond Pattern, 230
  Sharps and Hankins, Model 1862, Army, 238
  Sharps and Hankins, Model 1862, Navy, 238
  Shotgun, 230
  Smith, 240-241
  Spencer, 241-243
  Spencer, Model 1865, 241, 243
  Starr, 243
  Triplett and Scott, 243-244
Carbine boot, 68
Carbine box, 37
Carte de visite, 352-373
Cartridge 136-161
  .28 Plant Revolver, 144
  .32 National Revolver, 144
  .35 Maynard, 144
  .36 caliber, 148
  .36 Colt Pocket Revolver, 144
  .44 Colt Revolver, 144
  .44 Henry Rifle, 144
  .50 Maynard, 145-146
  .50 Smith, 146

.52 Sharps, 146
.52 Spencer, 146
.54 Burnside,146
.54 Gallagher, 148
.54 Starr, 143, 148
.54 Model 1841, 146
.54 Starr, 149
.58 rifled 149
.69 ball, 149
.69 buck and ball, 149
.69 caliber, 150
7 mm pinfire, 149
12 mm, French, 160
15 mm, French pinfire, 161
Minié, 151-153
Cartridge box, 30-32, 34-42, 120,
  122, 124, 127, 134
.58 Rifle, 32, 34
.58 Rifle Enfield, 32
.58 Rifle Mann's Patent, 32
Carbine Model 1855, 38
Day's Patent, 41
Maynard, 36
Model 1855, 32
Model 1861, 32
Model 1863, 32
Model 1864, 34
Pistol, 41
Revolver, 41-42
Cartridge packages, 155-160
.31 Colt Pocket Revolver, 155
.35 Maynard, 155
.36 Colt Police Revolver, 155
.36 Colt Revolver, 155
.36 Whitney Navy Revolver,
  155
.44 Colt Army, 156
.44 Colt Revolver, 157

.50 caliber, Gallagher, 158
.50 Gallager, 157
.50 Maynard, 157
.50 Smith, 157
.52 Sharps, 157
.52 Spencer, 159
.54 Burnside, 159
12 mm Pinfire, 159
Lefaucheaux, 160
Chapeau de Bras, 433
Chest, Medical, 342
Chevrons, U.S., 466
Chisel, 334
Coat, 436, 446, 450
  frock, officer's, 436, 447-448,
    451
  frock, officer's, cavalry, 448
  frock, officer,'s infantry, 447,
    451
  frock, officer,'s surgeon, 451
  militia officer's, 450
  officer's, 436
  overcoat, infantry, 454
  overcoat, mounted, 454-455
Concertina, 322
Container, 341
  medicine, 342
Cornet, 322
Corps badge, 463-466
Currency, 214-221
Cutlasses
  Confederate, 394
  Model 1860, 405

D

Drawers, 430, 458
Drum, 46-51, 54, 56, 309, 324-
  326, 328

bass, 328
infantry, 324
snare, 309, 325-326
Drumsticks, 327

E

Epaulettes, U.S., 467
Ephemera, 211-224

F

Fife, 327, 329
Firearms, 225-305
Flag, 306-321
    Confederate, 311-314
    Confederate, 1st National, 314
    Confederate, Regimental, 314
    U.S., 316, 319-320
    U.S., Naval, 319
    U.S., Regimental, 319
Forceps
    artery, 334
    bullet, 334
    bone, 335
    Sequestrum, 335
    side-cutting, 335
    tissue, 335
Fuse
    box, 44
    package, 5-Second, 169
    package, 8-Second, 169
    package, 10-Second, 169
    package, 12-Second, 172
    package, 20-Second, 172
    package, 25-Second, 172
    package, Naval, 169
    packet, 168, 170-174
    pouch, 43

G

Guidon
    Confederate, 1st National, 321
    Confederate, Texas, 321
    U.S., Regimental, 321
Gun tool, 33

H

Hat
    Enlisted Man, Sailor, 442
    infantry, 444
    Model 1858, 439, 442
    Officer, 440, 442
    Officer, Cavalry, 442
Hat Cord, 471
Hat Insignia, 471, 473-476
Headgear, 433, 437
Holster
    Model 1849 Colt, 66
    Model 1851, 61, 63, 66-67
    Model 1860, Colt, 66
    Revolver, 60
    Saddle, 67

I

Identification disc, 476-477
Identification tag, 477
Inkwell, 18
Insignia, 432, 434, 463, 466, 471,
    473-476

J

Jacket, 452-453, 456

K

Kepi
    chasseur, 445
    enlisted man, artillery, 433

general officer, 435
New York, Zouave, 445
officer, artillery, 435, 445
officer, cavalry, 446
officer, engineer, 446
officer, New York, infantry,
446
Knife, 76, 94, 98, 334

M

Medical, 330-447
bleeder, 332
chest, 338
instruments, 330, 343
set, Shepard and Dudley,
340
set, Wade and Ford, 340
set, military, Kolbe, 340
Music, sheet pouches, 307
Musket, .81, 85-86, 149, 162,
249-255, 257-266, 269-274,
277-284
.68 caliber, Potsdam, 283
hand-fabricated, 255
Model 1808, 257
Model 1809, conversion, 278
Model 1816, 86, 257-259,
278-279
Model 1816, conversion, 257,
259, 278-279
Model 1822, conversion, 260
Model 1842, 263, 265
Model 1842, Conversion,
278-279
Model 1848, Conversion, 279
Model 1861, 81, 85, 269, 273
rifled, .577 caliber, Enfield,
281

rifled, .58 caliber William Muir,
252
rifled, .69 caliber, Model 1842,
253
rifled, Model 1815, conversion,
278
rifled, Model 1816, 259, 261
rifled, Model 1816, conversion,
259, 279
rifled, Model 1842, 253, 264,
279
rifled, Model 1849, 280
rifled, Model 1853, Enfield,
280
rifled, Model 1854, Austrian
Lorenz, 282
rifled, Model 1855, 249, 266
rifled, Model 1858, 284
rifled, Model 1861, 251,
269-271
rifled, Model 1863, double,
272
rifled, Model 1863, type I, 274
rifled, Model 1863, type II, 274
rifled, P.S. Justice, 277
rifled, Richmond Armory, 251,
254
rifled, Springfield, 249
Musketoon, U.S., Model 1816,
244

P

Photographs, 348-390
Pike, 76, 94-96
Pistol, 41, 287-288, 291, 302, 305
Allen and Tuber, Bar Hammer,
291
Belgian, 305

boot, 287
Fayetteville Conversion, 288
France, pinfire, 302
Model 1836, 291
Remington-Elliot, Derringer,
  291
Plate, Cartridge Box
  Pattern of 1839, 122
  Pattern of 1841, 124, 127
  sling, Virginia, 120
  U.S., Volunteer Militia of
    Maine, 134
Plate, N.C.O. sling, Pattern of
  1839, 122
Powder flasks, 16
Projectile, 136, 142, 166, 175-
  178, 180-181, 184, 186-187
  .69 caliber, Enfield-Tower, 166
  4 lb, 178
  12 lb Bormann-type, 178
  12 lb Mortar, 178
  12 lb Side-loading, 178
  32 lb, 180
  23" Read, 178, 180
  3" Read-Broun, 180
  3" Read-Parrott, 180
  4.6" Read, 180
  Archer, 180
  Bolt, 175, 184
  Bolt, 2.35" Pattison, 184
  Caseshot, 175, 176, 187
  Grape shot, 175, 177, 187
  Parrott, 142, 184, 186
  solid shot, 177
Prosthetic leg, 333

R

Revolver
  Adams Patent percussion
    pocket, 291

Allen and Thurber, Pepperbox,
  292
Allen and Wheelock,
  "Providence Police," 292
Bacon, pocket, 292
Colt, First Model Dragoon, 292
Colt, Model 1851, navy,
  293-294
Colt, Model 1860, army, 285,
  294
Colt, Model 1862, police, 296
Colt, Third Model Dragoon,
  292
Colt 1851, navy, 295
Colt Model 1860, army, 285,
  294
England, Kerr, 304
France, LeFaucheaux, 304
Griswold, 289-290
L. Whitney, Navy, 296
Manhattan Arms Co., 296-297
Massachusetts Arms, American
  Adams pocket, 297
Model 1849 Colt pocket, 293
Model 1860, Colt army, 298
Moore's Patent, belt, 297
Moore's Patent, teat-fire, 297
Remington, New Model Army,
  299
Remington, New Model Navy,
  300
Remington Beals, navy, 299
Rogers and Spencer, army, 300
Smith and Wesson, Model 1,
  300-301
Smith and Wesson, Model 2,
  301
Springfield Arms, pocket, 301

Starr .44, Model 1858, 303
Starr Arms Co., Model 1858, army, 301
Starr Arms Co., Model 1863, army, Single Action, 302
Whitney, Navy, 2nd Model, 302
Rifle
C.B. Holden, 276
Greene, 275
Henry, 267
Joslyn, 276
L. G. Sturdivant, 256
Maynard, First Model, 276
Model 1817, conversion, 260
Model 1819, conversion, 260
Model 1841, 81, 85, 262 263
Model 1853, 264
Model 1855, Colt Revolving, 266
Model 1856, Enfield, 282
Model 1858, Enfield, 284
Model 1861, Navy, 268
Model 1863, Remington, 85, 272
New Model 1859, Sharps, 267
New Model 1863, Sharps, 272
New Model 1865, Sharps, 275
Read and Watson, 256
Spencer, 268
Whitney-Enfield, 277

S

Saber
Enlisted Man, artillery, 394
Enlisted Man, cavalry, 395
Model 1833, 407
Model 1840, 407-408, 410, 414-415
Model 1850, 424, 426
Model 1852, 428
Model 1860, 408-409, 411-412
officer, cavalry, 396-397
Confederate, 394
Saddle bags, medical, 342
Sash
officer, 469
U.S., 469
Saw
amputation, 335
Hey, 335
Metacarpal, 335
Scabbard, 406
Scales, apothecary, 344
Shako plate, 476
Shirt, infantry, 457
Shoulder scales, 478-479
Shoulder straps, 468-470, 472
Sling, 68, 71, 120, 122
Slingbuckle, 68
Solid shot, 177, 182, 188-189
4 lb, 188
12 lb, 188
18 lb, 188
24 lb, 189
32 lb, 189
spur, 72-75
State-issued buttons, 206
Stethoscope, 335
Surgeon's kit, 336, 339
Surgical set, 344-345
Sword, 117, 129, 132-134, 391-428
artillery, 400
Confederate, 397
field and staff officer's, 401, 403
foot officer, 398, 402

import, Model 1832, 413, 416
militia, officer, 413
Model 1830, 393
Model 1832, 397, 399, 413
Model 1832, artillery, 397
Model 1840, 416-418, 420
Model 1840, NCO, 416, 418
Model 1850, 418-419, 421-423, 427
Model 1850, foot officer, 418-419, 421
Model 1850, officer, field and staff, 421-423
Model 1852, officer, 423, 425
Model 1860, 425
officer, 397, 402, 404, 406
officer, Artillery, 397
officer, Field and Staff, 402, 404

T

Tenaculum, 335
Tintype
    1/2 plate, 386
    1/4 plate, 375, 377-379, 380, 382
    1/6 plate, 376, 380-384, 388-389
    1/8 plate, 376, 384
    1/9 plate, 377, 384-386
    full plate, 386
Tool
    bleeder, 346
    dental elevator, 346
    electric magneto, 346
    pill roller, 347
    saw, 347
    syringe, 347
    surgical, 347
Tourniquet, 335-336
Trepanning set, 340
Trephine, trepanning, 336
Trousers, 449, 455, 460
    buckskin, 449
    enlisted man, Zouave, 455
    officer's, 455, 460

U

Uniform, 429-479
    infantry, 458
    officer, 458

V

Vest
    enlisted man, 461
    infantry, 462
    officer, 437

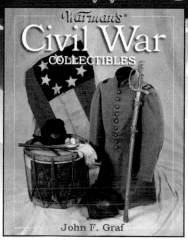
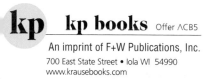